Voilà!

2

GWEN BERWICK AND SYDNEY THORNE
SERIES EDITOR: JULIE GREEN

Published in 2005 by:
Nelson Thornes Ltd
Delta Place
27 Bath Road
CHELTENHAM
GL53 7TH
United Kingdom

05 06 07 08 09 / 10 9 8 7 6 5 4 3 2 1

A catalogue record for this book is available from the British Library
ISBN 0 7487 9094 2

Series Editor: Julie Green

Illustrations by Mike Bastin, Tony Forbes and Melanie Sharp c/o Sylvie Poggio Artists
Agency; Angela Lumley; Beverly Curl; Dan Fletcher; Ian F. Jackson; Harry Venning;
Stefan Chabluk

Page make-up by eMC Design, www.emcdesign.org.uk

Printed in Croatia by Zrinski

Acknowledgements

The authors and publisher would like to thank the following people, without
whose support they could not have created *Voilà! 2*:

Marie-Thérèse Bougard for writing pages 61, 79 and 113, as well as for her detailed
advice on language and cultural matters.

Claire Bleasdale, Teresa Huntley and Stephen Jones for detailed advice throughout
the writing.
Steven Faux for providing the music and songs, with Emile Ratin, Alice Gouneau,
Lucie Deglane and Nicholas Mead.
Rachel Wood for editing the materials.
All the children who modelled for these pictures, especially Kelly Patard and Mehdi
Sobczak; their families and friends for their exceptional help; Monsieur Garcia, the
staff and pupils of College St Pierre – Troyes; and all the businesses featured that
provided locations and props.

Recorded at Air Edel, London with Daniel Pageon, Caroline Crier, Sophie Pageon,
Charles Sanders, Sabine Williams, Lélani Abey, Mathieu Hagg, Maxime Tokunaga,
Florian Coste; produced by Frances Ratchford, Grapevine Productions.

Welcome to Voilà! 2

- In *Voilà! 2*, you'll meet these two teenagers:

> **Salut! Je m'appelle Marine Cartier. J'habite à Bruxelles, en Belgique. Bruxelles, c'est la capitale de la Belgique.**

> **Bonjour! Je m'appelle Ali Amrani. J'habite à Alençon. C'est une assez grande ville en Normandie. Alençon, c'est génial!**

Calais ● Bruxelles ●
LA BELGIQUE

la Normandie

● Paris

Alençon ●

LA FRANCE

- **Most pages have the following features to help you:**

Grammaire:
Examples of how you put French words together to make sentences.

A list of the key words and phrases you'll need to do the activities.

🗬 Prononciation
Practice of French sounds to improve your pronunciation and spelling.

Stratégies!
Tips to help you learn better and remember more.

💿 Activities in which you'll listen to French.

🗨 Activities in which you'll practise speaking French.

📖 ✏ Activities in which you'll practise reading and writing in French.

extra! Activities which provide an extra challenge – have a go!

♻ Activities which give you the chance to recycle language from *Voilà! 1*.

- The *Sommaire* at the end of each unit lists the key words of the unit in French and English. Use it to look up any words you don't know!

> **Bonne chance!**

Table des matières *Contents*

Introduction
Ali et Marine

- meet the main characters in *Voilà! 2*
- revise some language from *Voilà! 1*
- revise the idea of gender (masculine and feminine)

1 a 💿 Écoute et lis.
Note les images A–E
dans le bon ordre.

> Salut! Je m'appelle Ali.
> J'ai treize ans. Je joue au football
> et au badminton. Je fais de la natation, et je
> fais du vélo. Je ne joue pas d'un instrument de musique.
>
> J'ai une copine qui s'appelle Marine.
> Elle habite à Bruxelles, en Belgique.

1 b 💬 Lis le texte:
A une phrase, B une phrase.
Attention à la prononciation!

2 a 💿 Listen and read. Then note
six things about the town where Ali lives.

> J'habite à Alençon, une ville de Normandie. J'aime
> Alençon: c'est génial!
>
> Il y a une piscine, une grande bibliothèque et un parc.
> Il y a aussi beaucoup de cafés et beaucoup de magasins.
> Le centre sportif près de ma maison est super!

2 b 🗣💬 **Prononciation**

💿 Listen again, then discuss
in class how these sounds are
pronounced:

ç – Alen**ç**on

é – g**é**nial, caf**é**s

è – biblioth**è**que, pr**è**s

on – Alen**ç**on, mais**on**

a – génial, parc

3 a 🔊 Écoute et lis. Puis note la bonne option.

1 Marine habite à Paris/Bruxelles.
2 Sa sœur s'appelle Estelle/Julien.
3 Marine a un animal/deux animaux.
4 Elle aime le sport/la géographie.

3 b ♻ Can you spot the factual mistake in what Marine says?

3 c ♻ Grammaire: gender

All French nouns are either **masculine** or **feminine**.

mon = 'my' + masculine word
ma = 'my' + feminine word

● What are the feminine forms of:
   1 *un*   2 *petit*   3 *blanc*   4 *le*   5 *il*
● Look in the text and check your answers!

> Bonjour! Je m'appelle Marine. J'habite à Bruxelles. Ma sœur s'appelle Estelle (elle a six ans), et mon frère s'appelle Julien. J'ai un petit lapin blanc et une petite gerbille blanche.
>
> J'aime le sport (par exemple, le cheval) et les sciences, mais je n'aime pas la géographie.
>
> J'ai un bon copain en France. Il s'appelle Ali, et il habite à Alençon, en Bretagne.

Ali téléphone souvent à Marine.

4 a 💿 Écoute Marine et Ali. Note les réponses (A–J): aime ✔   bof, ça va –   non ✗.

Exemple: A –

 A *le collège*

 B *les maths*

 C *le basket*

 D *les ordinateurs*

 E *l'histoire*

 F *les chiens*

 G *le fromage*

 H *le poisson*

 I *la politique*

J *le sport*

> Tu aimes le collège, Marine?

> Bof, ça va.

> Tu aimes les maths?

> Oui, j'aime les maths.

> Et toi, tu aimes le basket, Ali?

> Non, pas beaucoup!

4 b 💬 Pose les questions (A–J) à ton/ta partenaire.

Exemples: A Tu aimes le collège?
            B Bof, ça va.

            A Tu aimes les maths?
            B Oui, j'aime les maths.

            A Tu aimes le basket?
            B Non, pas beaucoup.

1 Ali au collège

1A Un cours d'histoire

- say what language is spoken in a country
- use *en* (or *au/aux*) to mean 'in' a country

J'adore l'histoire. Et toi?

Les anciennes colonies européennes
– dix exemples

A les États-Unis
B le Mexique
F l'Algérie
G le Sénégal
I le Pakistan
J l'Inde
D le Brésil
H le Mozambique
E l'Argentine
C la Nouvelle-Zélande

1 a 💿 **Écoute (1–10). Note les pays (A–J) dans le bon ordre.**

Exemple: **1 D le Brésil**

1 b 💬 ♻ **Prononciation:** *i* and *é*

💿 **Écoute et répète: i, é**; le Brésil, l'Algérie, les États-Unis, le Sénégal, le Mexique.

2 a 💿 **Écoute et lis le texte. C'est quoi en français?**

1 *What language do they speak?*
2 *they speak*
3 *because*
4 *it was*
5 *in India*
6 *and other languages too*

2 b 📖 **Vrai (V) ou faux (F)?**

1 Le Mozambique était une colonie espagnole.
2 L'Inde était une colonie britannique en 1950.
3 Au Mozambique on parle portugais.
4 En Inde on parle anglais, hindi, etc.

Les langues dans deux anciennes colonies

On parle quelle langue au Mozambique? On parle portugais. Pourquoi? Parce que c'était une colonie portugaise de 1505 à 1975.

L'Inde était une colonie britannique de 1757 à 1947: en Inde, on parle anglais et d'autres langues aussi – l'hindi, par exemple.

3 🖉 **Recopie et complète.**

Exemple: **1 au Brésil**

1	___	Brésil	4	___	Pakistan
2	___	États-Unis	5	___	Algérie (f)
3	___	Sénégal	6	___	Inde (f)

▶

> **Grammaire:** *en (au/aux)* + country
> - Many countries are feminine, and use *en*: *en* Algérie, *en* France, *en* Grande-Bretagne.
> - Use *au* with masculine countries: *au* Pakistan.
> - Use *aux* with plurals: *aux* États-Unis.

4 📖 **Quiz! Recopie et complète les phrases.**

Exemple: **1 Aux États-Unis on parle anglais.**

1 Aux États-Unis on parle...
2 Au Brésil on parle...
3 En Argentine on parle...
4 Au Mexique on parle...
5 En Algérie on parle...

espagnol

anglais

portugais

français

> ♻ **Grammaire: Languages and nationalities**
> 1 language (e.g. *le français*), never add an *-e*
> 2 adjective (e.g. *une colonie française*), add an *-e* if feminine

on parle quelle langue...	
au	Pakistan / Sénégal / Mexique / Brésil / Mozambique?
en	Inde / Algérie / Nouvelle-Zélande / Argentine?
aux	États-Unis?
on parle anglais / français / espagnol / portugais et d'autres langues aussi	
pourquoi?	
parce que c'était une colonie britannique / française / espagnole / portugaise	

5 💬 **Joue et adapte le dialogue.**

▶

Exemple: **A On parle quelle langue au Sénégal?**

   B On parle français, et d'autres langues aussi.

   A Pourquoi?

   B Parce que c'était une colonie française.

Pays	Langue	Colonie
Sénégal	français*	française (1638–1960)
Argentine	espagnol*	espagnole (1536–1816)
États-Unis	anglais*	britannique (1607–1783)
Brésil	portugais*	portugaise (1532–1822)
Algérie	arabe/français*	française (1830–1962)
Inde	hindi/anglais *	britannique (1757–1947)

* et d'autres langues, aussi

6 💿 **Écoute (1–6). Note la langue: français (fr), anglais (ang), espagnol (esp), portugais (port).**

Exemple: **1 esp**

1	au Pérou	4	en Bolivie
2	en Angola	5	au Canada
3	au Kenya	6	au Cameroun

7 a 🖉 **Recopie et adapte le dialogue de l'exercice 5 deux fois:**

1 le Brésil   2 l'Algérie

7 b 🖉 *extra!* **Recherche trois autres pays.**

Exemple: **1 Au Viêt Nam on parle...**

Le Mont Kenya

1B Un cours de géographie

- say countries and their capitals
- use *du/de la/des* to mean 'of (the)'
- apply a grammar rule one step at a time

> Copenhague est la capitale de quel pays?

> C'est la capitale du Danemark.

> Très bien! Et c'est où exactement, Copenhague?

> C'est dans l'est du Danemark.

> Oui, c'est ça.

la France **F**

la Grande-Bretagne **GB**

l'Allemagne (f) **D**

le Luxembourg **L**

le Danemark **DK**

les Pays-Bas **NL**

la Belgique **B**

la Suisse **CH**

---

1 a 💿 Écoute et répète les huit pays.

1 b 💿 Écoute les conversations (1–4) et lis la conversation 1 (du prof de géo). Note les pays.

Exemple: **1 le Danemark**

Grammaire: *du / de la / des* 'of (the)'

We say '**the** Netherlands': the French say 'the' with all countries.
So they say 'the capital of **the** France': *la capitale de **la** France*.

	masc. sing.	fém. sing.	masc. & fém. pl.
	du	*de la*	*des*
la capitale	*du* Brésil	*de la* France	*des* États-Unis
	(*de + le = du*)		(*de + les = des*)

Exception! French tries to avoid two vowels together, so if a singular noun begins with a vowel sound, use *de l'*: *de l'Allemagne*.

2 a ✏️ Écris les cinq questions et réponses.

Exemple: – Berne, c'est la capitale de quel pays?
– C'est la capitale de la Suisse.

Berne   Berlin
Copenhague
Amsterdam
Bruxelles

le Danemark
les Pays-Bas
la Belgique
l'Allemagne
la Suisse

2 b 💿 Écoute et vérifie tes réponses.

▶ **Stratégies!** *du, de la or des?*

Think one step at a time:

1 Is the country singular or plural?

singular   plural ➔ *des*

2 Is the country masculine or feminine?

masc. ➔ *du**   fem. ➔ *de la**

* Remember, if it starts with a vowel sound, use *de l'*.

3 a  Regarde la carte et écoute
le quiz. C'est quelle ville?

Exemple: **1** Strasbourg

3 b 💬 Pose des questions sur
les villes de France à ton/ta partenaire.

Exemple: **A** Bourges, c'est où?

B C'est dans le centre de la France.

3 c 💬 **extra!** Pose des questions
sur les trois autres pays.

(Attention! dans le centre **des** Pays-Bas.)

4 📖 Fais le quiz!

Quiz: monarchies et républiques

A Vrai ou faux?
1. La Grande-Bretagne a un président.
2. L'Allemagne a un roi et une reine.
3. La France a un président et un premier ministre.
4. Le Danemark a une reine.
5. La Belgique a un roi.

La reine Beatrix des Pays-Bas

*La Belgique a un **roi**, Albert II*

B
1. Qui est le premier ministre de la Grande-Bretagne en ce moment?
2. Qui est le président de la France?
3. Qui est le président des États-Unis?
4. La Grande-Bretagne est une monarchie. Comment s'appelle le roi/la reine?

Général de Gaulle, président de la France (1959–69)

Winston Churchill, premier ministre de la Grande-Bretagne (1940–45; 1951–55)

5 🖉 Invente un quiz (six questions) pour ton/ta partenaire.

Exemple:
- ... est la capitale de quel pays?
- C'est où?
- Qui est le président du/de la/des...?
- **extra!** On parle quelle langue au/en/aux... ?

la France	l'Allemagne	le Danemark
la Grande-Bretagne	la Suisse	les Pays-Bas
la Belgique	le Luxembourg	

... est la capitale de quel pays?		C'est où?
c'est la capitale		
c'est dans	le nord / le sud / l'est / l'ouest / le centre	du / de la / des...

1C En classe

- speak to the teacher in French
- understand instructions in *Voilà!*

1 a **L'élève parle au prof.**
Trouve les paires (1–5 et A–E).

1 I've finished!

2 Can you repeat that?

3 How do you spell that?

4 What's 'Scotland' in French?

5 I don't understand, sir!

un/une élève – *pupil*

A Ça s'écrit comment?

B J'ai fini!

C Monsieur, je ne comprends pas!

D Pouvez-vous répéter?

E C'est quoi en français, *Scotland*?

1 b Écoute cinq scénarios.
Note les lettres (A–E).

Je ne comprends pas.
J'ai fini.
Ça s'écrit comment?
Pouvez-vous répéter?
C'est quoi en français, ...?

1 c Regarde les photos d'Ali. Choisis et
recopie *quatre* phrases dans le bon ordre.

1

2 Brusselles? Bruxelles?

3 ?

x2

4

2 **Les instructions dans le livre.** Trouve les paires.

Exemple: **1 f**

1 Choisis le bon mot pour chaque personne.	**a** *Answer the questions.*
2 Quelle est la bonne réponse? Devine!	**b** *Find and correct the two mistakes.*
3 Trouve et corrige les deux erreurs.	**c** *Choose a word for each gap.*
4 Écris les phrases dans le bon ordre.	**d** *Write the sentences in the right order.*
5 Choisis un mot pour chaque blanc.	**e** *Which is the right answer? Guess!*
6 Réponds aux questions.	**f** *Choose the right word for each person.*

3 a 📖 Six cours de sciences. Fais les activités (1–6).

---

1 Choisis un mot pour chaque blanc. Devine!

1 La ___ est un chat.
2 Le ___ est un reptile.
3 Le ___ est un primate.

lézard   gorille   panthère

---

2 Choisis le bon symbole pour chaque élément.

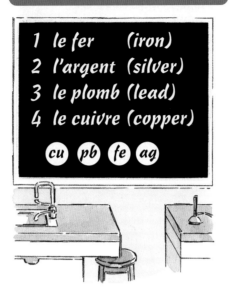

1 le fer   (iron)
2 l'argent (silver)
3 le plomb (lead)
4 le cuivre (copper)

cu   pb   fe   ag

---

3 Quatre définitions et trois images: quelle définition n'a pas d'image?

Feuille 3.2

A une pipette
B un circuit électrique
C un bec Bunsen
D une solution

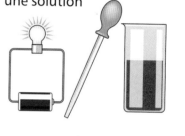

---

4 Réponds aux questions.

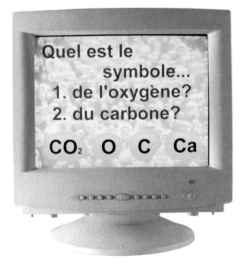

Quel est le symbole...
1. de l'oxygène?
2. du carbone?

CO_2 O   C   Ca

---

5 Écris les mots dans le bon ordre.

le papillon   le cocon

l'œuf   la chenille

---

6 Trouve et corrige les trois erreurs.

1 L'oxygène est un solide.
2 Le mercure est un gaz.
3 Le quartz est un liquide.

---

3 b 💿 Écoute et vérifie tes réponses.

3 c 📖 Trouve et recopie les cinq verbes en français.

Exemple: *find* – trouve

find   answer   guess   choose   correct

3 d ✏️ C'est quoi en français?

Exemple: **1** *words* – mots

1 *words*   3 *which*   5 *mistakes*
2 *each*   4 *gap*   6 *in the right order*

1D Les devoirs de géo

- make comparisons
- use a pattern to work out meaning

Ali fait ses devoirs de géographie

1 a 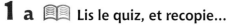 Lis le quiz, et recopie...

1 trois villes
2 deux sites touristiques à Paris
3 deux montagnes
4 quatre fleuves.

> un fleuve – *river*

1 b 💿 Écoute, vérifie et répète les réponses.

2 a Stratégies! *Working out meaning*

- *est plus* **haut** *que...* = is higher than...
  est plus **grand** *que...* = ?
  est plus **long** *que...* = ?

- What is the feminine form of *haut*? And of *long*?

2 b 💬 Fais les devoirs d'Ali!

Exemple:
A Numéro 1: La tour Eiffel est plus
haute que Notre-Dame.

B C'est faux?

A Non! C'est vrai!

Grammaire: comparisons

plus *grand* **que***...* = bigg**er than***...* ('more big than')
Remember: feminine adjectives take an *-e*.
Exception: *long* → *long**ue***

Vrai ou faux?

1 La tour Eiffel est plus
haute que Notre-Dame.

2 Édimbourg est plus
grand que Londres.

3 La Seine est plus
longue que l'Amazone.

4 Le mont Blanc est
plus haut que le
mont Everest.

5 Le Nil est plus
long que la
Tamise.

6 Paris est plus
petit que
Londres.

Londres	est plus	petit(e)	que...
Édimbourg		grand(e)	
la tour Eiffel		haut(e)	
la Tamise		long(ue)	

3 a ✏️ Écris des phrases correctes (1–5).

Exemple: **1** Le Nil est plus long que le Mississippi.

1 le Mississippi / le Nil / long

2 l'Inde / grande / la France

3 l'Amazone / la Seine / longue

4 haut / le mont Snowdon / Ben Nevis

5 Londres / petit / Édimbourg

3 b ✏️ Écris en français:

1 *Luxembourg is smaller than Denmark.*
2 *The Eiffel Tower is higher than Big Ben.*
3 *Switzerland is bigger than Belgium.*

4 💿 extra! Écoute les informations. Quel pays est plus grand?

1 le Sénégal
le Cameroun

2 la Suisse
le Danemark

3 le Mexique
l'Argentine

4 l'Allemagne
la France

L'histoire / History

on parle quelle langue?	*what language do they speak?*
on parle...	*they speak*
anglais/français	*English/French*
espagnol/portugais	*Spanish/Portuguese*
et d'autres langues aussi	*and other languages too*
pourquoi?	*why?*
parce que c'était...	*because it was...*
une colonie	
britannique	*a British colony*
française	*a French colony*
espagnole	*a Spanish colony*
portugaise	*a Portuguese colony*
au Brésil	*in Brazil*
au Mexique	*in Mexico*
au Pakistan	*in Pakistan*
au Mozambique	*in Mozambique*
au Sénégal	*in Senegal*
en Inde	*in India*
en Algérie	*in Algeria*
en Nouvelle-Zélande	*in New Zealand*
en Argentine	*in Argentina*
aux États-Unis	*in the United States*

La géographie / Geography

la France	*France*
la Grande-Bretagne	*Great Britain*
la Belgique	*Belgium*
l'Allemagne *f*	*Germany*
la Suisse	*Switzerland*
le Luxembourg	*Luxembourg*
le Danemark	*Denmark*
les Pays-Bas	*the Netherlands*
... est la capitale de quel pays?	*... is the capital of which country?*

c'est où?	*where is it?*
c'est dans...	*it's in...*
le nord/le sud	*the north/the south*
l'est/l'ouest	*the east/the west*
le centre	*the centre*
... du Danemark	*... of Denmark*

En classe / In class

un/une élève	*pupil*
je ne comprends pas	*I don't understand*
j'ai fini	*I've finished*
ça s'écrit comment?	*how do you spell that?*
pouvez-vous répéter?	*can you repeat that?*
c'est quoi en français, ...?	*what's... in French?*
choisis le bon mot pour chaque personne	*choose the right word for each person*
quelle est la bonne réponse? devine!	*what is the right answer? guess!*
trouve et corrige les deux erreurs	*find and correct the two mistakes*
écris les phrases dans le bon ordre	*write the sentences in the right order*
choisis un mot pour chaque blanc	*choose a word for each gap*
réponds aux questions	*answer the questions*

Les devoirs de géo / Geography homework

Londres/Édimbourg	*London/Edinburgh*
la Tamise	*the Thames*
la tour Eiffel	*the Eiffel Tower*
est plus petit(e) que	*is smaller than*
est plus grand(e) que	*is bigger than*
est plus haut(e) que	*is higher than*
est plus long(ue) que	*is longer than*

Grammaire

	masc. sing.	fém. sing.	masc. & fém. pl.
in + country	*au* Brésil	*en* France	*aux* États-Unis
of (the)	*du* Brésil	*de la* France	*des* États-Unis
		(de l'Allemagne)	

***plus* grand *que*...** = bigg**er than**... (more big than)

cross-topic words

c'était – *it was*
pourquoi? – *why*

Stratégies!

★ pronunciation: *i* and *é*

★ applying a grammar rule one step at a time (**Step 1** sing. or plural? **Step 2** masc. or fem.?)

★ using a pattern to work out meaning (e.g. *plus... que*)

2 Les activités de Marine

2A Les activités

- say what you did recently
- compare the present tense and the past tense

Marine habite à Bruxelles

The present tense

1 a 📖 **Les phrases sont *fausses*! Corrige les phrases.**

Exemple: **1 Je joue au football.**

1 Je joue au télé.
2 Je surfe sur musique.
3 J'invite des football.
4 Je loue une Internet.
5 Je regarde la copains.
6 J'écoute de la vidéo.

1 b 💿 **Écoute et vérifie.**

1 c ✏️ **Écris une phrase pour chaque image (A–F).**

Exemple: **A Je regarde la télé.**

2 💬 **A écrit une activité (en secret!). B devine.**

Exemple: **B Tu regardes la télé?**
A Non.

1–3 questions: victoire pour B!

4–6 questions: victoire pour A!

The past tense

3 a 💿 **Stratégies!** *Listening for clues about tense*

The verbs **above** are in the present tense. Now you're going to hear them in the past tense too (*le passé*).

- What differences do you hear? Tell your teacher.

3 b 💿 **Écoute et lis les phrases. Le passé, c'est a ou b?**

Exemple: **1 b**

1 **a** Je joue souvent au football.   **b** J'ai joué au football lundi dernier.
2 **a** Je surfe sur Internet.   **b** Hier, j'ai surfé sur Internet.
3 **a** Samedi, j'ai invité des copains.   **b** J'invite des copains le vendredi.
4 **a** Normalement, j'écoute du rap.   **b** Vendredi dernier, j'ai écouté des CD de hard rock.
5 **a** Lundi dernier, j'ai loué un DVD.   **b** Normalement, je loue des vidéos.

♻️ **Grammaire: *le passé* (the past tense)**

There are two forms of the past in English but just one in French:

j'ai joué	I played *or* I have played
j'ai surfé	I surfed *or* I have surfed

4 a 📖 Lis le texte. Qui parle au passé?

4 b 📖 Regarde les images. C'est qui?

Exemple: **A** Laura + Jérémy

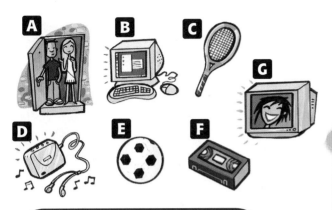

Qu'est-ce que tu as fait le week-end dernier?

Samedi dernier, j'ai joué au tennis avec ma sœur. C'était bien. Le soir, j'ai loué une vidéo amusante, et j'ai invité des copains. Dimanche après-midi, j'ai regardé un bon film à la télé. Dimanche soir, j'ai écouté de la musique.

Laura

Normalement, j'invite des copains ou je loue une vidéo, mais mes copains sont en vacances en ce moment.

Jérémy

Vendredi soir, j'ai surfé sur Internet. J'ai trouvé un site web très intéressant sur le judo. Samedi, j'ai joué au football dans le parc avec des copains. Et dimanche, j'ai écouté des CD dans ma chambre.

Anthony

Grammaire: *le passé*

This is how you form the past tense:

present		past
je joue	je'ai joug é	j'**ai** jou**é**
I play		I played

5 a 💿 Écoute les dix phrases. C'est le passé ou le présent?

Exemple: **1** le passé

5 b ✏️ Recopie et complète les phrases (1–6) au passé.

1 Lundi dernier, j'ai ___ 🖼️

2 Mardi dernier, ___ invité des copains.

3 Mercredi dernier, j'ai ___ ⚽

4 Jeudi, j'ai ___ 🎧

5 Vendredi, j'ai ___ sur Internet.

6 Samedi dernier, ___ loué une vidéo.

6 a ✏️ Écris six jours et six activités (en secret).

Exemple: **lundi – j'ai loué une vidéo**

6 b 💬 Compare avec ton/ta partenaire. Activité identique? Deux points!

Exemple: **A** Qu'est-ce que tu as fait lundi?

B J'ai invité des copains. Et toi?

A Moi aussi. Deux points!

ou **A** Moi, j'ai loué une vidéo. Zut! Zéro points!

lundi	dernier,	j'ai	écouté	de la musique
mardi			surfé	sur Internet
mercredi			joué	au football
jeudi			loué	une vidéo
vendredi			regardé	la télé
samedi			invité	des copains
dimanche				

2B Le week-end dernier

- say what you did last weekend
- use the past tense

Marine téléphone à son corres, Ali

1 a 💿 **Écoute (1–8). Regarde les photos et note les lettres (A–H) dans le bon ordre.**

Exemple: **1 C**

> Le week-end dernier, c'était bien, Marine? Qu'est-ce que tu as fait?

> Bof...

A J'ai retrouvé des copains en ville.

B J'ai mangé des frites.

C J'ai acheté des vêtements.

D J'ai envoyé des textos.

E J'ai invité des copains.

F J'ai réparé mon vélo.

G J'ai promené mon chien.

H J'ai rangé ma chambre.

1 b 💿 **Réécoute (1–8) et note la bonne expression de temps.**

Exemple: **1 SA**

temps – *time*

Expressions de temps: quand?

| samedi après-midi (SA) | dimanche matin (DM) |
| samedi soir (SS) | dimanche après-midi (DA) |

1 c 💬 **A dit une expression de temps et commence une des phrases (A–H). B complète la phrase.**

Exemple: **A** Samedi après-midi, j'ai rangé...
B ... ma chambre.

2 a ✏️ **Écris huit phrases.**

Exemple: **Dimanche matin, j'ai mangé une glace.**

2 b ✏️ *extra!* **Écris d'autres phrases.**

Exemple: *Lundi matin,* j'ai mangé *du chocolat.*

Samedi après-midi,	j'ai mangé	**ma cousine**
		mon skateboard
Samedi soir,	j'ai retrouvé	**un e-mail** *ma hi-fi*
		une glace *une lettre*
Dimanche matin,	j'ai réparé	**une copine**
Dimanche soir,	j'ai envoyé	**un sandwich au jambon**

3 ✏️ Détective de langues! Écris les verbes *au présent*.

1 j'ai rangé 3 j'ai retrouvé 5 j'ai invité
2 j'ai mangé 4 j'ai réparé   6 j'ai surfé

samedi dimanche soir	matin après-midi

j'ai	retrouvé	des copains en ville
	mangé	des frites
	acheté	des vêtements
	envoyé	des textos
	invité	des copains
	réparé	mon vélo
	promené	mon chien
	rangé	ma chambre

♻️ Grammaire: *le passé*

Remember how you form the past tense?

present		**past**
je répare	~~je 'ai répare é~~	j'**ai** répar**é**
I repair		I repaired

4 a 💿 Stratégies! *Linking sentences*

Read and listen to Ali's letter.

● *Parce que* and *mais* are used to connect sentences. Can you work out what these words mean?

Barfleur, le 15 octobre

Chère Marine

Ça va? Moi, ça va.

Samedi, c'était bien, parce que j'ai acheté des vêtements en ville: un jean et un T-shirt. C'est pour mon anniversaire. Samedi après-midi, j'ai retrouvé des copains au club des jeunes. Samedi soir, j'ai réparé mon vélo avec mon père.

Dimanche matin, j'ai promené le chien avec ma sœur dans le parc. L'après-midi, j'ai envoyé beaucoup de textos.

J'aime ça. Mais dimanche soir, j'ai rangé ma chambre – c'était très ennuyeux!

Écris-moi bientôt!

Ali

4 b 📖 Relis la lettre. Recopie la grille et note les détails pour les six activités.

activité	avec qui?	quand?	où?
acheté des vêtements	–	samedi	en ville

4 c 💬 A joue Marine et pose des questions à Ali. B joue Ali et répond aux questions.

Exemple: **Marine** Tu as fait quoi samedi, Ali?
           Ali J'ai acheté un jean et un T-shirt.
           Marine Et tu as fait quoi samedi après-midi?
           Ali J'ai...
           Marine Avec qui?...

5 a ✏️ Écris huit phrases.

Invente des détails: avec qui? quand? où?

Exemples: 1 J'ai réparé mon vélo dans le jardin avec ma mère.

          2 Samedi matin, j'ai rangé ma chambre.

j'ai	réparé ● acheté ● retrouvé promené ● rangé ● invité envoyé ● mangé

5 b ✏️ extra! Écris une lettre à Marine. Adapte la lettre d'Ali: change dix détails (mais ne change pas les verbes!).

2C Une visite à Waterloo

- talk about a visit in the past
- predict how words are pronounced
- find words in the dictionary

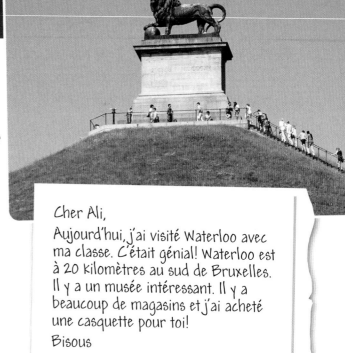

Le lion de Waterloo

1 a 🔘 Lis et écoute les cartes postales. C'est quoi en français?

1	today	**6**	because
2	it was brilliant	**7**	it was boring
3	an interesting museum	**8**	it's rubbish
4	a cap	**9**	a bar of chocolate
5	for you	**10**	a small shop

> Cher Ali,
> Aujourd'hui, j'ai visité Waterloo avec ma classe. C'était génial! Waterloo est à 20 kilomètres au sud de Bruxelles. Il y a un musée intéressant. Il y a beaucoup de magasins et j'ai acheté une casquette pour toi!
> Bisous
> Marine

1 b 📖 Mini-test d'histoire!

1 La bataille de Waterloo, c'était en…

    a 1815   **b** 1945

2 C'était une bataille entre…

    a Jules César et Astérix   **b** Wellington et Napoléon

2 ✏️ Trouve les paires.

Exemple: **c'était… – it was…**

> c'était… nul
> intéressant génial
> barbant

> brilliant it was…
> boring rubbish
> interesting

> Chère Anaïs,
> Ça va? Moi pas, parce que j'ai visité Waterloo aujourd'hui, et c'était barbant. Il y a un musée: c'est nul aussi. Mais j'ai acheté une tablette de chocolat dans un petit magasin.
> À bientôt
> Raphaël

3 a 🔘 Stratégies! *Pronouncing French*

- Discuss how the items below should be pronounced.
- Now listen carefully to a French person saying the words: see if you were right.
- Finally, listen again and repeat the words. Try to sound as French as possible – exaggerate if you like!

Une casquette

A une carte postale

B un paquet de chewing-gums

> Dans le magasin j'ai acheté…

C une tablette de chocolat

D un paquet de bonbons

E une casquette

3 b 🔘 Les élèves ont acheté… quoi? Écoute (1–5) et note les deux lettres (A–E).

extra! Note d'autres détails aussi.

Exemple: **1** C, E (*extra!* musée – nul)

4 🔘 **Écoute, puis joue et adapte le dialogue.**

A Papa, aujourd'hui j'ai visité Waterloo.
B C'était bien?
A Oui, c'était génial.
B Il y a beaucoup de magasins?
A Oui. J'ai acheté une casquette et un paquet de bonbons.

cher *(boy)* / chère *(girl)*		
aujourd'hui, j'ai visité...		
c'était génial / nul / intéressant / barbant		
il y a beaucoup de magasins?		
j'ai acheté	un paquet de	bonbons chewing-gums
	une tablette de	chocolat
	une carte postale et une casquette	

5 a 🔘 **Écoute et lis le texte.**

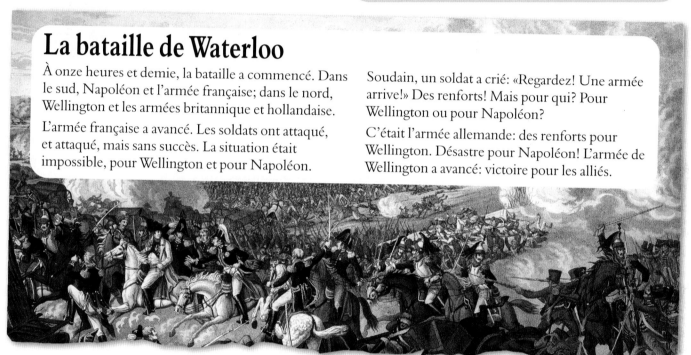

La bataille de Waterloo

À onze heures et demie, la bataille a commencé. Dans le sud, Napoléon et l'armée française; dans le nord, Wellington et les armées britannique et hollandaise.

L'armée française a avancé. Les soldats ont attaqué, et attaqué, mais sans succès. La situation était impossible, pour Wellington et pour Napoléon.

Soudain, un soldat a crié: «Regardez! Une armée arrive!» Des renforts! Mais pour qui? Pour Wellington ou pour Napoléon?

C'était l'armée allemande: des renforts pour Wellington. Désastre pour Napoléon! L'armée de Wellington a avancé: victoire pour les alliés.

5 b Stratégies! *Finding words in the dictionary*

● Look at the words at the top of the dictionary page.

> **sage – sapin**

Will you find *sans* on this page? And *soudain*?

In the dictionary you'll usually find:
– nouns in the singular
– adjectives in the masculine form
– verbs in the infinitive.

● Race to look up these words:
  1 *renforts*   **2** *sans*   **3** *attaqué*   **4** *soudain*   **5** *allemande*

5 c 📖 ***Write down three things you've learnt about the Battle of Waterloo.***

5 d 🔘 **Écoute un soldat à la bataille de Waterloo. Note le maximum de détails.**

Exemple: il est français, ...

6 ✏️ **Imagine une visite et écris une carte postale.**
● Préparation: discutez en classe des adaptations possibles des cartes de la page 20.
● Écris ta carte.
● extra! Invente d'autres détails.

2D Quand?

- use time phrases
- use *avoir* to form the past tense

1 a 📖 **Trouve les paires: mots anglais – mots en rouge.**

Exemple: *yesterday* – hier

> today
>
> yesterday evening
>
> yesterday
>
> last weekend
>
> last week

> Le week-end dernier, j'ai acheté des vêtements.

> Hier soir, j'ai promené mon chien.

> Aujourd'hui, j'ai envoyé des textos.

> Hier, j'ai rangé ma chambre.

> La semaine dernière, j'ai invité des copains.

Hier soir, j'ai acheté des vêtements

1 b ✏️ **Recopie les phrases dans l'ordre *chronologique*.**

2 a 💬 **Teste ton/ta partenaire sur le verbe *avoir*.**

2 b ✏️ **Recopie et complète les phrases.**
1. Hier soir, elle ___ rangé sa chambre.
2. Mardi dernier, nous ___ invité des copains.
3. Vous ___ surfé sur Internet aujourd'hui?
4. Ils ___ loué une vidéo hier.
5. Tu ___ regardé la télé samedi dernier?
6. Samedi, Élise ___ acheté des vêtements.

3 💿 **Écoute (1–6) et note les participes passés.**

extra! **Note d'autres détails aussi.**

Exemple: **1** invité (*extra!* **samedi, des copains**)

4 💬 **Invente six dialogues différents.**
- **A** Tu as passé un bon week-end?
- **B** Oui. J'ai... et j'ai...   (*extra!* Nous avons...)

| la semaine dernière / hier / hier soir | j'ai | rangé... |
| aujourd'hui / le week-end dernier | il a / elle a | envoyé... / promené... |

> ♻️ **Grammaire:** *avoir* (to have) *et le passé*
>
> Remember the verb *avoir*? It's important for the past tense:
>
> | | | |
> |---|---|---|
> | j' ai | nous | avons |
> | tu as | vous | avez |
> | il/elle a | ils/elles | ont |
>
> To form the past tense, you need two things:
> 1. the right form of *avoir*
> 2. the verb ending in -é – the 'past participle'
>
> | | |
> |---|---|
> | *j'ai joué* | I played |
> | *il a mangé* | he ate |
> | *elle a mangé* | she ate |
> | *Martin a visité* | Martin visited* |
>
> *With a name, use *a*, as after *il* or *elle*.

Nous avons loué un lion!

Les activités	Activities
lundi dernier	*last Monday*
mardi dernier	*last Tuesday*
mercredi dernier	*last Wednesday*
jeudi dernier	*last Thursday*
vendredi dernier	*last Friday*
samedi dernier	*last Saturday*
dimanche dernier	*last Sunday*
j'ai écouté de la musique	*I listened to music*
j'ai surfé sur Internet	*I surfed the internet*
j'ai joué au football	*I played football*
j'ai loué une vidéo	*I hired a video*
j'ai regardé la télé	*I watched TV*
j'ai invité des copains	*I invited some friends*

Le week-end dernier	Last weekend
samedi matin	*Saturday morning*
samedi après-midi	*Saturday afternoon*
samedi soir	*Saturday evening*
j'ai retrouvé des copains en ville	*I met some friends in town*
j'ai mangé des frites	*I ate some chips*
j'ai acheté des vêtements	*I bought some clothes*
j'ai envoyé des textos	*I sent some text messages*
j'ai réparé mon vélo	*I repaired my bike*
j'ai promené mon chien	*I walked my dog*
j'ai rangé ma chambre	*I tidied my room*

Une visite	A visit
cher	*dear... (boy/man)*
chère	*dear... (girl/woman)*
aujourd'hui	*today*
j'ai visité...	*I visited...*
c'était...	*it was...*
génial	*brilliant*
nul	*rubbish*
intéressant	*interesting*
barbant	*boring*
j'ai acheté...	*I bought...*
un paquet de...	*a packet of...*
bonbons/ chewing-gums	*sweets/ chewing gum*
une tablette de chocolat	*a bar of chocolate*
une casquette	*a cap*
une carte postale	*a postcard*

Quand?	When?
aujourd'hui	*today*
hier soir	*yesterday evening*
hier	*yesterday*
le week-end dernier	*last weekend*
la semaine dernière	*last week*
il a envoyé...	*he sent...*
elle a envoyé...	*she sent...*

Grammaire: *the past tense*

j'ai	joué	nous avons	envoyé
tu as	travaillé	vous avez	invité
il/elle/Martin a	regardé	ils/elles ont	surfé

Stratégies!

★ listening for clues about tense: sounds which tell you it's the past tense

★ finding words in the dictionary:
  – using the words at the top of the page
  – finding alternative forms of the word you're looking up

★ recognising *parce que* and *mais*, used to connect sentences

★ predicting the pronunciation of new words

Cross-topic words

parce que – *because*
mais – *but*

3 La semaine du goût

3A Miam-miam! J'adore ça!

- talk about foods you love and hate
- use regular -er verbs

En octobre en France, c'est la semaine du goût. Dans la classe d'Ali, il y a une discussion.

la semaine du goût – 'food-tasting week'

A Moi, je déteste le poisson. Berk!

B Tu aimes la viande?

C Madame, vous aimez l'ail? Moi, je déteste ça.

D Je n'aime pas les œufs brouillés.

E Mes parents aiment les plats épicés; moi pas.

F Mon frère n'aime pas le fromage, mais moi, j'adore ça.

G La cuisine indienne? Je ne sais pas: je n'ai jamais goûté ça.

H J'adore la ratatouille! Miam-miam!

I Mon père adore les oignons crus. Berk!

La ratatouille est une spécialité du sud de la France: tomates, aubergines, courgettes, oignons, ail.

1 a 🔘 Écoute les phrases. Note les lettres (A–I) dans le bon ordre.

Exemple: **H, ...**

1 b 📖 Trouve les paires: photos et phrases.

Exemple: **1 D**

2 🔘 Écoute les neuf conversations. Note la bonne photo et l'opinion.

Exemple: **7** ❓

😋 = j'adore ça

😞 = je déteste ça

❓ = je ne sais pas, je n'ai jamais goûté ça

3 a 🗨 **Pose neuf questions à ton/ta partenaire.**

Exemple: **A** Tu aimes les oignons crus?
            B Non, je déteste ça! Berk!

j'aime / j'adore...	tu aimes...?
je n'aime pas...	

le fromage / l'ail / le poisson / la viande
la ratatouille / la cuisine indienne / les plats
épicés / les oignons crus / les œufs brouillés

miam-miam! j'adore ça / j'aime ça
berk! je n'aime pas ça / je déteste ça
je ne sais pas: je n'ai jamais goûté ça

3 b 🖊 **Écris neuf phrases.**

Exemple: J'adore les plats épicés.
            La ratatouille, je ne sais pas: je n'ai
            jamais goûté ça...

4 🖊 **Recopie et complète les phrases.**

Exemple: **1** Mes parents préparent le dîner.

1 Mes parents ___ le dîner. (*préparer*)
2 Vous ___ à quelle heure? (*manger*)
3 Nous ___ à 19h. (*dîner*)
4 Je ___ à midi et quart. (*déjeuner*)
5 Philippe ___ dans un café. (*travailler*)
6 Tu ___ les plats épicés? (*aimer*)

> ♻ **Grammaire:** *les verbes réguliers*
>
> Many verbs end in *-er* in the infinitive, for example
> *détester* (to hate). They have the following endings
> in the present tense:
>
> je détest**e**   nous détest**ons**
> tu détest**es**   vous détest**ez**
> il/elle détest**e**   ils/elles détest**ent**

Chacun ses goûts!

Personnellement, je déteste les plats épicés, mais mes parents adorent ça. Adam, mon copain anglais, adore la cuisine indienne, mais moi, je n'ai jamais goûté ça. Il y a beaucoup de restaurants indiens en Angleterre, mais pas en France.

Robin

Moi, je ne mange jamais de viande, parce que je suis végétarien. Je déteste ça. Manger des animaux, c'est cruel! Mais ma sœur adore la viande. Elle mange de la viande juste pour m'irriter!

Nicolas

Mes grands-parents adorent la ratatouille – Mamie prépare ça pour nous chaque dimanche. Berk! C'est horrible! Ma copine, Camille, aime le fromage. Moi, je déteste ça, donc Camille mange mon fromage à la cantine du collège.

Sandrine

5 a 📖 **Lis l'article et écris six phrases.**

Exemple: Robin déteste les plats épicés.

5 b 🖊 *extra!* **Tes goûts: écris une lettre au magazine.**

Robin		
Les parents de Robin	adore	le...
Nicolas	adorent	la...
La sœur de Nicolas	déteste	les...
Les grands-parents de Sandrine	détestent	
Sandrine		

3B Un paquet de chewing-gums

- say different quantities of foods
- pronounce -ille
- recycle words you've learnt before
- give a presentation

1 a 💿 Écoute. Note l'article.

Exemple: **1 C – chips**

1 b 💿 Réécoute. Le prix est correct?

Exemple: **1 oui**

prix – price

un paquet	de chips de chewing-gums
un kilo	de pommes d'oranges
100g (cent grammes)	de pâté
une bouteille	d'eau minérale
une boîte	de tomates
un litre	de lait
quatre-vingts centimes un euro cinquante	

Grammaire: *quantité + de*

With quantities, use *de*, or *d'* if it's followed by a vowel sound (can you tell your teacher why?):

*un paquet **de** chips*
*un kilo **d'**oranges*

2 💬 A dit une phrase – logique ou pas logique! B donne son opinion.

Exemple: **A** Cent grammes de lait.

B Ce n'est pas logique!

Extramarché

A 100g de pâté ~~1,60€~~ **1,10€**

B un paquet de chewing-gums ~~0,60€~~ **0,40€**

C un paquet de chips ~~0,50€~~ **0,35€**

D une boîte de tomates ~~1,10€~~ **0,75€**

E une bouteille d'eau minérale ~~1,45€~~ **1,25€**

F un kilo de pommes ~~2,40€~~ **2,00€**

G un kilo d'oranges ~~1,65€~~ **1,30€**

H un litre de lait ~~0,95€~~ **0,80€**

3 🗣️💬 **Prononciation: -ille**

- In French, -ille is usually pronounced as a 'y' sound, not as a 'l'! (Exceptions: *ville, Lille*.)

 Écoute et répète.
1 Une bouteille de jus d'orange.
2 Je n'ai jamais goûté la ratatouille.
3 Tu aimes les œufs brouillés?
4 Je n'ai jamais visité Marseille.

4 ♻️ 💬 **Tu trouves combien d'exemples pour chaque quantité? Vérifie avec ton/ta partenaire.**

le jambon ● le fromage ● la limonade ● le jus d'orange
● les oignons ● le thé ● le café ● la viande ● le poisson ● etc.

▶ **Stratégies!** *Recycling words*

Where possible in your French lessons, bring in words you've learnt before (e.g. *un litre de* **coca**).

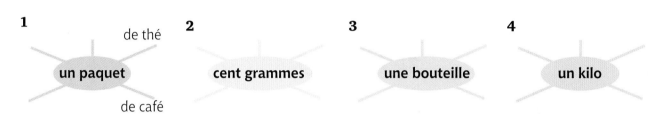

1 de thé / un paquet / de café   **2** cent grammes   **3** une bouteille   **4** un kilo

5 **Stratégies!** *Giving a presentation*

Your aim is to say a few sentences about likes and dislikes in your family.

Step 1 Find some useful model sentences, for example on pages 26–7:

Step 2 Adapt the model sentences, so that you say what *you* want to say, for example:

> Moi, je déteste le ~~poisson~~. Berk! ⟶ Moi, je déteste le **pâté**. Berk!
> ~~Mes parents~~ aiment ~~les plats épicés~~; moi pas. ⟶ **Ma sœur** aime **le lait**; moi pas.

Moi, je déteste le poisson. Berk!

Mes parents aiment les plats épicés; moi pas.

Step 3 Write your sentences in full. Read them: can you add any more information?

Step 4 Read your presentation aloud, to practise your pronunciation.
  Try:
  – reading it to your partner;
  – recording yourself, then listening to see how you could sound more French.

Step 5 Practise giving your presentation from memory. Write down a few key words: you might find it helpful to look at them when you give your presentation, just to jog your memory.

You're ready! Say the sentences you have prepared.
Tip: don't speak too quickly!

3C On fait des courses

- buy food and understand a recipe
- understand instructions
- use words from the dictionary

Pour la semaine du goût, les copains d'Ali préparent un punch aux fruits. Ils vont au marché.

1 a 💿 Écoute et lis le dialogue.

1 b 💿 Écoute (1–5).
Qu'est-ce qu'on achète?

Exemple: **1 100g de pâté, ...**

2 a 💬 Joue les dialogues A, B et C.
Ton modèle: l'exercice 1a.

- Bonjour, monsieur. Un kilo de pommes, s'il vous plaît.
- Voilà. Et avec ça?
- Deux kilos d'oranges.
- C'est tout?
- Oui, c'est tout. C'est combien?
- Trois euros soixante.
- Merci. Au revoir.

bonjour, madame / monsieur
..., s'il vous plaît
voilà
et avec ça?
c'est tout?
c'est combien?
merci
au revoir

2 b 💬 Invente deux autres dialogues.

2 c ✏️ Écris les dialogues A et C.

3 a 📖 Trouve les paires: liste et scénario.

(Attention: un scénario n'a pas de liste!)

A Monsieur Simonet prépare une soupe pour le dîner.

B Chloé invite des copines à une fête pour son anniversaire.

C La famille Tayeb va faire un pique-nique à la campagne.

D Alexandre prépare une pizza pour ce soir.

E Ali va faire un punch aux fruits.

3 b ✏️ extra! Écris une liste pour le scénario qui n'a pas de liste.

1
1 paquet de biscuits
2 bouteilles de limonade
10 paquets de chips
1 litre de coca
1 paquet de café

2
300g de pâté
2 baguettes
1 kg de pommes
200g de fromage
6 œufs
3 bouteilles d'eau minérale

3
1 kg de carottes
500g d'oignons
1 gousse d'ail
une boîte de tomates

4
1 kg d'oranges
1 pomme
2 pêches
1 kiwi
1 litre de jus d'orange

Le punch aux fruits

Ingrédients

un litre de jus d'orange

une bouteille de limonade

une banane

un kiwi

une pêche

une pomme

une orange

1 Lave la pomme et la pêche. Pèle la banane et le kiwi.

2 Coupe la pêche, la pomme, la banane et le kiwi en petits morceaux.

3 Mets les fruits dans un grand bol.

4 Ajoute le jus d'orange et la limonade.

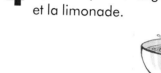

5 Coupe une orange en tranches comme décoration.

4 📖 **C'est quoi en français?**

Exemple: **1 *wash* – lave**

1 *wash*	4 *pieces*	7 *add*
2 *peel*	5 *put*	8 *slices*
3 *cut*	6 *bowl*	

5 📖 **Find five verbs in Voilà! which give you instructions.**

6 ✏️ **Invente une recette de punch aux fruits. (Utilise les verbes de l'exercice 4.)**

Stratégies! *Using words from a dictionary*

You'll need to look up words for the fruit. Check the gender, and use the correct words: *un/une, le/la/l'*.

pear *n* poire *f* → *une* poire → *pèle **la** poire*

apricot *n* abricot *m* → *un* abricot → *lave l'abricot*

Grammaire: *les instructions*

● With instructions, most verbs don't have an -s ending:
  lave les fruits   **pèle** les pommes
  ajoute le jus   **coupe** une orange en morceaux

● But some irregular verbs *do* have an -s ending:
  mets les fruits dans un bol   **écris** une phrase

lave	
pèle	
ajoute	les fruits
coupe	
mets les fruits dans un bol	

3D Une page de casse-têtes!

- practise thinking skills
- give reasons in French

Attention: plus d'une réponse est parfois possible!

1 ⌕ Paires logiques! Trouve les mots.

Exemple: *eau* et *bouteille*, ça correspond à *chips* et *paquet*

1 eau: bouteille ⟶ chips: **?**

2 mère: sœur ⟶ père: **?**

3 Allemagne: Berlin ⟶ Grande-Bretagne: **?**

4 je: joue ⟶ j'ai: **?**

5 litre: lait ⟶ boîte: **?**

6 tu: aimes ⟶ vous: **?**

7 lundi: janvier ⟶ mardi: **?**

8 un: le ⟶ une: **?**

2 a ⌕ Trouve l'intrus. Compare avec ton/ta partenaire et justifie ta réponse!

Exemple:

> pomme
> kiwi petite sœur
> poire

"Kiwi", c'est masculin.

"Kiwi", ça ne commence pas par "p".

"Petite sœur" – il y a deux mots.

"Petite sœur", c'est un thème différent.

> ça correspond à...
> c'est un thème différent
> c'est masculin / féminin
> ça ne commence pas par...
> il y a deux / trois mots

1
> américain
> amusant
> français
> anglais

2
> cochon d'Inde
> perruche
> cinéma
> chat

3
> frère
> copain
> père
> sœur

4
> Pays-Bas
> Suisse
> grand-mère
> Grande-Bretagne

5
> piscine cinéma
> collège
> centre sportif

2 b ✎ extra! Invente des jeux similaires pour ton/ta partenaire.

3 a ⌕ En classe! Vous inventez combien de phrases pour la photo?

Exemple: Il s'appelle Olivier.
          C'est en juillet.
          Il va à la bibliothèque.

3 b ✎ extra! Écris six phrases. Invente!

Exemple: Il va à la bibliothèque parce qu'il aime louer des vidéos.

Miam! J'adore ça!	**Yum! I love that!**
tu aimes...?	*do you like...?*
le fromage	*cheese*
l'ail *m*	*garlic*
le poisson	*fish*
la viande	*meat*
la ratatouille	*ratatouille*
la cuisine indienne	*Indian food*
les plats épicés *mpl*	*spicy dishes*
les oignons crus *mpl*	*raw onions*
les œufs brouillés *mpl*	*scrambled eggs*
miam-miam!	*yum-yum!*
berk!	*yuck!*
j'adore ça	*I love it/them*
j'aime ça	*I like it/them*
je n'aime pas ça	*I don't like it/them*
je déteste ça	*I hate it/them*
je ne sais pas	*I don't know*
je n'ai jamais goûté ça	*I've never tasted it/them*

Un paquet de chewing-gums	**A packet of chewing gum**
cent grammes de pâté	*100g of pâté*
un kilo de pommes	*1 kg of apples*
un kilo d'oranges	*1 kg of oranges*
un paquet de chips	*a packet of crisps*
un paquet de chewing-gums	*a packet of chewing gum*
un litre de lait	*1 litre of milk*
une bouteille d'eau minérale	*a bottle of mineral water*

une boîte de tomates	*a tin of tomatoes*
un euro	*1 euro*
20 centimes	*20 cents*

On fait des courses	**Going shopping**
bonjour, madame	*hello (to woman)*
bonjour, monsieur	*hello (to man)*
s'il vous plaît	*please*
voilà	*here you are*
et avec ça?	*anything else with that?*
c'est tout?	*is that everything?*
c'est combien?	*how much is that?*
merci	*thank you*
au revoir	*goodbye*
lave	*wash*
pèle	*peel*
coupe en morceaux	*cut*
mets les fruits dans un bol	*put the fruit into a bowl*
ajoute	*add*

Une page de casse-têtes	**A page of brain-teasers**
ça correspond à…	*that corresponds to…*
c'est un thème différent	*it's a different topic*
c'est masculin/féminin	*it's masculine/feminine*
ça ne commence pas par "c"	*it doesn't start with a 'c'*
il y a deux/trois mots	*there are two/three words*

Grammaire:

- Regular -*er* verbs:

je détest**e**	nous détest**ons**
tu détest**es**	vous détest**ez**
il/elle détest**e**	ils/elles détest**ent**

- Quantity + *de* (or *d'* if followed by a vowel sound): *un litre **de** lait*

- Instructions: *lave, pèle, joue, écris*, etc.

Cross-topic words

jamais – *never*
avec – *with*

Stratégies!

★ pronunciation: *-ille* (a 'y' sound!)

★ recycling words you've learnt before

★ giving a short presentation

★ using the right words (*un/une* or *le/la*) with words you've looked up in the dictionary

4 À Bruxelles

4A En ville

- ask if a place is nearby
- give directions
- the four aspects of learning nouns

1 ♻ Stratégies! MSSG

Remember the four aspects of learning nouns?

Ⓜ = meaning

Ⓢ = sound

Ⓢ = spelling

Ⓖ = gender

Get the MⓔSⓢaⓖⓔ?

Il y a un arrêt de bus près d'ici? means 'Is there a bus stop near here?' **Ⓜ**

- Can you work out what the other questions mean? Write them in both French and English.

1 Pardon, monsieur. Il y a un arrêt de bus près d'ici?

2 Pardon, madame. Il y a une pharmacie près d'ici?

3 Pardon, monsieur. Il y a une banque près d'ici?

4 Pardon, madame. Il y a une poste près d'ici?

5 Pardon. Il y a des toilettes publiques près d'ici?

2 💿 Ⓢ Écoute et répète les questions (1–5).
Imite la prononciation française!

3 ♻ Stratégies! Ⓢpelling and Ⓖender of nouns

- Can you remember the spelling and gender of words from *Voilà 1*? Make a class list of as many place words as you can!

Example: *(un? une?) piscine, ...*

**2 points par mot:
s = 1 point, G = 1 point
La classe arrive à 20 points?**

🗣 **Prononciation**
pardon: il y a un son nasal
arrêt: ne prononce pas la consonne finale!

4 a 💿 Écoute et lis.

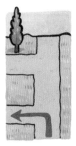
Prenez la première rue à gauche.

Prenez la deuxième rue à droite.

Prenez la troisième rue à gauche.

Allez tout droit.

4 b 💿 Écoute (1–6) et note la bonne lettre.

Exemple: **1 F**

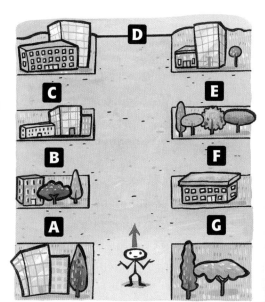

Grammaire: les nombres ordinaux

2nd = 2ème deuxième   Exception:

3rd = 3ème troisième   1st = 1er premier *m*

4th = 4ème quatrième   1ère première *f*

5th = 5ème cinquième   ⟶ la **première** rue

5 🖊 **Tu comprends le système?**

a 6th = ?   c 20th = ?

b 10th = ?   d 100th = ?

6 a 💿 **Écoute et lis.**

A Pardon, monsieur. Il y a une banque près d'ici?

B Je n'ai pas compris. Pouvez-vous répéter?

A Il y a une banque près d'ici?

B Une pharmacie?

A Non, une banque!

B Ah, une banque!

A Oui, il y a une banque près d'ici?

B Oui. Prenez la deuxième rue à gauche et puis
   la première rue à droite, allez tout droit, et puis…

A Pardon, pouvez-vous répéter? Je n'ai pas compris!

6 b 💬 **Joue et adapte le dialogue.**

prendre *v to take*

(vous) prenez
verbe irrégulier ▶▶ p. 143

7 a 🖊 **Écris quatre dialogues. Ton modèle: l'exercice 6a.**

  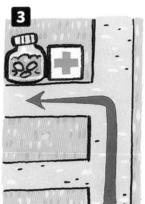 

7 b 🖊 **extra! Écris deux dialogues similaires.**

● Choisis deux autres destinations.

   Exemple: *the butcher's*

● Cherche les mots dans le dictionnaire.
   Attention: *m* ou *f*?

   butcher's (shop) boucherie f

   f ➤ **une** boucherie

8 💿 **Écoute des infos sur la poste de Bruxelles.
Note des détails en anglais.**

pardon, monsieur / madame			
il y a	une poste une banque une pharmacie un arrêt de bus des toilettes publiques		près d'ici?
prenez	la première la deuxième la troisième	rue	à droite à gauche
allez tout droit, et puis…			
je n'ai pas compris. pouvez-vous répéter?			

4B Bruxelles

- ask the way to known places
- use *un/une*, *le/la* correctly
- pronunciation of *th*

1

C'est sur la Grand-Place.

Pardon, madame. C'est où, **l'hôtel de ville**?

2

la cathédrale
(sur la place Sainte-Gudule)

3

le parc Mini-Europe
(à Bruparck)

4

le musée de la BD
(dans la rue des Sables)

5

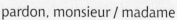

le théâtre de la Monnaie
(dans la rue Léopold)

1 a 💿 Écoute (1–8). C'est où? Vrai ou faux?

Exemple: **1 faux**

1 b 💬 Joue huit petits dialogues.

Exemple: **A** Pardon, c'est où, l'hôtel de ville?
B C'est dans la Grand-Place.

2 a 🗣💬 **Prononciation:** *th*

- En français, la prononciation *th* = *t*.
- **Prononce:** la cathédrale, le thé, le théâtre, la bibliothèque, Catherine, Mathieu.

2 b 💿 Écoute et vérifie.

3 a 💿 Écoute (1–4) et note la destination + la lettre de la réponse finale (A–D).

Exemple: **1 le théâtre + C**

3 b 💬 Joue quatre dialogues. Ton modèle: les dialogues à droite.

3 c ✏ Écris deux dialogues.

pardon, monsieur / madame		
c'est où,	le musée / le théâtre / le parc la cathédrale / la gare / la piscine l'hôtel de ville?	
c'est loin?	oui, non,	c'est	dans la rue... sur la place...

Pardon, monsieur/madame. C'est où, le/la/l'... ?

C'est dans...

C'est loin?

Non.

A Prenez la troisième rue à gauche.

D Prenez la deuxième rue à droite.

B Allez tout droit.

C Prenez la première rue à droite.

6 la piscine Océade
(à Bruparck)

7 la gare
du Midi
(dans la rue
de France)

8 l'Atomium
(près de Bruparck)

4 a ✎ Écris des phrases.

Exemple: *une* banque ⟶ C'est où, *la* banque?

1 une poste   **3** une pharmacie
2 un arrêt de bus   **4** un café

♻ Grammaire: *les articles*

	the	a
masc. sing.	le / l'	un
fém. sing.	?	?
masc. & fém. pl.	les	des (some)

4 b ✎ Écris encore des phrases.

Exemple: *le* palais ⟶ Il y a *un* palais
                        près d'ici?

1 le théâtre   **3** le musée
2 la gare   **4** la piscine

5 a 📖 Lis le texte. Trouve...

1 deux langues
2 quatre choses à manger
3 la date de l'Ommegang
4 deux instruments de musique
5 une nationalité
6 dix adjectifs

5 b 📖 extra! *Give evidence for the following statements from the text:*

Example: **1** *Unofficial capital of the European Union, ...*

1 Bruxelles est internationale.
2 On mange bien.
3 Les fêtes sont spectaculaires.

Bruxelles

Rome est plus ancienne, Paris est plus grande... Eh bien, quoi? Bruxelles, capitale internationale, est jeune, dynamique, cosmopolitaine.

À Bruxelles, capitale non-officielle de l'Union européenne, on parle français, on parle flamand... et beaucoup d'autres langues aussi! 30% des habitants de Bruxelles sont des étrangers ou d'origine étrangère!

On mange bien. Dans les petites rues près de la Grand-Place, il y a beaucoup de restaurants. Moules et frites? Gaufres de Bruxelles? Miam-miam!

Les fêtes sont spectaculaires! Le premier jeudi du mois de juillet, c'est la fête de l'Ommegang: une procession folklorique de 600 personnes en costumes de 1594!

Tu aimes les BD? Il y a *deux* musées de la BD! Tu aimes la musique? Le musée des Instruments de Musique a 1500 instruments, du violon au saxophone (inventé par un Belge, Adolphe Saxe!).

Fatigué? Relaxe-toi dans un des cafés de la Grand-Place – et puis achète une petite boîte de chocolats belges. Irrésistibles!

l'étranger *m* – foreigner   la fête – *festival*
les moules *fpl* – *mussels*   la BD – *cartoon strip*
la gaufre – *waffle*

4C Mini-Europe

- say where places are
- use your general knowledge

1  Écoute et lis. Choisis la bonne option: a ou b.

1 Bruparck **a** est **b** n'est pas dans le centre de Bruxelles.

2 Marine **a** aime **b** n'aime pas Mini-Europe.

3 Les trains à Mini-Europe sont **a** mobiles **b** immobiles.

4 Marine a mangé **a** à 12h **b** à 13h.

5 Le Kinépolis, c'est **a** un musée **b** un cinéma.

6 Les toboggans plus faciles **a** sont bleus **b** sont jaunes.

2 Stratégies!
Applying your general knowledge

- Regarde la carte de Mini-Europe à la page 39. C'est quoi en anglais, A–L?

  Exemple: A – *Brussels town hall*

3 a 📖 Regarde le plan de Mini-Europe à la page 39. C'est vrai (V) ou faux (F)?

1 Le palais de Westminster est près de la Place Saint-Marc à Venise.

2 Le château de Douvres est en face de la tour Eiffel.

3 La côte de l'Algarve au Portugal est près des canaux d'Amsterdam.

4 L'Acropole d'Athènes est près de l'arène de Séville, en Espagne.

5 La tour de Pise est en face du Vésuve.

6 L'hôtel de ville de Bruxelles est près de l'arc de Triomphe à Paris.

3 b ✏️ extra! Corrige les phrases fausses!

Cher Ali,

Ça va? Moi, ça va bien. Hier, j'ai visité Bruparck, près de l'Atomium, à l'ouest de Bruxelles.

D'abord, on a visité Mini-Europe. C'est génial! Il y a quinze pays, avec des bâtiments en format réduit (1/25ème). C'est amusant: Big Ben est en face de la tour Eiffel, et la tour de Pise est près du centre de Paris! Les trains, les autos, tout est en mouvement!

À midi, on a mangé dans "le Village". Il y a des rues avec des cafés et des restaurants. En face des cafés, il y a un grand carrousel – c'est amusant!

Le Kinépolis est près du "Village". J'ai regardé un film sur les planètes, dans la salle IMAX. Les images sont énormes: hautes de sept étages!!

Après le film, la piscine Océade! Il y a dix toboggans. Les toboggans bleus sont pour toute la famille. Les toboggans jaunes s'appellent Kamikaze et Niagara: on descend 80 mètres en sept secondes!!

A+

Marine

le bâtiment – *building*
l'étage m – *floor, storey*

Grammaire: *près/en face du, de la, etc.*

masc. sing.	fém. sing.	masc. & fém. pl.
en face **du** en face **de l'** + vowel sound	en face **de la**	en face **des**

le musée ⟶ près **du** musée
la tour ⟶ en face **de la** tour
l'hotel ⟶ en face **de l'**hôtel
les cafés ⟶ près **des** cafés

Remember?
La capitale **du** Danemark
de la France

◄◄ p.10

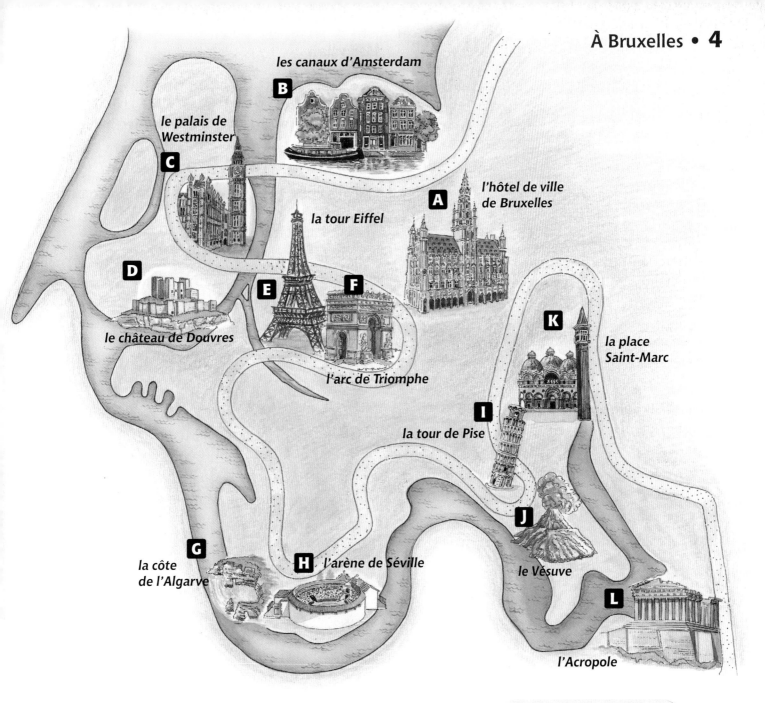

les canaux d'Amsterdam **B**

le palais de Westminster **C**

A l'hôtel de ville de Bruxelles

la tour Eiffel

D

le château de Douvres

E

F

l'arc de Triomphe

K la place Saint-Marc

I

la tour de Pise

J

le Vésuve

G

la côte de l'Algarve

H l'arène de Séville

L

l'Acropole

4 💿 **Écoute (1–6). On se retrouve où?**

extra! Et à quelle heure?

Exemple: **1** en face du cinéma (**extra!** 10h30)

5 a 💬 **Pose des questions à ton/ta partenaire.**

Exemple: **A** C'est où, la tour Eiffel?
    B C'est près/en face d...

5 b ✏️ **Écris trois dialogues.**
Ton modèle: l'exercice 5a.

6 ✏️ **extra!** Décris la visite d'un parc
d'attractions. Ton modèle: la lettre de Marine.

> C'est où, le / la / l'… ?
> C'est près de / en face de…

♻️ **Stratégies!** *du, de la or des?*

Think one step at a time:

1 Is the place singular or plural?

| singular | plural | → | *des* |

2 Is the place masculine or feminine?

| masc. | → | *du** | fem. | → | *de la** |

* If it starts with a vowel sound, use *de l'*.

4D Ta ville/Ton village

- describe your town or village
- recycle the MSSG message for nouns

Une école

Mon village

J'habite à Beersel. C'est un assez grand village près de Bruxelles. Les touristes aiment le château du Moyen Âge. Il y a un grand parking pour les touristes en face du château.

Beersel, c'est bien mais c'est assez barbant le soir. Il y a beaucoup de magasins, et il y a aussi un petit supermarché près de l'église.
Il y a une église et une poste, mais il n'y a pas de gare.
Il y a une école primaire, mais il n'y a pas de collège.
Il n'y a pas grand-chose pour les jeunes. Il y a un centre sportif près de Beersel, mais c'est nul. Il n'y a pas de patinoire.

Louis

1 a 🔴 Écoute et lis le texte.

1 b ♻️ Stratégies! 🅜🅢🅢🅖 (◀◀ p. 34)
- With a partner, find the words for 11 places in a town.
- Decide on their meaning and sound.
- Then write them down with the correct gender.

Example: *le château (m) – castle*

1 c 📖 Trouve et recopie deux opinions.

1 d ✏️ Adapte **les deux phrases du texte pour ta ville/ton village.**
1   Il y a beaucoup de magasins, et il y a aussi un petit supermarché près de l'église.
2   Il y a une école, mais il n'y a pas de collège.

2 🔴 Écoute Julien et Virginie. Il y a quoi:
1 à Genappe?   2 à Nivelles?

Exemple: **1** une école, ...

Stratégies! *Une présentation de ta ville/ton village*
- Relis les suggestions à la page 29.

3 a ✏️ Écris 8–10 phrases.

3 b 💬 Prépare et donne ta présentation.

Une église

Un château – le château de Beersel

♻️ **Grammaire:** *il y a/il n'y a pas de*
il y a	there is, there are	*il y a **une** gare*
il n'y a pas de = ??		*il n'y a pas **de** gare* (you don't say *une*!)

j'habite à…	
c'est un village / une ville près de…	
c'est	nul / assez bien / barbant
il n'y a pas grand-chose pour les jeunes	
il y a et il y a aussi	un supermarché / un château une église / une école beaucoup de magasins
il n'y a pas de	collège / piscine

En ville	**In town**
pardon, monsieur	*excuse me* (to man)
pardon, madame	*excuse me* (to woman)
il y a une poste près d'ici?	*is there a post office near here?*
une banque	*a bank*
une pharmacie	*a chemist's*
un arrêt de bus	*a bus stop*
des toilettes publiques	*public toilets*
prenez...	*take...*
la première rue à droite	*the first road on the right*
la deuxième rue à gauche	*the second road on the left*
la troisième rue	*the third road*
allez tout droit	*go straight on*
et puis...	*and then...*
je n'ai pas compris	*I didn't understand*
pouvez-vous répéter?	*can you repeat that?*

Bruxelles	**Brussels**
c'est où, ...	*where's...*
le musée?	*the museum?*
le théâtre?	*the theatre?*
le parc?	*the park?*
l'hôtel de ville?	*the town hall?*
la cathédrale?	*the cathedral?*
la gare?	*the station?*
la piscine?	*the swimming pool?*
c'est loin?	*is it far?*
c'est dans la rue X	*it's in X Street*
c'est sur la place X	*it's in X Square*

Mini-Europe	**Mini-Europe**
près de	*near*
en face de	*opposite*

Ta ville/Ton village	**Your town/village**
j'habite à...	*I live in...*
c'est un village/une ville	*it's a village/a town*
près de Bruxelles	*near Brussels*
c'est...	*it's...*
nul/barbant	*rubbish/boring*
assez bien	*quite good*
il n'y a pas grand-chose pour les jeunes	*there isn't much for young people*
il y a...	*there is...*
un supermarché	*a supermarket*
un château	*a castle*
une église	*a church*
beaucoup de magasins	*lots of shops*
il y a aussi une école	*there's also a school*
mais il n'y a pas de collège	*but there isn't a (secondary) school*

Grammaire:

● a, the, some

masc. sing.	**un** a	**le, l'** the
fém. sing.	**une** a	**la, l'** the
masc. & fém. pl.	**des** some	**les** the

● near, opposite

masc. sing.	*près, en face du / de l'*
fém. sing.	*près, en face de la / de l'*
masc. & fém. pl.	*près, en face des*

● *il y a un château* there is a castle   *il n'y a pas **de** château* there isn't a castle

Stratégies!

★ learning nouns: **m**eaning, **s**ound, **s**pelling, **g**ender

★ pronouncing *th* in French: *théâtre, cathédrale*, etc.

★ thinking one step at a time to work out *du, de la, des*, etc.

★ preparing, practising and giving a presentation

Cross-topic words

près – near   **loin** – far

Unité 3 (Des problèmes? Consulte la page 33.)

1 a Écoute (1–5). Note les bonnes lettres (A–E).
Le prix est correct: oui ou non?

Exemple: **1 C – oui**

1 b Joue les cinq dialogues (A–E).

Exemple: **(A)** – Bonjour, madame. Cent grammes
de pâté, s'il vous plaît.
– Voilà. Et avec ça?
– C'est tout. C'est combien?
– Un euro dix.
– Merci, madame. Au revoir.

2 a Lis le texte. Vrai ou faux?

Exemple: **1 vrai**

1 Les parents de Marion aiment la viande.
2 Marion aime la cuisine indienne.
3 Marion déteste les fruits.
4 Élodie est végétarienne.
5 Marion adore le fromage.
6 Élodie et Marion aiment les chips.

> Moi, je déteste la viande, mais papa aime la viande, et maman aussi. Et je n'aime pas les plats épicés, comme la cuisine indienne par exemple. Mais j'aime bien les pommes, les oranges, les bananes. Ma sœur Élodie aime beaucoup le jambon et le fromage. Personnellement, je déteste ça. Mais ma sœur et moi, nous aimons les chips et les biscuits.
>
> **Marion**

2 b Écris 4 – 6 phrases comme Marion.

Idées:
j'aime…
mon frère déteste…
mes parents adorent…
mon copain n'aime pas…

Stratégies! *Revising a verb pattern*

- Say the verb out loud: *je joue, tu joues, il joue,* etc.
- Write the whole verb. Underline letters that aren't pronounced: *je jou<u>e</u>, tu jou<u>es</u>,* etc.

Unité 4 (Des problèmes? Consulte la page 41.)

3 Écris huit phrases correctes.

Exemple: **1 Allez tout droit.**

Allez…	près d'ici?
Prenez…	répéter?
C'est…	loin?
C'est où, …	compris.
Pouvez-vous…	tout droit.
Je n'ai pas…	monsieur.
Pardon,…	la cathédrale?
Il y a une poste…	la première rue à droite.

4 a Écris cinq questions (A–E).

Exemple: **A Il y a une pharmacie près d'ici?**

4 b Écris cinq phrases avec *en face du/de la,* etc.

Exemple: **A La pharmacie est en face de la gare.**

La Belgique

A. Une nation... trois langues officielles

En Belgique, on parle français dans le sud, et on parle flamand dans le nord. Bruxelles, au centre, est une ville bilingue.

Une petite minorité belge parle allemand dans l'est du pays, près de la frontière allemande.

> **8** ◄ Dottignies Dottenijs

Le flamand est un dialecte néerlandais.

one	een	ein
two	twee	zwei
three	drie	drei
four	vier	vier
five	vijf	fünf
six	zes	sechs
seven	seven	sieben
eight	acht	acht
nine	negen	neun
ten	tien	zehn

- La Belgique et les Pays-Bas sont entre l'Allemagne et l'Angleterre. Le néerlandais est entre l'allemand et l'anglais.

B. Deux spécialités belges

Les **chocolats** belges sont célèbres et délicieux. Le secret de la haute qualité: ils sont faits avec du beurre de cacao pur.

Les Belges aiment beaucoup le chocolat: il y a beaucoup de "chocolateries" dans chaque ville belge!

La Belgique produit beaucoup de **bières** blondes et brunes différentes (une bière blonde s'appelle "*lager*" en anglais). "Stella Artois" est une bière belge.

C. L'histoire de la Belgique

L'histoire de la Belgique, c'est une histoire d'occupations par d'autres nations européennes.

L'indépendance de la Belgique: 1830.

les Espagnols	**1493–1713**
les Autrichiens	**1713–1794**
les Français	**1794–1815**
les Hollandais	**1815–1830**
les Allemands	**1914–1918 1940–1945**

1 a C'est quel paragraphe: A, B ou C?

Exemple: **1 C**

1 L'armée française entre en Belgique.
2 Il y a des Belges qui parlent allemand.
3 Achète ça quand tu es en Belgique!
4 De un à dix en trois langues.
5 La Belgique et les occupations militaires.
6 L'ingrédient spécial: le beurre de cacao.

1 b Donne ton opinion. Quel paragraphe est le plus intéressant, A, B ou C?

2 Les occupations militaires. Qui était en Belgique en...

1 1820?   3 1800?   5 1916?
2 1560?   4 1750?

Exemple: **1 les Hollandais**

5 Les copains et les stars

5A Les copains d'Ali

- describe friends
- use masculine and feminine adjectives
- raise the level of your French

> J'ai une amie qui s'appelle Pauline. Elle est sympa: bavarde et très amusante. Elle est grande et assez sportive. Elle aime beaucoup les animaux, et les ordinateurs aussi.

> J'ai aussi un ami qui s'appelle Ibrahim. Il est petit et très amusant. Il aime le collège (mais il n'aime pas le prof de maths!). Il aime beaucoup les voitures.

1 a 🔘 Écoute et lis.
Regarde les images (1–6).
C'est qui?

Exemple:
1 Ibrahim et Pauline

> Et j'ai un ami qui s'appelle Thomas. Il aime beaucoup les voitures, la musique et la politique. Il est très sportif et très intelligent, mais il n'aime pas beaucoup le collège.

1 b 📖 Dans les textes, trouve et recopie sept adjectifs en français et en anglais.

Exemple: **bavarde – *chatty***

1 c 📖 Trouve les équivalents dans les textes:

Exemple: **1 un copain = un ami**

1 un copain	3 une copine	5 les chiens, les chats, etc.
2 les autos	4 elle parle beaucoup	

1 d 💬 Vérifie tes réponses aux exercices 1b et 1c avec ton/ta partenaire.

> ♻️ **Grammaire:** *les adjectifs au masculin et au féminin (1)*
>
> | | masculin | féminin |
> |---|---|---|
> | The basic rule is: if an adjective is feminine, add an -e: | *il est petit* | *elle est petit**e*** |
> | Explain to your teacher why these two are exceptions: | *il est sportif* | *elle est sportive* |
> | | *il est sympa* | *elle est sympa* |

2 a 🖉 Recopie et complète les phrases. Vérifie avec ton/ta partenaire.

Exemple: **1 Caroline est amusante, et elle aime la politique.**

1 Caroline est (*amusant*), et elle aime la politique.
2 Paul est (*grand*), et il aime la musique.
3 Sarah est (*sportif*), et elle aime le basket.
4 Charlotte est (*intelligent*), mais elle n'aime pas le collège.
5 David est (*sympa*), et il aime les animaux.
6 Lucie est (*bavard*). Elle n'aime pas les ordinateurs.

2 b Stratégies! *Raise the level of your French*

Make your language more precise by using words like *très* (very), *assez* (quite) and *beaucoup* (very much). Practise by inserting these words into sentences 1–6, for example:

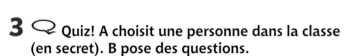

très   beaucoup
Caroline est⁄amusante, et elle aime⁄la politique.

Max est très sportif

3 🗩 Quiz! A choisit une personne dans la classe (en secret). B pose des questions.

Exemple: **A C'est un garçon ou une fille?**
    B Une fille.
    A Elle est petite?
    B Assez petite.
    A Elle aime les voitures?
    B Je ne sais pas.
    A Elle aime Man Utd?
    B Oui.
    A Elle est amusante?
    B Oui, très amusante.
    A C'est Amy!

j'ai un ami / une amie qui s'appelle...		
il / elle est	très assez	grand(e) amusant(e) intelligent(e) petit(e) bavard(e)
		sympa sportif (sportive)
il / elle aime il / elle n'aime pas	beaucoup	les animaux les ordinateurs les voitures le collège la politique la musique

4 💿 Écoute cinq descriptions. Note trois détails pour chaque personne.

Exemple: **1 très sportive; aime beaucoup la musique; anniversaire le 3 mai**

5 🖉 Décris trois ami(e)s. Ton modèle: les descriptions des amis d'Ali (exercice 1).

extra! Ajoute d'autres détails.

Exemple: **Il adore la cuisine indienne.**

▶ Stratégies! *Linking sentences*

Make your language more fluent by linking sentences where possible, for example:

*Elle est sympa **et** très amusante.*

*Elle aime beaucoup les animaux **mais** elle n'aime pas...*

5B Ma star préférée

- talk about your favourite star
- use more masculine and feminine adjectives
- learn ways of remembering words

Ma star préférée, c'est...

A Il est acteur.

B Elle est actrice.

C Il est chanteur.

D Elle est chanteuse.

E Il est footballeur.

1 🔘 Écoute (1–5) et note la bonne lettre (A–E).

il est chanteur – *he is a singer*
(You don't use the word 'a' in French.)

2 a Stratégies! *Some ways of remembering words*

Here are some words you might use to describe your favourite stars and some tips for remembering them.

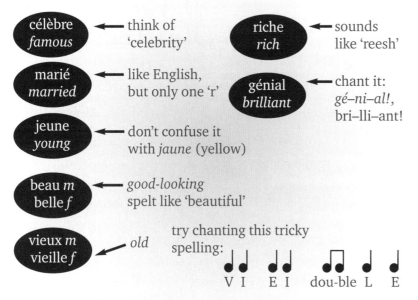

célèbre *famous* ← think of 'celebrity'

riche *rich* ← sounds like 'reesh'

marié *married* ← like English, but only one 'r'

génial *brilliant* ← chant it: *gé–ni–al!*, *bri–lli–ant!*

jeune *young* ← don't confuse it with *jaune* (yellow)

beau *m* **belle** *f* ← *good-looking* spelt like 'beautiful'

vieux *m* **vieille** *f* ← *old* try chanting this tricky spelling:
♪♪ ♪♪ ♪♪ ♪ ♪
V I E I dou-ble L E

Examples: *Elle est belle et célèbre.*
Il est beau, riche et marié.

2 b 🔘 Écoute le quiz. Réponds aux questions avec le bon adjectif.

Exemple: **1** jeune

3 ♻ 💬 Avec un/une partenaire, tu peux écrire combien d'adjectifs? 10? 15? 20? Plus?!

Exemples: génial, rouge, barbant, irlandais, bavard, ...

Ma star préférée, c'est Virginie Ledoyen. C'est une star du cinéma français.

4 a ✏ Écris six phrases.

Exemple: **1 Julie est belle.**

1 Julie *(good-looking)*
2 Kévin *(famous)*
3 Alice *(young)*
4 Mme Lefèvre *(very old)*
5 M. Guy *(rich)*
6 Marc *(good-looking)*

▶

4 b ✏ *extra!* Invente six phrases au féminin avec des adjectifs de l'exercice 3.

Exemple: J'ai une amie irlandaise.

♻ Grammaire: *les adjectifs au masculin et au féminin (2)*

Do you remember the key rule about masculine and feminine adjectives?

But note:

● no second e if the masculine adjective ends in -e:
il est jeune, elle est jeune.
(but: *marié* ➝ *elle est marié**e***)

● *(masc.)* -eux ➝ *(fém.)* -euse: *elle est ennuy**euse**.*

● two irregular adjectives: *il est vieux, elle est vieille;*
il est beau, elle est belle

---

5 a 📖 Lis les descriptions et identifie les stars.

Star A

Ma star préférée, c'est ⭐. Elle est américaine. Elle est très célèbre et très, très riche aussi. Elle est chanteuse et actrice, et elle a beaucoup de talent. Je la trouve belle. Elle est géniale!

Star B

Ma star préférée, c'est ⭐. Il est écossais et assez vieux – il est né en 1930. Il est acteur et il a joué le rôle de James Bond. Je le trouve génial!

Star C

⭐ est ma star préférée. Il est acteur. Il est anglais. Je le trouve beau. Très jeune, il a joué le rôle principal dans des films très populaires!

Kylie Minogue
Robbie Williams
Kate Winslet
Daniel Radcliffe
Madonna
Sean Connery
Brad Pitt

je le trouve beau – *I think he's good-looking*
je la trouve belle – *I think she's good-looking*

5 b ✏ Regarde le texte A et recopie les mots qui changent pour une star masculine.

Exemple: elle ➝ il; américaine ➝ américain

6 💿 Identités mystères! Écoute et prends des notes. Identifie les quatre personnages historiques ou de fiction.

Exemple: **1 anglaise, belle, ...**

7 💬 Donne une présentation: "Ma star préférée".

● Consulte les idées de la page 29.
● Écris 8–10 phrases: adapte les phrases de l'exercice 5a.

Exemples: ~~elle est américaine~~ ➝ **il est américain**

● Donne ta présentation.

Exemple:

> Ma star préférée, c'est Robbie Williams. Il est riche et jeune, et il est très, très beau. Son anniversaire, c'est le 13 février. Il est chanteur. Mon album préféré, c'est...

ma star préférée, c'est...	
il est	acteur / chanteur / footballeur
elle est	actrice / chanteuse
il / elle est	jeune / riche / célèbre / marié(e) génial(e) / américain(e) / anglais(e) écossais(e) beau / belle, vieux / vieille

- say where you went
- use *au/à la/aux* to mean 'to the'
- apply a grammar rule one step at a time

Lino Lenoir est chanteur.
C'est une star célèbre.

1 a 🔘 Écoute et lis. Lino aime les paparazzi?

Lundi dernier, je suis allé aux studios.

J'ai travaillé jusqu'à une heure.

Les paparazzi étaient là!

Je suis allé au restaurant où j'ai mangé avec mon agent. J'ai mangé un gros steak et lui, il a mangé du poisson. Il est très bavard. Les paparazzi étaient là!

Après ça, je suis allé à l'hôpital et j'ai parlé avec des enfants malades. Les paparazzi étaient là.

Puis, je suis allé à l'hôtel Magnifique et j'ai donné une interview à la journaliste d'un magazine de musique. (Ses questions étaient stupides!) Les paparazzi étaient là aussi.

puis – *then*   après ça – *after that*

Après ça, je suis allé à la poste... et les paparazzi étaient là! Oh là là!

1 b 🔘 Écoute. Il y a une différence? Lève la main.

1 c 💬 Lis le texte: A une phrase, B une phrase. Attention à la prononciation!

C'est ridicule!
Je déteste les paparazzi!

Grammaire: *je suis allé(e)...*

- Most past tense verbs use *j'ai*: *j'ai mangé.*
- 'I went' is an exception: *je **suis** allé.*
- Unlike verbs that take *j'ai*, you add an -e for female: (male) *je suis allé*
  (female) *je suis allée*

→ *Je suis allée à l'hôpital* I went to the hospital *(girl or woman speaking)*

... au / à la / à l' / aux

au	= 'to the' + masculine noun	*au* café
à la	= 'to the' + feminine noun	*à la* gare
aux	= 'to the' + plural noun (masculine or feminine)	*aux* studios

Exception! If a singular noun (*m* or *f*) begins with a vowel sound, use *à l'*: *à l'*hôtel

2 🖊 Écris des phrases (1–8).

Exemple: **1 Je suis allé à la poste.**

Félix
Je suis allé...

poste *f*   café *m*   studios *mpl*   hôpital *m*

Anne
Je suis allée...

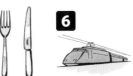

restaurant *m*   gare *f*   hôtel *m*   toilettes *fpl*

Stratégies! *au, à la or aux?*

As with *du/de la/des* (◀◀ p. 10), think one step at a time:

1 Is the place singular or plural?
singular   plural → *aux*

2 Is the place masculine or feminine?
masc. → *au**   fem. → *à la**

* if it starts with a vowel sound, use *à l'*.

je suis allé(e)	au restaurant
	à la poste
	à l'hôpital
	à l'hôtel
	aux studios

3 🖊 Tu trouves combien d'exemples? Fais deux listes avec ton/ta partenaire.

au Je suis allé(e)... au magasin au collège, etc.

à la Je suis allé(e)... à la campagne à la mer, etc.

4 💬 Tu es un/une collègue de la star, Lino Lenoir. Pose des questions à Lino (partenaire B).

Exemple: **A Lundi matin, tu es allé à la poste?**
B Non, lundi matin, je suis allé aux studios.

1 Lundi matin, tu es allé à la poste?
2 Tu as travaillé jusqu'à cinq heures?
3 Et puis, tu es allé où?
4 Les paparazzi étaient là? etc.

5 💿 **extra!** Écoute (1–4): c'est quelle profession?

acteur   employé dans un supermarché

footballeur   professeur   chanteur   médecin

5D Tu es une star!

- talk about a day in the past
- use the past tense
- understand a factual text

Lundi dernier, je suis allée aux studios. J'ai travaillé jusqu'à une heure et demie. Après ça, j'ai envoyé des textos, puis je suis allée au restaurant. J'ai mangé du poisson. L'après-midi, j'ai retrouvé des amies en ville.

1 a 📖 Lis le texte et recopie deux phrases avec *je suis -ée* et quatre phrases avec *j'ai -é*.

Exemple: **1** Je suis allée aux studios.

1 b 💿 Écoute et note cinq autres détails.

2 ♻️ 💬 Avec ton/ta partenaire, invente trois phrases pour chaque verbe.

Exemple: J'ai mangé avec ma sœur/au café...

> j'ai mangé ● j'ai travaillé ● j'ai retrouvé

3 a ✏️ Imagine: tu es une star! Décris mardi dernier. Adapte les phrases de la page 48.

3 b 💬 **extra!** A lit sa description à B. B interrompt:

> Et puis?   Et après ça?   Oh là là!

Stratégies! *Adapting model sentences*

~~Lundi~~ dernier, je suis ~~allé aux studios~~.
Mardi dernier, je suis allée au théâtre.
Puis, je suis ~~allé au restaurant~~.
Puis, je suis allée à la gare.

puis après ça	je suis allé(e) au / à la / à l' / aux...
	j'ai mangé... / j'ai retrouvé...
	j'ai travaillé jusqu'à...

4 a 📖 *Can you guess what the article is about from the title, the picture and from glancing at the text?*

4 b 📖 *Explain in English what these figures refer to in the text.*

a	20€	**c**	4,80€	**e**	4,10€
b	7,20€	**d**	3,90€	**f**	0,50€–1,30€

Les profits d'un CD

Si tu achètes un CD à 20€, voici comment se répartit cette somme:

- 💿 **7,20€** pour le producteur de l'album
- 💿 **4,80€** pour le distributeur qui se charge de la promotion
- 💿 **3,90€** pour le magasin où tu l'achètes
- 💿 **4,10€** de taxes pour l'État.
- 💿 Et l'artiste? C'est le producteur qui paie l'artiste: entre **0,50€** et **1,30€** par CD (ça dépend du contrat).

Les copains d'Ali — *Ali's friends*

j'ai un ami/une amie qui s'appelle...	*I've got a (male/female) friend called...*
il/elle est	*he/she is*
très	*very*
assez	*quite*
grand(e)	*tall*
petit(e)	*small*
amusant(e)	*funny*
bavard(e)	*chatty*
intelligent(e)	*clever*
sympa	*nice*
sportif *m* sportive *f*	*sporty*
il/elle aime (beaucoup)...	*he/she likes... (a lot)*
il/elle n'aime pas (beaucoup)...	*he/she doesn't like... (very much)*
les animaux	*animals*
les ordinateurs	*computers*
les voitures	*cars*
le collège	*school*
la politique	*politics*
la musique	*music*

Ma star préférée — *My favourite star*

ma star préférée, c'est...	*My favourite star is...*
il est...	*he's...*
acteur	*an actor*
chanteur	*a singer*
footballeur	*a footballer*
elle est...	*she's...*
actrice	*an actress*
chanteuse	*a singer*
il/elle est...	*he/she is...*
marié(e)	*married*
génial(e)	*brilliant*
américain(e)	*American*
jeune	*young*
riche	*rich*
célèbre	*famous*
vieux *m*, vieille *f*	*old*
beau *m*, belle *f*	*good-looking*

Les stars et les paparazzi — *Stars and the paparazzi*

je suis allé...	*I went... (male)*
je suis allée...	*I went... (female)*
au restaurant	*to the restaurant*
à la poste	*to the post office*
à l'hôpital	*to the hospital*
à l'hôtel	*to the hotel*
aux studios	*to the studios*

Tu es une star! — *You're a star!*

puis	*then*
après ça	*after that*
je suis allé(e) au/à la/à l'/aux...	*I went to...*
j'ai mangé	*I ate*
j'ai travaillé jusqu'à...	*I worked until...*
j'ai retrouvé	*I met*

Grammaire

- Masculine and feminine adjectives
  - Rule: if an adjective is feminine, add an -e.
  - Exception: if the adjective ends in -e, don't add another one.
  - Irregular adjectives: *sympa* (no -e), *sportif/sportive*, *vieux/vieille*, *beau/belle*
- I went to the...
  je suis allé (male)/*je suis allée* (female)
  au + masc. sing. (**à l'** before vowel sound)
  à la + fém. sing. (**à l'** before vowel sound)
  aux + pl.

Stratégies!

★ making your language more precise (*très*, *assez*, etc.)

★ linking sentences to make language more fluent

★ ways of remembering words

★ applying a grammar rule one step at a time

★ adapting model sentences

cross-topic words

puis – *then*
après ça – *after that*

6B En famille

- say what you do as a family
- use sentences with 'never' and 'nothing'
- adapt useful phrases from a text

Vous faites quoi en famille le week-end?

① Nous mangeons ensemble.
Véronique, Québec

② Nous regardons la télé le soir.
Nathalie, Guadeloupe

③ Le dimanche, nous sortons ensemble.
Catherine, Martinique

④ Nous allons au centre commercial.
Benjamin, Guyane

⑤ Nous discutons.
Karima, Belgique

⑥ Nous restons à la maison.
Martin, France

⑦ Nous ne mangeons jamais ensemble.
Antoine, Suisse

⑧ Nous ne discutons pas souvent.
Yann, Réunion

⑨ Nous n'allons jamais au centre commercial.
Fabienne, Congo

⑩ Nous ne faisons rien ensemble.
Étienne, Côte d'Ivoire

1 a 💿 Écoute et lis. C'est quoi en français?
Écris les expressions en anglais et en français.

1 together
2 we go out
3 nothing
4 we discuss
5 we stay
6 never

1 b 💿 Écoute. C'est qui?

Exemple: **1 Nathalie**

1 c 💿 Écoute. Note le détail ajouté.

Exemple: **1 à midi, ou le soir**

> **Grammaire:** *les phrases négatives: ne … rien/jamais*
>
> *ne … rien* = nothing   *nous **ne** faisons **rien***
>
> *ne … jamais* = never   *nous **ne** regardons **jamais** la télé*
>
> - *ne … rien* } go around the verb like *ne … pas.*
>   *ne … jamais*

2 ✏️ Écris les phrases 1–6 (Véronique, Nathalie, etc.) avec *ne … jamais.*

Exemple: **1 Nous ne mangeons jamais ensemble.**

3 a 💿 Écoute (1–5). Note les bonnes lettres (A–F).

Exemple: **1 D, A, B**

A

B

C

D

E

F

3 b 💬 Joue six petits dialogues (A–F).

Exemple: **(A) A Vous faites quoi en famille le week-end?**

B Nous regardons souvent la télé ensemble.

4 a 🖉 Trouve les possibilités pour chaque verbe (1–3).

Exemple: **1 Nous jouons au basket, aux jeux vidéo, …**

1 Nous jouons…
2 Nous allons…
3 Nous faisons…

… du vélo   … les devoirs   … au basket   … en ville   … de la danse   … aux jeux vidéo
… de la guitare   … au collège   … des excursions   … à la bibliothèque

4 b 🖉 extra! Écris d'autres possibilités pour chaque verbe.

Exemple: **1 Nous jouons au tennis, …**

4 c 🖉 Écris des phrases avec les six formes du verbe *faire*.

Exemple: **1 Vous faites parfois des excursions?**

> ♻ **Grammaire:** *le verbe faire*
>
> | je **fais** | nous **faisons** |
> | tu **fais** | vous **faites** |
> | il/elle **fait** | ils/elles **font** |

5 a 📖 Lis le texte. C'est la famille de qui?

Exemple: **1 la famille de Nadège**

1 Ils sortent en auto.
2 Les enfants invitent des copains.
3 Ils mangent en famille.
4 Ils parlent beaucoup le soir.
5 La famille aime le sport.
6 Les parents et les enfants ne sont pas ensemble le week-end.

vous faites quoi en famille le week-end?		
nous mangeons / sortons / discutons		ensemble
nous regardons nous allons nous restons	(parfois) (souvent)	la télé au centre commercial à la maison
nous ne faisons rien		nous n'allons jamais en ville

Vous faites quoi en famille le week-end?

Ça dépend. Parfois nous regardons le football à la télé, parfois nous allons au stade, s'il y a un bon match.
Farouk

C'est stupide: nous ne faisons rien en famille. Mes parents travaillent le week-end. Ma sœur et moi, nous faisons nos devoirs. Parfois nous invitons des amis.
Jordane

Le samedi, nous allons souvent chez mes grands-parents. Mais parfois, quand il fait beau, nous faisons des excursions en voiture.
Nadège

Normalement, le dimanche, nous allons à l'église, et puis nous déjeunons ensemble. Nous discutons beaucoup, par exemple le soir, quand nous jouons aux cartes.
Stéfan

5 b 💿 Écoute. Il y a une différence? Lève la main.

6 a 🖉 Écris ta réponse au magazine. (Tu peux inventer les détails!) Ton modèle: Farouk, Nadège, etc.

▶ **Stratégies!** *Taking and adapting phrases from a text*

You can adapt sentences to describe what your family does:

Nous allons ~~au stade~~ ➡ *Nous allons à la piscine.*

~~*Parfois*~~ *nous invitons…* ➡ *Souvent, nous…*

6 b extra! Fais une présentation: "Mon week-end". (◀◀ p. 29)

6C Le Cameroun et la Réunion

- learn about French-speaking countries
- choose the right word in the dictionary
- *on*, meaning 'they'

Le Cameroun

La Réunion

Le Cameroun est en Afrique, près de l'équateur. À midi, il fait très chaud et on ne travaille pas: on fait la sieste.

Au Cameroun, on cultive le riz, le cacao, le café, le coton, les bananes et le tabac.

On parle français, anglais – et 240 langues africaines! On roule à droite.

1 a 💿 **La classe de Marine étudie le Cameroun. Écoute Marine et lis.**

1 b Stratégies! *Choosing the right word in a dictionary*

If a word has two meanings, choose the one that makes sense in the sentence!

| **café** *m* 1 *café* 2 *coffee* |

- *On cultive le café.* = They grow ❓
- *Choisis l'option correcte pour le texte.*

1	**rouler** *v* 1 *to roll* 2 *to drive*
2	**langue** *nf* 1 *tongue* 2 *language*
3	**tabac** *nm* 1 *tobacco* 2 *tobacconist*

On cultive les cafés!

2 💿 **Écoute les phrases (1–8). C'est le Cameroun? Écris *oui* ou *non*.**

Exemple: **1 oui**

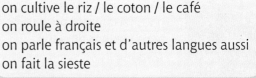

on cultive le riz / le coton / le café
on roule à droite
on parle français et d'autres langues aussi
on fait la sieste

3 a ✏️ **Écris une phrase pour chaque image (1–6).**

Exemple: **1 On cultive le riz.**

3 b 💬 **Vérifie avec ton/ta partenaire.**

4 🎧 **Écoute les informations (1–6) sur le Cameroun.**

Note la catégorie: agriculture (Ag), climat (Cl), langue (La), autre (Au).

Exemple: **1 Ag**

Grammaire: *on* (they)

On can mean 'they' (or 'people'):
on roule à droite they drive on the right

On can also mean 'we': *on regarde = nous regardons*
It takes the same part of the verb as *il/elle.*

---

5 ✏️ **Compare le Cameroun et la Grande-Bretagne.**

Exemple:

1 *Au Cameroun* **on cultive les bananes,** *mais en Grande-Bretagne* **on cultive les pommes.**

1 On cultive les bananes.

2 On roule à droite.

3 On parle français, anglais et des langues africaines.

4 On fait la sieste.

6 a 📖 **Lis l'article sur la Réunion et note les détails importants.** ▶

Exemple: **1 dans l'océan Indien, …**

1 la situation géographique

2 le climat

3 l'agriculture

4 les langues

6 b 📖 **extra! Lis le texte sur le cyclone. Décris…** ▶

1 le danger

2 les préparations

3 le résultat

7 💬 **Interviewe ton/ta partenaire.**

A On cultive quoi en Algérie?

B On cultive…

A On parle quelles langues?

B On…

A On roule à droite ou à gauche?

B On…

A Et quel temps-fait il?

B Il…

La Réunion

L'île de la Réunion est une petite île volcanique dans l'océan Indien, à 800 kilomètres de Madagascar.

Il fait chaud en été, du mois de novembre à avril. C'est la saison des cyclones. En hiver, de mai à octobre, il pleut dans l'est de l'île, mais il ne pleut pas dans l'ouest. On cultive la canne à sucre, le thé, le café, la vanille et les fleurs (géraniums).

Beaucoup de races différentes habitent à la Réunion. On parle créole et français. Et la monnaie de cette île, située à 10 000 km de l'Europe? L'euro!

extra! *Alerte! Un cyclone arrive!*

Le 12 février, nous entrons en alerte orange. Gerry, un cyclone tropical intense (vents de 180km/h!) s'approche de la Réunion. Les écoles ferment. Toutes les heures, la radio diffuse un flash d'informations. Au supermarché, on achète des bouteilles d'eau, des lampes à gaz, du riz, des pâtes. À la maison, on fait des réserves d'eau.

Mais le 13 février à 16h, la météo annonce que l'alerte orange est levée. Gerry passe à 280km au nord-est de la Réunion. Ouf!

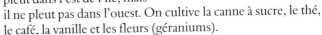

en Algérie	au Canada
les fruits	le blé (wheat)
arabe, français + autres	anglais, français
droite	droite
très chaud; pleut pas	hiver – froid; été – chaud

6D Une présentation

- **research information**
- **give a presentation**

le Sénégal

Voici une présentation du Sénégal.

A La capitale **est** Dakar, dans l'ouest du pays.

B La population **est de** dix millions d'habitants.

C On cultive l'arachide, le maïs, le riz, le coton et le mil.

D On parle français. 80% des habitants parlent aussi wolof, et il y a d'autres langues africaines.

E On roule à droite.

F Le climat? Il pleut dans le sud en été, mais il ne pleut pas beaucoup dans le nord. Il fait chaud, et on fait la sieste.

> l'arachide *f – groundnut*
> le mil – *millet*

Le drapeau national

D'autres idées

G On joue au football. Le rallye Paris–Dakar est célèbre. Les plages sont idéales pour le surf.

H On mange du riz au poisson, et de la viande à la sauce à l'arachide.

I Les religions: musulmans (90%), chrétiens (5%), animistes (5%).

J Le drapeau est vert, jaune et rouge.

1 a 💿 Écoute et lis les informations.

1 b ✏️ Écris les phrases correctes (1–5).

▶

1	On cultive	parlent wolof.
2	80% des habitants	dans le nord.
3	Il ne pleut pas beaucoup	sont idéales pour le surf.
4	On mange	du riz au poisson.
5	Les plages	le riz, le coton et le mil.

1 c 💿 Écoute (1–6) et regarde les phrases A–F ci-dessus. C'est quelle phrase?

1 d ✏️ Avec un/une partenaire, change un élément dans chaque phrase (A–F).

extra! Change aussi G–J.

Exemple: **A** La capitale est dans *le nord* du pays.

2 a 📖 Fais des recherches sur un autre pays francophone:

- sur Internet?
- à la bibliothèque?
- dans une encyclopédie?

2 b *Stratégies!* *Preparing, practising and giving a presentation*

- Write a first version: adapt sentences A–F (*extra!* A–J).
- Ask your partner to check your draft: make any corrections.
- Write a few key words to jog your memory while you speak.
- Practise your pronunciation, for example record yourself.
- When you give your presentation, look your audience in the eye!

> voici une présentation de…
> la capitale, c'est…
> la population est de… millions d'habitants
> le climat: il pleut / il fait chaud
> on cultive (le maïs)
> on roule (à droite)
> on parle (français)
> on mange (du riz)
> on joue au (foot)

Bonne chance!
Good luck!

Le temps	**The weather**
quel temps fait-il?	*what's the weather like?*
il fait beau	*it's nice*
il fait mauvais	*it's bad*
il fait (assez) chaud	*it's (quite) hot*
il fait (très) chaud	*it's (very) hot*
il fait froid	*it's cold*
il pleut	*it's raining/it rains*
il neige	*it's snowing/it snows*
mais parfois	*but sometimes*
il y a du soleil	*it's sunny*
en été	*in summer*
en automne	*in autumn*
en hiver	*in winter*
au printemps	*in spring*
il fait (souvent) beau	*it's (often) nice*
il ne fait pas beau	*it isn't nice*

En famille	**In the family**
vous faites quoi en famille?	*what do you do as a family?*
le week-end	*at the weekend*
nous discutons	*we discuss (things)*
nous mangeons	*we eat*
nous sortons	*we go out*
nous allons au centre commercial	*we go to the shopping centre*
nous restons à la maison	*we stay at home*

nous regardons la télé	*we watch TV*
ensemble	*together*
nous ne faisons rien	*we don't do anything*
nous n'allons jamais en ville	*we never go to town*

Le Cameroun	**Cameroon**
on cultive...	*they grow...*
le riz	*rice*
le coton	*cotton*
le café	*coffee*
on roule à droite	*they drive on the right*
on parle français	*they speak French*
et d'autres langues aussi	*and other languages too*
on fait la sieste	*they have a midday rest*

Une présentation	**A presentation**
voici	*here is*
une présentation de...	*a presentation on...*
la capitale, c'est...	*the capital city is...*
la population est de... millions d'habitants	*the population is... million inhabitants*
le climat	*the climate*
on cultive le maïs	*they grow maize/corn*
on mange du riz	*they eat rice*
on joue au foot	*they play football*

Grammaire

● Negative sentences: *ne ... pas: il **ne** pleut **pas**; il fait beau/il **ne** fait **pas** beau*
                            ne ... rien (nothing): *nous **ne** faisons **rien***
                            ne ... jamais (never): *je **ne** discute **jamais** avec ma mère*

● *On* meaning 'they' or 'people': *on roule à droite* they drive on the right

Stratégies!

★ using sounds and actions to help you remember new language

★ giving additional, contrasting information with *mais parfois...*

★ taking and adapting phrases from a text

★ words with two meaning: choosing the right meaning when looking in a dictionary

★ practising, learning and giving a presentation

Cross-topic words

quel *m*	*– which, what*
quelle *f*	*– which, what*

Révision

Unité 5 (Des problèmes? Consulte la page 51.)

1 a 📖 Trouve les paires et écris les phrases.

1 b 💿 Écoute et vérifie.

Exemple: **1 d** Ma star préférée, c'est un chanteur.

1 Ma star préférée, …	**a** pas beaucoup le collège.
2 J'ai une amie…	**b** une heure.
3 Mohamed aime beaucoup…	**c** très vieille.
4 Émilie n'aime…	**d** c'est un chanteur.
5 Philippe Lebon est très célèbre…	**e** les voitures.
6 Madame Cresson est…	**f** allé au restaurant.
7 Lundi dernier, je suis…	**g** et assez riche.
8 J'ai travaillé jusqu'à…	**h** qui s'appelle Myriam.

2 ✏️ Écris huit phrases (A–H).

Attention! les garçons  je suis allé   les filles  je suis allée

 **A**  **B**

Exemple: **A** Je suis allé au théâtre./Je suis allée au théâtre.

C  **D**  **E**  **F** **G** **H**

Unité 6 (Des problèmes? Consulte la page 59.)

3 a 💿 Écoute (1–7). Note la bonne lettre (A–G).

Exemple: **1 D**

3 b ✏️ Écris une phrase pour chaque image.

Exemple: **A** Il fait mauvais.

3 c ✏️ Écris les phrases (A–G) à la forme négative.

Exemple: **A** Il *ne* fait *pas* mauvais.

E  **F**  **G**

4 💬 Joue six petits dialogues.

Exemple: **A** Vous faites quoi en famille le week-end?

B Nous mangeons ensemble.

manger sortir regarder
discuter aller faire

Stratégies! *Revision*

How do you revise words? Do you…

● write words on cards? ● work with a partner? ● make a word web? ● say the words aloud?

Use the method that works best for *you*!

Cheb Mami

La ville d'origine de Cheb Mami, c'est Saïda, dans l'ouest de l'Algérie. En hiver, il fait froid dans la région de Saïda. En été, il fait très chaud et il ne pleut pas.

Cheb Mami aime beaucoup Saïda, mais maintenant il habite en France. Il est chanteur et ses inspirations sont multiples. Il y a bien sûr le raï, une musique d'Algérie. Il y a aussi la soul, le funk et le reggae.

Cheb Mami donne des concerts dans le monde entier: en Algérie, en France, en Angleterre ou aux États-Unis. Il chante en duo avec Sting, avec la chanteuse de hip hop américaine Baby Girl, avec le groupe de reggae Aswad, ou avec le rappeur franco-algérien K Mel. C'est un chanteur international!

> maintenant – *now*
> bien sûr – *of course*
> dans le monde entier – *throughout the world*

1 *In the first paragraph, find the French for:*
   1 *two seasons*
   2 *three weather phrases*
   3 *the name of a French-speaking country in Africa.*
   Write the English translation next to each French word or phrase.

2 Vrai ou faux?
   1 Saïda est dans le sud de l'Algérie.
   2 À Saïda, il fait froid en hiver et il pleut en été.
   3 Cheb Mami habite en Algérie.
   4 Le raï est une musique d'Algérie.
   5 Cheb Mami est un chanteur international.

3 Trouve les paires.

1	le raï	**a**	Baby Girl
2	le rap	**b**	Aswad
3	le hip hop	**c**	K Mel
4	le reggae	**d**	Cheb Mami

L'Algérie

la capitale: Alger
la population:
   32,8 millions d'habitants
la langue officielle: l'arabe
le drapeau: vert, blanc et rouge

7B Suggestions

- suggest activities with *tu veux?* (do you want to?), and respond to other people's suggestions
- bring in words you've learnt before

> Zut! C'est fermé!

Ali:	Tu veux aller à la patinoire ce matin?
Marine:	Non, je n'ai pas envie. C'est barbant.
Ali:	Alors, tu veux jouer à un jeu vidéo?
Marine:	Bof...
Ali:	Tu veux faire du karting?
Marine:	D'accord, je veux bien.

1 a 💿 Écoute et lis le dialogue.

1 b 📖 C'est quoi en français?

1 *do you want to... ?* 5 *well then, …*
2 *this morning* 6 *OK, I'd like to*
3 *I don't feel like it* 7 *oh no!*
4 *it's boring*

1 c 💿 Écoute Ali. Lis le rôle de Marine. Puis change de rôle.

2 a 📖 Trouve les paires (phrases 1–6 et images A–F).

> ce matin – *this morning*
> cet après-midi – *this afternoon*
> ce soir – *this evening*

Exemple: **1 D**

1 Tu veux faire du karting cet après-midi?
2 Ali, tu veux aller en ville ce matin?
3 Tu veux faire du vélo ce soir?
4 Marine, tu veux aller à la patinoire ce matin?
5 Tu veux jouer à un jeu vidéo ce soir?
6 Est-ce que tu veux faire du kayak cet après-midi?

2 b 💿 Écoute et vérifie.

3 💬 Adapte et joue le dialogue de l'exercice 1. Change les questions.

Exemple: **Tu veux aller *en ville cet après-midi*?**

4 a Grammaire:

- ***l'infinitif***
  Ton modèle: la grammaire, page 63!
  - The infinitive is the ___ of the verb.
  - It's the form you find in the ___.
  - ***-er*** is ___ like **é**.

- ***je veux, tu veux***
  je veux = I want to
  tu veux… ? = do you want to… ?

- *je/tu veux* + *l'infinitif:*
  Tu veux **aller** en ville?

4 b ✏️ Écris des questions avec *tu veux.*

Exemple: **1 Tu veux surfer sur Internet cet après-midi?**

> surf- mang- envoy- visit- jou- invit-

5 💿 **Écoute les dialogues (1–4). Choisis a ou b.**

1 Ali veut...
   a surfer sur Internet   **b** aller en ville.

2 Ils vont visiter la cathédrale de Rouen...
   a ce matin   **b** cet après-midi.

3 Marine veut...
   a aller à la patinoire   **b** faire du karting.

4 Ils vont jouer à un jeu vidéo...
   a cet après-midi   **b** ce soir.

6 a *Stratégies!* ***Bring in words you know***
Look at how you could bring in some language you've met before.

● Practise the dialogue in pairs, bringing in the phrases in blue.

– Tu veux faire du vélo ce matin?   *Il pleut.*
– Non, je n'ai pas envie. C'est barbant.
– Alors, tu veux faire du kayak?   *Je n'aime pas ça.*
– Bof...
– Tu veux aller en ville?   *On se retrouve à quelle heure? À onze heures.*
– D'accord, je veux bien.

		du karting?
tu veux	faire	du vélo?
		du kayak?
	jouer	à un jeu vidéo?
	aller	à la patinoire?
		en ville?

ce matin / cet après-midi / ce soir
non, je n'ai pas envie / c'est barbant
alors, tu veux...?
d'accord, je veux bien

6 b 💬 **Avec ton/ta partenaire, invente deux dialogues, et ajoute d'autres expressions. Puis joue les dialogues.**

J'adore ça!   Oui, génial!   Il fait très froid!   Bof, je ne sais pas.   Tu aimes ça?   C'est loin?

extra!   Je n'ai jamais essayé ça. *I've never tried it.*   On y va en bus? *Are we going there by bus?*

7 a 📖 ***Read the magazine article.***
● *Why has Isabelle written to the magazine for help?*
● *What do you think* Tourne la page *means here?*

7 b 📖 **Note les sept solutions de Djamel, Louis et Clément.**

Exemple: **1** écrire, ...

Problème:
"Ma meilleure amie Éva va habiter en Australie! Désastre! Aide-moi!"
Isabelle, 15 ans

"Tourne la page, Isabelle! Tu peux écrire des lettres et téléphoner à Éva. Mais tu as d'autres copines au collège, non? Invite tes copines le week-end!"
Djamel, 12 ans et demi (Paris)

"Moi, j'habite à New York et je suis en contact avec mes copains français grâce à Internet. Tu as une webcam? C'est pratique, et c'est amusant!"
Louis, 14 ans (New York)

"Eh oui, c'est difficile. Mais la copine d'Isabelle peut venir en vacances en France. Et toi, Isabelle, tu peux aller lui rendre visite en Australie!"
Clément, 12 ans (Essonne)

7C Excuses

- **make excuses: say what you have to do**
- **use the verbs *je peux*, *tu veux*, *je dois***

Est-ce que je peux parler à Ali?

Oui, un moment... Ali, c'est Sophie pour toi.

Bonjour, Sophie. Ça va?

Tu veux venir chez moi ce soir?

Oh, zut!

Euh... je ne peux pas, parce que je dois... euh... je dois...

...laver mon hamster!

Ah oui! Je dois laver mon hamster!

Quoi?!

1 a  Écoute et lis.

1 Ali aime/n'aime pas Sophie?

2 Son excuse est amusante/stupide/raisonnable?

1 b Joue le dialogue.

2 a Écris une phrase pour chaque image (A–F).

Exemple: A Je dois promener le chien.

Je dois	faire	la voiture
	promener	la vaisselle
	aller	mon chien
	laver	les courses
		chez mes grands-parents
		mes devoirs

2 b  Écoute et vérifie.

3 a Écoute les dialogues (1–4).
Travaillez à trois: A note la première excuse, B la deuxième excuse, C la troisième.

Exemple: (A) laver la voiture; (B) aller...

3 b Joue le dialogue. Puis, continue le dialogue: demain soir, mardi, mercredi.

Dialogue 1

– Tu veux venir chez moi cet après-midi?
– Je ne peux pas. Je dois laver la voiture.
– Et ce soir?
– Je dois aller chez mes grands-parents.
– Alors, demain?
– Je ne peux pas. Je dois promener mon chien.

tu veux venir chez moi? et demain? alors, lundi?		
	faire	mes devoirs / la vaisselle / les courses
je ne peux pas, parce que je dois	promener	mon chien
	laver	la voiture
	aller	chez mes grands-parents

Cher Mustafa,

Merci pour l'invitation à ta soirée, jeudi. Je regrette, mais je ne peux pas venir parce que je dois aller chez ma grand-mère. C'est son anniversaire.

Bisous

Jessica

Salut, Franck

Je ne peux pas venir à la teuf chez toi demain soir. D'abord, je dois laver ma girafe, puis je dois aller chez Britney Spears.

Joyeux anniversaire!

Nico

la teuf = la fête = la soirée

Chère Carole

Je suis désolé, mais je ne peux pas venir à ton barbecue samedi soir parce que je dois promener ma gerbille. Peut-être l'année prochaine?

Ludovic

Sandra,

Je ne peux pas venir chez toi ce soir. Je dois aller à l'hôpital, pour rendre visite à ma tante Agnès et son nouveau bébé. À demain!

Andréa

4 a 📖 **Lis les quatre lettres.**

1 Qui refuse une invitation à...

  a une fête?

  b un barbecue?

2 Qui doit...

  a aller à l'hôpital?

  b aller à l'anniversaire de sa grand-mère?

4 b 📖 **Ton opinion sur chaque excuse: c'est une bonne/une mauvaise excuse?**

4 c 📖 extra! **C'est vrai ou faux?**

1 Carole va faire un barbecue samedi.

2 Andréa doit aller au théâtre ce soir.

3 Nico est invité chez Franck demain soir.

4 Jessica ne peut pas venir parce que jeudi, c'est l'anniversaire de sa grand-mère.

Grammaire: *je peux, je veux, je dois*

can	want to	have to, must	
je **peux**	je **veux**	je **dois**	
tu **peux**	tu **veux**	tu **dois**	+ l'**infinitif**
il/elle **peut**	il/elle **veut**	il/elle **doit**	

▼

5 a **Recopie les phrases (1–5) avec la bonne option.**

Exemple: **Je regrette: je ne** *peux* **pas venir...**

1 Je regrette: je ne (**peux/dois**) pas venir chez toi. Tu (**veux/dois**) venir chez moi?

2 J'aime le cinéma. Je (**veux/dois**) aller au cinéma lundi, mais je ne (**dois/peux**) pas.

3 Tu (**dois/peux**) venir chez moi ce soir?

4 Je (**peux/dois**) laver la voiture, mais je ne (**veux/peux**) pas – c'est barbant!

5 Tu (**veux/dois**) venir à ma soirée?

5 b 💬 **Vérifie avec ton/ta partenaire.**

6 a 🖊 **Réponds à Mustafa et à Carole avec des excuses amusantes! Ton modèle: l'exercice 4a.**

Exemple: **Je ne peux pas venir à ta soirée parce que je dois promener mon éléphant.**

6 b 💬 **Joue un dialogue avec des excuses amusantes. Ton modèle: l'exercice 3b.**

▼

Stratégies! *Bring in words you know*

How long can you keep going before you run out of excuses?!

7D Un sketch et une lettre

- write and act out a sketch
- write a thank you letter

Coralie: Je peux avoir des biscuits?

Mme Brion: Oui, bien sûr, Coralie. Tu veux faire du vélo ce matin? Il fait très beau.

Coralie: Non, je n'ai pas envie.

Mme Brion: Alors tu veux faire du kayak? Il y a un grand lac près d'ici.

Coralie: Non, je n'aime pas le kayak, moi.

Mme Brion: Tu veux jouer à un jeu vidéo peut-être?

Coralie: Non, pas vraiment. C'est ennuyeux, ça.

Mme Brion: Tu préfères faire du karting?

Coralie: Ah non! Le karting, c'est trop difficile.

1 Écoute Coralie et Mme Brion et trois autres conversations (1–4). Identifie la situation (a–d).

Exemple: **1** d

L'invité...

a est impatient

b est très enthousiaste

c ne parle pas beaucoup

d n'aime rien

2 À deux, inventez un sketch comique:

L'invité(e) difficile

- Écrivez un script amusant. Adaptez les phrases du dialogue.
- Jouez le sketch devant la classe.

◀ **Stratégies!** *Writing a funny sketch*

- Adapt the sentences from the dialogue above.
- Your host or hostess could be really strict:
  – *Je peux avoir une pomme?*
  – *Non!!*
- The guest could be *too* polite:
  – *Tu veux aller à la patinoire?*
  – *Oh oui! J'adore ça!! C'est super!!!*

3 a Écoute et lis.

Au revoir, Marine.

Au revoir, et merci beaucoup.

Et deux jours plus tard...

31 rue Alfred de Musset
B-1050 Bruxelles
le 4 mai

Chers Monsieur et Madame Amrani, et Ali,

Merci beaucoup pour mon week-end à Alençon. C'était fantastique! J'ai beaucoup aimé le pique-nique. Ali, est-ce que tu peux envoyer les photos de la soirée chez Justine? Merci!

Et, Ali, tu veux venir chez moi en juillet? Pour mon anniversaire peut-être? (C'est le 15 juillet!)

Amitiés

Marine

3 b Tu as passé un week-end chez Monsieur et Madame Leclerc et Sabrina à Marseille. Écris une lettre: dis merci.

Ton modèle: la lettre de Marine, mais choisis d'autres mots pour *fantastique*, *pique-nique*, *juillet*, etc.

chers Monsieur et Madame X
merci beaucoup pour (mon week-end)
c'était fantastique
j'ai beaucoup aimé...
(est-ce que) tu peux (envoyer les photos?)
amitiés

En classe / **In class**

pardon, madame — *excuse me, Miss*
pardon, monsieur — *excuse me, Sir*
est-ce que je peux... — *can I...*
  ouvrir la fenêtre? — *open the window?*
  fermer la fenêtre? — *close the window?*
  aller aux toilettes? — *go to the toilet?*
  aller voir Mme X? — *go and see Mrs X?*
  avoir une feuille de papier? — *have a sheet of paper?*
oui, bien sûr — *yes, of course*
non, assieds-toi — *no, sit down*
tais-toi! — *be quiet!*

Suggestions / **Suggestions**

tu veux... — *do you want to...*
  faire du vélo? — *go cycling?*
  faire du kayak? — *go kayaking?*
  faire du karting? — *go go-karting?*
  jouer à un jeu vidéo? — *play a video game?*
  aller à la patinoire? — *go to the ice-rink?*
  aller en ville? — *go into town?*
ce matin — *this morning*
cet après-midi — *this afternoon*
ce soir — *this evening*
bof... — *pfff... (i.e. not enthusiastic!)*
non, je n'ai pas envie — *no, I don't feel like it*
c'est barbant — *it's boring*
alors, tu veux...? — *well then, do you want to...?*
d'accord — *OK*
je veux bien — *I'd like to*

Excuses / **Excuses**

tu veux venir chez moi? — *do you want to come to my house?*
je ne peux pas — *I can't*
je dois... — *I have to...*
  faire mes devoirs — *do my homework*
  faire la vaisselle — *do the dishes*
  faire les courses — *do the shopping*
  promener mon chien — *walk my dog*
  laver la voiture — *wash the car*
  aller chez mes grands-parents — *go to my grandparents' house*
et demain? — *what about tomorrow?*
alors, lundi? — *Monday, then?*

Un sketch et une lettre / **A sketch and a letter**

chers Monsieur et Madame Amrani — *dear Mr and Mrs Amrani*
merci beaucoup pour mon week-end — *thank you very much for my weekend*
c'était fantastique! — *it was great!*
j'ai beaucoup aimé... — *I really liked...*
(est-ce que) tu peux envoyer les photos? — *can you send the photos?*
amitiés — *best wishes*

Stratégies!

★ pronunciation: practising a longer phrase (e.g. *est-ce que...*) until it trips off your tongue
★ saying words as you write them to practise and remember the pronunciation
★ bringing in words you've learnt before
★ starting a letter with *Cher* (to a boy), *Chère* (to a girl)
★ writing a funny sketch

Grammaire: *je peux, je veux, je dois*

can	want to	have to, must	
je peux	*je veux*	*je dois*	
tu peux	*tu veux*	*tu dois*	+ *l'infinitif*
il/elle peut	*il/elle veut*	*il/elle doit*	

bien sûr – *of course*
d'accord – *OK*

8 Ma routine et mon look

8A Hier

- say what you did yesterday
- revise the past tense
- practise changing parts of sentences

Marine parle d'hier, mercredi:

3 «À midi, j'ai mangé un hamburger. C'était délicieux (ha! ha!)»

4 «L'après-midi, je suis allée en ville et j'ai acheté un T-shirt.»

5 «Après ça, j'ai bu deux cocas! Puis je suis allée à la maison.»

6 «Le soir, j'ai fait mes devoirs dans ma chambre. C'était barbant!»

1 a 🔵 Écoute et lis (1–6). La photo correspond à quelle phrase?

1 «Hier matin, j'ai parlé avec mon copain dans le bus. C'était amusant.»

2 «À dix heures, j'ai eu histoire. C'était assez intéressant.»

1 b 🔵 Écoute (1–6). Note les mots différents.

Exemple: **1** ma sœur

1 c 📖 Recopie les expressions de temps en français et en anglais.

temps – *1* time   *2* weather

Exemple: **1** hier matin – *yesterday morning*

♻ Grammaire: *le passé* (the past tense)

1 The regular past participle is -é: *j'ai joué*, *j'ai acheté*, etc.
   Note three exceptions: *j'ai **eu***, *j'ai **bu***, *j'ai **fait***.
2 *je suis allé* (male)/*je suis allée* (female) = I went
3 *c'était* = it was

1 d 📖 Détective de langues! Regarde les phrases 2, 5 et 6. C'est quoi en anglais?
1 j'ai eu
2 j'ai bu
3 j'ai fait

2 a ♻ ✏ Change deux éléments dans chaque phrase.

Exemple: **1** *L'après-midi*, j'ai eu dessin – c'était *intéressant*.

1 Hier matin,	j'ai eu	dessin –	c'était ennuyeux.
2 Après ça,	j'ai parlé	avec une copine	dans le tram.
3 À midi,	j'ai acheté	un livre	en ville.
4 Puis	j'ai mangé	un croque-monsieur	dans un café – c'était délicieux.
5 L'après-midi,	j'ai bu	un thé au citron	avec mon cousin.

2 b 💬 En groupes, chaque personne change un ou deux éléments d'une phrase de l'exercice 1.

Exemples: **A** À midi, j'ai mangé *une pizza*.
B À midi, j'ai *bu un coca*.
C À *une heure*, j'ai bu un coca.

3 🎧 **Écoute la description. Écris les verbes dans le bon ordre.**

> j'ai acheté   j'ai bu   j'ai eu   j'ai fait   j'ai mangé   j'ai parlé

4 a 📖 **Lis les deux textes.**

Marine

Hier, dimanche, j'ai promené les chiens à dix heures. C'était assez bien.

À onze heures, j'ai fait mes devoirs. C'était assez ennuyeux.

Je suis allée dans un restaurant marocain avec ma famille à midi. C'était vraiment délicieux – miam-miam! J'ai mangé une tajine et j'ai bu du thé à la menthe. J'adore la cuisine marocaine.

L'après-midi, à deux heures, j'ai regardé un film de science-fiction, mais c'était vraiment stupide! Quelle perte de temps!

À quatre heures, j'ai retrouvé des copains au centre sportif et j'ai joué au badminton avec eux. C'était assez amusant. Après ça, j'ai fait de la danse. C'était super bien!

> Quelle perte de temps! – *What a waste of time!*

Ali

Hier, c'était mercredi. Le matin, à dix heures, j'ai eu éducation physique. C'était assez bien; j'ai joué au handball. Puis, à onze heures, j'ai eu un contrôle de sciences. C'était assez difficile!

À midi, j'ai mangé du poisson et des frites à la cantine et j'ai parlé avec des copains. C'était très amusant.

À deux heures, j'ai réparé mon vélo – c'était barbant! Puis, à trois heures, j'ai fait du vélo avec trois copains. Il faisait très chaud, c'était vraiment génial!

À cinq heures, à la maison, j'ai rangé ma chambre. Je déteste ça, mais c'était pour faire plaisir à ma mère!

> le contrôle – *exam*

Le graphique d'émotions, c'est pour Ali ou Marine? ▶

Graphique d'émotions

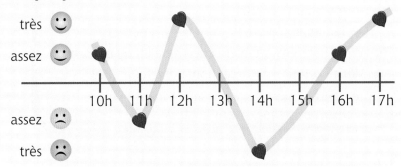

4 b 📖 **Recopie les verbes au passé et note l'anglais.**

Exemple: **j'ai eu** – *I had*

4 c 📖 **Fais un graphique d'émotions pour l'autre personne.**

5 a ✏️ **Décris tes activités d'hier. Note l'heure et l'activité.**

Exemple: **Hier matin à huit heures et demie, …**
À… heures…   Après ça/Puis…

5 b 🗣️ extra!

- *Read and record your description.*
- *Listen to it and learn it off by heart.*
- *Give your presentation in class (see page 29 for tips).*

hier matin, l'après-midi, le soir, à midi, après ça, puis	j'ai	acheté / parlé / mangé / eu fait / bu
	je suis	allé / allée
	c'était (assez)	intéressant / barbant / amusant / délicieux

8B Les vêtements

- talk about clothes and colours
- use adjectives correctly
- work out the meaning of new words

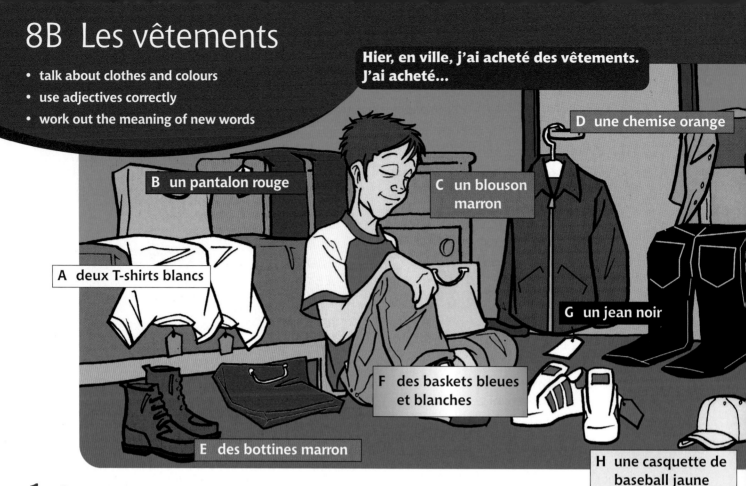

Hier, en ville, j'ai acheté des vêtements. J'ai acheté...

A deux T-shirts blancs

B un pantalon rouge

C un blouson marron

D une chemise orange

E des bottines marron

F des baskets bleues et blanches

G un jean noir

H une casquette de baseball jaune

1 Écoute. Note les lettres (A–H) dans le bon ordre.

Exemple: **G, ...**

2 a Grammaire: *les adjectifs*

Can you remember the rule for adjectives (e.g. colours)?

- What letters do you add for:
  - feminine singular?
  - masculine plural?
  - feminine plural?
- What happens when an adjective already ends in -e?
- Which colour is an exception in the feminine?

Note: *marron* (brown) – no -e in feminine;
marron, orange – no -s in plural.

2 b A écrit un vêtement et la couleur en secret. B devine le vêtement, puis la couleur.

Exemple: B Tu as acheté des bottines? A Non.
B Tu as acheté une chemise? A Oui.
B Tu as acheté une chemise verte? A Non.

Prononciation: *les adjectifs*

- Attention à la prononciation: vert/verte
- On ne prononce pas les "s" au pluriel: des T-shirts rouges

3 a Joue au loto! Jeux 1 et 2: note *trois vêtements*. Puis écoute le dialogue, et coche (✔) les vêtements sur ta liste.

3 b Loto! Jeux 3 et 4: note *trois couleurs*.

3 c extra! Écoute. Écris un résumé de l'incident en anglais.

un pantalon / un jean / un T-shirt / un blouson
une chemise / une casquette de baseball
des bottines / des baskets / des vêtements

bleu(e) / vert(e) / noir(e)
blanc (blanche)
rouge / jaune / orange / marron

Et aujourd'hui, je suis fauché!!

4 🖉 **Regarde l'image et écris 12 phrases.**

Exemple: **Dans le magasin, il y a trois T-shirts jaunes.**

5 a 📖 Lis le texte.

Stratégies! *New words*

- Copy the words below (1–10). Note the method you used to understand each one, and write the English.

Methods:

- looks like English
- use picture
- guess from context
- look in glossary

Example: 1 *cagoule* →
use picture → balaclava/hood

1 *cagoule*
2 *feu*
3 *casque*
4 *résister*
5 *gants*
6 *cuir*
7 *semelles*
8 *renforts*
9 *métalliques*
10 *absorber*

5 b 📖 Note, en anglais, cinq détails du texte.

Les vêtements d'un pilote de Formule 1

La Formule 1 est un sport difficile et dangereux. Il y a des vêtements spéciaux pour réduire les dangers.

La cagoule

La cagoule et les sous-vêtements sont en Nomex, un tissu spécial résistant au feu.

Le casque

Le casque pèse 1,3 kg mais peut résister à des chocs très violents (accidents!!) et tenir 45 secondes exposé à une chaleur de 800°C.

Les gants

On recouvre les gants en cuir pour la flexibilité. Résultat: le pilote peut bien contrôler la voiture.

La combinaison

Chaque pilote a sa combinaison individuelle et unique. Le tissu est léger et très résistant au feu.

Les bottines

Les semelles ont des renforts métalliques pour absorber les vibrations de la voiture (par exemple, à 300 km/h).

la cagoule · le casque · les gants · la combinaison · les bottines

8C Un débat

- say what you think of designer clothes
- have an argument in French
- revise the verb *être* (to be)

1 🔘 **Écoute et lis le dialogue. Trouve les paires (1–6 et A–F).**

A *In my opinion they're too expensive. They're a rip-off!*

B *They're not too expensive. They're better quality! They're great!*

C *Do you like designer clothes?*

D *You're stupid, you are!*

E *Why?*

F *I don't agree.*

Tu aimes les vêtements de marque[1], Marine?
Non.
Pourquoi?[2]
À mon avis, ils sont trop chers. C'est du vol![3]
Je ne suis pas d'accord.[4]
Non?
Ils ne sont pas trop chers. Ils sont de meilleure qualité! C'est le top![5]
Tu es bête, toi![6]

2 a ✏️ **Lis les phrases 1–5. Fais deux listes:**
A pour (*for*); **B contre** (*against*).

1 Les vêtements de marque sont trop chers.

2 Je suis d'accord. Ils sont le top!

3 À mon avis, ils ne sont pas trop chers.

4 C'est du vol!

5 Ils sont de meilleure qualité!

2 b 🔘 **Écoute les conversations (1–5). Les deux personnes sont d'accord (✔) ou pas d'accord (X)?**

Exemple: **1 X**

2 c 💬 **A dit une des phrases (1–5); B dit *Tu es bête* + le contraire!**

Exemple: **A** C'est du vol!
B Tu es bête!
Ce n'est pas du vol!

ne ... pas = negative
(◀◀ p. 53)

3 ♻️ **Grammaire: être (to be)**

Recopie et complète le verbe. (Trouve les formes du verbe sur cette page!)

je ___ *I am*   nous sommes *we are*
tu ___ *you are*   vous êtes *you are*
il /elle/c'___ *he/she/it is*   ils/elles ___ *they are*

tu aimes les vêtements de marque?	
pourquoi?	
je suis d'accord	
je ne suis pas d'accord	
tu es bête!	
à mon avis, ...	
ils sont	trop chers
ils ne sont pas	de meilleure qualité
c'est	le top!
ce n'est pas	du vol!

Tu aimes les vêtements de marque?

Moi, personnellement, je n'aime pas les vêtements de marque. Ils sont trop chers, beaucoup trop chers!
Habib

J'aime les vêtements de marque parce qu'ils sont plus intéressants. Bon, ils sont chers (trop chers pour moi!), mais ils sont beaux.
Raoul

Je pense que les vêtements de marque sont super. Moi, j'ai des baskets Nike. Mes copines sont jalouses, c'est bien!
Claudia

C'est une question intéressante. Moi, je pense que les vêtements de marque sont un peu ennuyeux. Moi, je préfère avoir un look individuel.
Aurélia

Moi, je pense que les vêtements de marque sont ridicules. Payer plus cher pour avoir le nom Adidas, Lacoste, etc.? Non, c'est bête!
Sébastien

Avec des vêtements de marque, par exemple mes T-shirts, je peux montrer ma personnalité. C'est génial.
Violaine

Super, ton pull! C'est quelle marque?

Fait par ma grand-mère!

Oh! C'est une marque américaine?

fait par – *made by*

4 a 💿 **Écoute et lis les textes. Puis, lis les questions et écris un, deux ou trois noms.**

Exemple: **1** Raoul, ...

1 Qui aime les vêtements de marque?

2 Qui n'aime pas les vêtements de marque?

3 Qui préfère un style plus individuel?

4 Qui trouve les vêtements de marque ridicules?

extra!

5 Qui a des vêtements de marque?

6 Qui n'aime pas le prix des vêtements de marque?

7 Qui aime l'admiration de ses amis?

8 Qui trouve les vêtements de marque importants pour montrer son caractère?

4 b Stratégies! *Taking and using expressions from a text*

Make your language richer by picking up useful expressions from reading texts. For example, copy four expressions, in French and English, that you will be able to use in exercises 4c and 5 below.

Example: *Moi, personnellement, ...* – Me, personally, ...

4 c ✏️ **Écris une lettre au magazine. Ton modèle: l'exercice 4a. Ajoute des expressions du magazine!**

Exemple: **Moi, j'aime/je n'aime pas les vêtements de marque. À mon avis, ...**

5 💬 **Compare ton opinion avec cinq camarades de classe.**

Exemple: **A** Je pense que les vêtements de marque sont... Et toi?
B Moi, personnellement, je...

8D Tu aimes ça?

- give your opinion about different clothes
- use adjectives in the plural

Tu aimes les pulls larges?

Oui. C'est le top!

Tu aimes les chemises blanches?

Bof, ça dépend.

Tu aimes les pantalons à pattes d'éléphant?

Oui. C'est le top.

Tu aimes les cravates?

Non. C'est bête!

Tu aimes les T-shirts avec des slogans?

Non. C'est bête!

1 a 💿 Écoute et lis. Tu es d'accord? Écris *oui* ou *non*.

1 b 💿 Écoute (1–6). Note les vêtements et les opinions. ◀

Exemple: **1 pantalons larges/c'est bête**

♻️ **Grammaire:** *adjectifs au pluriel*

Remember to add an -*s* to plural adjectives:
*Tu aimes les pull**s** large**s**?*
*Je n'aime pas les chemise**s** blanche**s**.*

2 a ✏️ Regarde les mots (1–6). Écris les questions. Puis écris ta réponse/ton opinion.

Exemple: – **Tu aimes les bottines rouges?**
– **Oui, c'est le top!/Non, c'est bête./Bof, ça dépend.**

 **1** les bottines *f* (rouge)

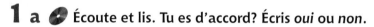 **2** les pulls *m* (bleu)

 **3** les chemises *f* (large)

4 les jeans à pattes d'éléphant *m*

5 les baskets *f* (rouge et blanc)

6 les casquettes de baseball *f*

2 b 💬 Pose les questions 1–6 à ton/ta partenaire.

extra! Pose six autres questions, et donne une variété de réponses (◀◀ p. 75, ex. 4b).

Exemple: – **Tu aimes les T-shirts rouges?**
– **Moi, je pense que c'est ridicule!**

tu aimes… ?
  les pulls larges
  les chemises blanches
  les pantalons à pattes d'éléphant
  les cravates
  les T-shirts avec des slogans

oui, non,	c'est	le top! bête!
bof, ça dépend		

Hier	**Yesterday**
hier matin	*yesterday morning*
l'après-midi	*in the afternoon*
le soir	*in the evening*
à midi	*at midday*
après ça	*after that*
puis	*then*
j'ai acheté...	*I bought...*
j'ai mangé...	*I ate...*
j'ai parlé...	*I talked...*
j'ai eu...	*I had...*
j'ai bu...	*I drank...*
j'ai fait...	*I did...*
je suis allé	*I went* (male)
je suis allée	*I went* (female)
c'était (assez)...	*it was (quite)...*
intéressant	*interesting*
barbant	*boring*
amusant	*fun*
délicieux	*delicious*

Les vêtements	**Clothes**
un pantalon	*a pair of trousers*
un jean	*a pair of jeans*
un T-shirt	*a T-shirt*
un blouson	*a blouson jacket*
une chemise	*a shirt*
une casquette de baseball	*a baseball cap*
des bottines *fpl*	*(ankle) boots*
des baskets *fpl*	*trainers*

des vêtements *mpl*	*clothes*
blanc *m* blanche *f*	*white*
marron	*brown*
rouge/jaune/orange	*red/yellow/orange*
bleu(e)/vert(e)/noir(e)	*blue/green/black*

Un débat	**A debate**
tu aimes les vêtements de marque?	*do you like designer clothes?*
pourquoi?	*why?*
je suis d'accord	*I agree*
je ne suis pas d'accord	*I don't agree*
à mon avis, ils sont...	*in my opinion, they're...*
ils ne sont pas...	*they aren't...*
trop chers	*too expensive*
de meilleure qualité	*better quality*
c'est du vol!	*it's a rip-off!*
ce n'est pas du vol	*it isn't a rip-off*
c'est le top!	*they're brilliant!*

Tu aimes ça?	**Do you like that?**
les pulls larges	*baggy jumpers*
les chemises blanches	*white shirts*
les pantalons à pattes d'éléphant	*flared trousers*
les cravates	*ties*
les T-shirts avec des slogans	*T-shirts with slogans on them*
bof, ça dépend	*it depends*
c'est bête	*they're stupid*

Grammaire:

- *le passé*
  - regular past participle: *-é: j'ai joué*
  - three exceptions: *j'ai **eu**, j'ai **bu**, j'ai **fait**.*
- *les adjectifs masculins et féminins*

fém. sing:	+ e	Don't add an -e if
masc. pl.:	+ s	the adjective already
fém. pl.:	+ es	ends in -e.

- *le verbe **être** (to be)*

je **suis**	nous **sommes**
tu **es**	vous **êtes**
il/elle **est**	ils/elles **sont**

- *les adjectifs au pluriel*
  Remember to add an -s to plural adjectives:
  *Les pulls large**s**? Ils sont bête**s**.*
  *Les cravate**s**? Elles sont bête**s**.*

Stratégies!

★ ways of understanding new words: looks like English; guess from context; use picture; use glossary

★ making your language richer by taking and using expressions from a reading text

Cross-topic words

trop – *too*
pourquoi? – *why?*

Unité 7 (Des problèmes? Consulte la page 69.)

1 💿 Écoute (1–5). C'est quelle image?

A
B
C
D
E

2 a ✏️ Recopie et complète le dialogue.

> bien   cet   chez   faire   je
> lundi   mes   ne   pas   soir

– Tu veux ___**1** du kayak ___**2** après-midi?

– Non, je n'ai ___**3** envie.

– Et samedi?

– Samedi, ___**4** dois aller ___**5** mes grands-parents.

– Alors, ___**6**?

– Lundi, je ___**7** peux pas. Je dois faire ___**8** devoirs.

– Et mardi ___**9**?

– D'accord, je veux ___**10**.

2 b 💬 Joue le dialogue.

Unité 8 (Des problèmes? Consulte la page 77.)

3 ✏️ Écris six phrases correctes.

1 Tu aimes les vêtements...	pantalons à pattes d'éléphant.
2 À mon avis, ils sont...	de marque?
3 Les vêtements de marque...	pas d'accord.
4 Je ne suis...	trop chers.
5 Je n'aime pas les...	slogans, c'est le top!
6 Les T-shirts avec des...	sont de meilleure qualité.

4 📖 Recopie et complète les phrases.

> acheté   allé   bu   eu   fait   joué   mangé   regardé

1 Mercredi matin, j'ai ___ français et histoire.

2 À midi, j'ai ___ à la cantine.

3 Après ça, je suis ___ en ville.

4 J'ai ___ un pantalon.

5 Puis, j'ai ___ un coca dans un café.

6 Le soir, chez moi, j'ai ___ mes devoirs.

7 Puis, j'ai ___ à un jeu vidéo.

8 À 21h, j'ai ___ un film avec ma mère.

Stratégies! *Revision*

● Read through a section of the *Sommaire* page.

● Cover the English words and read the French. Try to say the English words from memory.

● Now look at the English only and say the French from memory.

Vive la différence!

1

Mon copain Lucas,
il est très sympa
et super marrant!
Mais pour les vêtements,
euh... ben... ça dépend!

Je sais, toi, tu adores!

Moi, je ne suis pas d'accord!

Mais quelle importance?

Vive la différence!

2

Hier après-midi,
à quatre heures et demie,
dans un magasin
qui est super bien,
Lucas a acheté
Un petit pull rayé.

Je sais, toi, tu adores!

Moi, je ne suis pas d'accord!

Mais quelle importance?

Vive la différence!

3

Et Lucas a dit:
"Moi, à mon avis,
le T-shirt est cher,
mais il est super!
Et le pantalon,
C'est oui ou c'est non?"

Je sais, toi, tu adores!

Moi, je ne suis pas d'accord!

Mais quelle importance?

Vive la différence!

4

Le pull rose et blanc,
oui, il est marrant!
Mais le T-shirt noir,
il est très bizarre!
Et le pantalon,
non, non, non, et non!

Je sais, toi, tu adores!

Moi, je ne suis pas d'accord!

Mais quelle importance?

Vive la différence!

marrant – *good fun*
quelle importance? – *does it matter?*
vive la différence! – *hooray for variety!*
rayé – *striped*

1 *Which verse describes:*
  1 *what Lucas did yesterday?*
  2 *what the singer thinks of Lucas?*
  3 *what Lucas thought of the T-shirt?*
  4 *what the singer thinks of the clothes?*

2 1 *What does the singer like about Lucas?*
  2 *What is the one thing they rarely agree on?*
  3 *Where did Lucas go yesterday afternoon?*
  4 *In the singer's opinion, which item should Lucas definitely not buy?*

3 Trouve les mots qui riment.
  1 Lucas   a d'accord
  2 adores   b marrant
  3 vêtements   c bizarre
  4 magasin   d sympa
  5 noir   e bien
  6 pantalon   f non

4 *According to the chorus, the fact that Lucas and his friend don't like the same clothes is:*
  1 *sad*   2 *annoying*   3 *unimportant.*

9B Au centre d'activités

- discuss which activities you're going to do
- discuss issues of French pronunciation
- focus on high-frequency words *et* and *ou*

Ali et ses copains sont dans un centre d'activités en Normandie.

Programme pour la semaine prochaine

S'il fait beau, nous allons...

faire du cheval

faire du VTT

faire de la voile

faire de l'escalade

faire du théâtre

faire du tir à l'arc

faire du patin à glace

faire de la poterie

1 a Écoute (1–8). C'est une activité s'il fait beau ou s'il fait mauvais?

Exemple: **1** s'il fait mauvais

1 b **Prononciation**

Discuss in class: is there anything tricky about the pronunciation of the eight activities?

Example: *cheval – ch* in French is 'sh' not 'tch'

1 c Les phrases en silence! Partenaire A "dit" une phrase – mais sans le son! Partenaire B devine et dit la phrase.

dit – *says*   sans le son – *without a sound*

2 Écoute (1–6). Note les deux activités mentionnées. La personne va faire *une* activité ou *deux*?

Exemple: **1** A ou C →   une activité

Attention:
X **et** Y (*and*) = 2 activités
X **ou** Y (*or*) = 1 activité

A

B

C

D

E

F

G

H

3 a 📖 *Find the French words in Maxime's postcard for:* **1** *fun* **2** *tiring* **3** *exciting.*

Clues: the English words 'amusing', 'fatigue', 'passion'.

3 b 📖 **Lis les trois textes. Trouve et note:**
1 six activités 2 dix opinions

Exemple: **1** tir à l'arc, ...   **2** J'aime bien, ...

> Chère Tante Nicole,
>
> Je suis arrivé au centre d'activités ce matin. Demain, s'il fait mauvais, nous allons faire du tir à l'arc. J'aime bien: c'est amusant. S'il fait beau, nous allons faire de la voile. J'adore ça: c'est fatigant, mais c'est passionnant.
> Grosses bises,
> Maxime

> Cher Rachid,
>
> Ça va? Me voici au centre d'activités. C'est bien. Cet après-midi, nous allons faire du patin à glace ou de l'escalade. Moi, je préfère le patin à glace: c'est facile. L'escalade, c'est peut-être dangereux!?!
> À bientôt!
> Ton copain, Théo

> Chère Hélène,
>
> Je t'écris du centre d'activités. C'est génial: il y a beaucoup d'activités différentes. Demain, nous allons probablement faire du cheval (j'adore ça!), et puis nous allons faire de la poterie. Je n'ai jamais fait ça!
> Dis bonjour à Estelle!
> Grosses bises, Chloé

4 a 💿 **Écoute et lis le dialogue.**

A Qu'est-ce que nous allons faire lundi?

B Ça dépend. S'il fait beau, nous allons probablement faire de la voile.

A Génial! J'adore ça. Et s'il fait mauvais?

B S'il fait mauvais, nous allons faire du tir à l'arc.

A Je n'ai jamais fait ça, moi.

B C'est génial, et ce n'est pas difficile.

	s'il fait beau	s'il fait mauvais
lundi	voile	tir à l'arc
mardi	escalade	poterie
mercredi	VTT	théâtre
jeudi	cheval	patin à glace

4 b **Joue le dialogue. Puis adapte le dialogue pour mardi, mercredi et jeudi.** ▶

qu'est-ce que nous allons faire demain / lundi?	
s'il fait beau / mauvais...	
nous allons faire	du tir à l'arc / du théâtre / du cheval / du VTT du patin à glace / de la poterie / de la voile / de l'escalade
c'est ce n'est pas	amusant / génial / passionnant / facile / fatigant / difficile
je n'ai jamais fait ça, moi	

5 a ✏ **Tu es Paul. Écris une carte postale à ton oncle Henri avec les détails de ton texto!**

- Commence: *Cher Oncle Henri*
- Écris des phrases complètes.
- Finis par *À bientôt.*

5 b ✏ extra! **Écris un texto à un/une partenaire.**

bjr Suis centre d'act.
2m1: (beau) cheval -
jamais fait ça;
(mauvais) poterie -
difficile!
@ 2m1
Paul

2m1 = demain (en langue texto!)

9C Planète Futuroscope

- describe a planned school trip
- read about a French theme park
- use a dictionary

COLLÈGE LOUIS BOURDON
ALENÇON

Excursion au Futuroscope le jeudi 23 avril

- Le car va partir à 7h00.
- Nous allons arriver vers 10h30.
- Le matin, nous allons voir un film au cinéma 360°.
- À midi, nous allons manger dans un café.
- Après ça, s'il fait beau, nous allons peut-être voir le spectacle "Mélodies Aquatiques".
- Nous allons rentrer au collège vers 20h30.

> Cool! Jeudi, nous allons aller au Futuroscope. J'ai une lettre pour mes parents.

à onze heures

vers onze heures

1 Écoute et lis. Détective de langues: c'est quoi en anglais *partir, arriver, voir, rentrer*?

♻ **Grammaire:** *aller* (to go)

je	**vais**	I am going
tu	**vas**	you are going
il/elle	**va**	he /she is going
nous	**allons**	we are going
vous	**allez**	you are going
ils/elles	**vont**	they are going

2 Recopie et complète les phrases.

Marc – je – mes parents – vous – ma mère et moi, nous – tu

1 ___ allez manger à midi?
2 Demain matin, ___ va partir à sept heures, probablement.
3 Lundi, ___ allons voir un film au cinéma en ville.
4 L'après-midi, ___ vais faire mes devoirs.
5 ___ vas arriver à quelle heure?
6 Ce soir, ___ vont rentrer vers huit heures.

3 Écoute les informations sur trois autres excursions.

Les élèves vont **a** partir **b** arriver **c** rentrer à quelle heure?

extra! Tu peux noter combien d'autres détails?

Exemple: **1 a** 8h30 **b**... (*extra!* à Bayeux; ...)

4 Ali a perdu sa lettre de l'exercice 1!
A joue le père/la mère d'Ali, et pose des questions à Ali.
B joue Ali.

A Vous allez | partir à quelle heure?
arriver à quelle heure?
faire quoi?
manger où?
rentrer à quelle heure?

B Nous allons partir à 7h00.

	partir	à 7h30
nous allons	arriver	vers 10h
	rentrer	
le matin,		manger dans un café
à midi,	nous allons	voir un spectacle
après ça,		voir un film

Le Futuroscope

Avec ses cinémas Imax, ses films en 3D, ses effets spéciaux sensationnels, le Futuroscope est un parc d'attractions pas comme les autres!

Quelques attractions...

Métropole Défi – un jeu interactif en 3D

Tu prends les commandes de véhicules, et tu dois traverser la ville. Attention aux obstacles: trampoline, labyrinthe, barrières magnétiques...

Sur les traces du Panda

Tu es en Chine. Tu veux voir le panda géant, un des animaux les plus rares de la planète. L'expédition est probablement dangereuse...

Le 360°

Dans le cinéma circulaire, tu vas voir le film fascinant *Couleurs du Brésil*. Couleurs intenses, danses rythmiques, le carnaval splendide de Rio...

Cyber Avenue

60 jeux d'arcades (ski extrême, Formule 1, Foot, Jet Ski). Sensations extraordinaires!

prendre – *take*   le jeu (*pl* jeux) – *game*   traverser – *cross*

5 a 📖 *Imagine you are at Futuroscope. Which attraction would you choose first? Why?*

5 b *In French, the adjective usually comes <u>after</u> the noun. In English, the adjective usually comes <u>before</u> the noun.*

📖 *Recopie dix exemples en français, et écris aussi l'expression en anglais.*

Exemple: **1 effets spéciaux – *special effects***

6 a Stratégies! *Using the English section of the dictionary.*

For example, if you need the word for 'theme park':

> **theme** *n* thème *m*;
> ~ **park** *n* parc *m* d'attractions

- The ~ sign stands for the main word (in bold), so:
  ~ park = theme park
- *m* shows the word is masculine: *Nous allons aller à **un** parc d'attractions* (to a...)

● Look in the dictionary, then write down the French for:
  a to a leisure centre   **b** in a department store

6 b 🖉 Imagine: ta classe va faire une excursion. Écris à un ami en France: invente les détails.

Exemple:

> Samedi, nous allons visiter Alton Towers.
> Le matin, nous allons partir à...
> S'il fait beau, nous allons...

Stratégies! *Decribing a day out*

Think of the trip as six steps:
1 leaving
2 arriving at destination
3 morning activity
4 lunch
5 afternoon activity
6 return

Then write one sentence for each step.

9D Une page de casse-têtes!

- practise thinking skills
- read a story in French

1 a 💬 Paires logiques! Trouve les paires.

Exemple: **A** "Gauche" va avec "droite".
         B Oui, c'est ça!

> gauche   bavard
> c'est combien?
> et avec ça?   bonjour
> aller   la   c'est loin?
> faire   des

> je vais   aux
> c'est tout   de la voile
> deux euros trente
> sympa   au revoir
> une   droite
> c'est près du marché

1 b ✏️ extra! Explique les paires de l'exercice 1a.

- Ce sont deux mots au pluriel.
- Ce sont deux adjectifs.
- Ce sont deux mots féminins.
- C'est la réponse à la question.
- C'est le même contexte.
- C'est le même verbe.

> "gauche" va avec… – *"left" goes with…*
> c'est ça – *that's right*
> c'est le même verbe – *it's the same verb*
> ce sont deux mots – *they're two words*

1 c ✏️ Invente un jeu similaire pour ton/ta partenaire.

2 📖 Lis le mystère. Puis réponds aux questions.

Maman rentre du supermarché. Surprise: la porte est ouverte…
"Sabine! Sandrine! La porte est ouverte! Et où est le chien?" demande maman.
"Oh là, là! Je ne sais pas," dit Sabine.
"Qui a laissé la porte ouverte?" demande maman.
"Pas moi," dit Sabine. "Je suis rentrée à 4 heures, et Sandrine est rentrée après moi."
"Non, ce n'est pas vrai!" dit Sandrine. "Je suis rentrée à 4 heures, et Sabine est rentrée à 4h30."

Succès, maman!

Nous avons retrouvé le chien!

Cinq minutes plus tard…
Sabine et Sandrine rentrent du jardin – avec le chien!
"Succès, maman!" dit Sandrine.
"Nous avons retrouvé le chien!" dit Sabine.
"Bravo!" dit Maman. "Et moi, je sais qui est rentrée la dernière et a laissé la porte ouverte. C'est…❓"

> je sais – *I know*
> je ne sais pas – *I don't know*
> laisser la porte ouverte – *to leave the door open*

- **Qui a laissé la porte ouverte?**
- **Maman sait qui – comment? (*how?*)**
  (Réponse à la page 148!)

Pendant les vacances	**During the holidays**
qu'est-ce que tu vas faire…?	what are you going to do…?
la semaine prochaine	next week
pendant les vacances	during the holidays
ça dépend	it depends
je vais aller…	I'm going to go…
à Paris	to Paris
chez ma tante	to my aunt's
chez mon oncle	to my uncle's
chez mes cousins	to my cousins'
au cinéma	to the cinema
à la plage	to the beach
aux halles	to the covered market
peut-être	perhaps
probablement	probably
avec qui?	with whom?
avec ma famille	with my family
quand?	when?
le week-end	at the weekend

Au centre d'activités	**At the activity centre**
qu'est-ce que nous allons faire…?	what are we going to do…?
demain	tomorrow
lundi	on Monday
s'il fait beau	if the weather is good
s'il fait mauvais	if the weather is bad

nous allons faire…	we're going to…
du tir à l'arc	do archery
du théâtre	do drama
du cheval	go horse-riding
du VTT	go mountain-biking
du patin à glace	go ice-skating
de la poterie	do pottery
de la voile	go sailing
de l'escalade	go rock climbing
c'est amusant/génial	it's fun/great
c'est passionnant	it's exciting
c'est facile/difficile	it's easy/difficult
ce n'est pas fatigant	it isn't tiring
je n'ai jamais fait ça	I've never done that

Planète Futuroscope	**Planet Futuroscope**
le matin	in the morning
à midi	at midday
après ça	after that
nous allons…	we're going to…
partir à 7h30	leave at 7.30
arriver	arrive
rentrer vers 10h	return around 10.00
nous allons…	we're going to…
manger dans un café	eat in a café
voir un film	see a film
voir un spectacle	see a show

Les casse-têtes	**Brain-teasers**
"gauche" va avec…	'left' goes with…
c'est ça	that's right
c'est le même verbe	it's the same verb
ce sont deux mots	they're two words

♻ **Grammaire:**

- For events in the future, use *aller* + infinitive:

  je **vais** partir   I'm going to leave
  tu **vas** partir   you are going to leave
  il/elle **va** partir   he/she is going to leave

  nous **allons** partir   we are going to leave
  vous **allez** partir   you are going to leave
  ils/elles **vont** partir   they are going to leave

- 'to' in French:

  à + **named town**: *à Paris*   to Paris
  chez + **people**: *chez ma tante*   to my aunt's
  au/à la/ à l'/aux = 'to the' + **place**: *au café (m), à la plage (f), aux halles (pl)*

Stratégies!

- ★ keeping a conversation going: asking questions, saying more than the bare minimum
- ★ using the English section of the dictionary: headword represented by ~ symbol
- ★ focusing on high-frequency words *et* and *ou*
- ★ describing a day out

Cross-topic words

ça dépend – *it depends*
peut-être – *perhaps*

10 Des excursions

10A Le parc safari

- use the past tense to describe a visit
- predict how words will be pronounced

1 a 🔵 **Écoute et lis. Puis trouve et recopie les mots:**

a six animaux

b quatre choses à manger

c cinq choses à acheter à la boutique

Exemple: a girafes, …
           b hamburgers, …
           c peluches, …

1 b *Stratégies!*

Predicting how new words will be pronounced

- Les 15 mots de l'exercice 1a se prononcent comment?

Discute avec ton/ta partenaire.

Exemple:

> 'Girafes' – **g** comme **j**oue; on ne prononce pas le **s**.

- 🔵 Écoute les mots. Tu as bien deviné?

2 📖 **Relis le texte, et réponds aux questions.**

1 Les touristes visitent le parc safari en auto ou à pied?
Ils visitent…

2 La saison des films en 3D est de mars à août?   *Non, de… à…*

3 Où est la boutique?   *Elle est…*

4 Où est le parc safari?   *Il est…*

le choix – *choice*
la peluche – *cuddly toy*

Le parc safari

MONDE SAUVAGE

- **Visite du parc safari en voiture ou petit train. Les girafes, autruches, rhinocéros, zèbres, hippopotames, éléphants, etc. sont en semi-liberté.**

- **Cinéma 3D: films 3D du 01/05 au 30/09. Accès au cinéma sans supplément de prix.**

- **Restaurant: hamburgers, frites, croques-monsieur, desserts, etc.; café, thé, limonade, etc.**

- **Boutique, située à l'entrée du restaurant, avec un grand choix de souvenirs: peluches, cartes postales, T-shirts, casquettes, jeux…**

- **Monde Sauvage est situé dans le sud de la Belgique, à 20km au sud de Liège.**

Tarif: adultes 12,00€, enfants de 3 à 12 ans 8,00€

3 a  Écoute et lis la lettre de Marine. Puis, trouve dans la lettre et écris en français et en anglais:

a quatre expressions de temps

Exemple: **1** hier – *yesterday*, 2...

b six verbes au passé

Exemple: **1** j'ai visité – *I visited*, 2...

3 b ♻ **Grammaire:** *le passé*
- Le participe passé régulier: -**é**
  j'ai visit**é**, j'ai mang**é**, etc.
- Exceptions: j'ai **bu**, etc.   ◀◀ p. 70
- C'est quoi en anglais?
  a j'ai vu – *'I took'* or *'I saw'*?
  b j'ai pris – *'I took'* or *'I saw'*?

4 a  Écoute, puis joue le dialogue avec ton/ta partenaire.

A Tu as vu quels animaux?
B J'ai vu des éléphants.
A Tu as mangé un hamburger?
B Non, j'ai mangé une glace.
A Tu as bu un coca?
B Oui, j'ai bu un coca.
A Tu as pris beaucoup de photos?
B Bof, j'ai pris trois ou quatre photos.

4 b Recopie la grille. Puis écoute (1–4) et complète la grille.

4 c Joue les dialogues A–D. Ton modèle: l'exercice 4a.

Exemple: **A** Tu as vu quels animaux?
          B J'ai vu des autruches.

	j'ai vu	j'ai mangé	j'ai bu	photos
A	des autruches	une glace au chocolat	un coca	2–3
B	des rhinocéros	un sandwich au fromage	un café	5–6
C	des zèbres	un hamburger	une limonade	10
D	des girafes	des frites	un jus d'orange	7–8

5 a 🖊 Recopie le texte et invente les détails.

Hier, j'ai visité un parc safari. C'était ___. J'ai vu des ___ et des ___. J'ai pris beaucoup de ___!
À midi, j'ai ___ un hamburger et des ___. J'ai ___ un café. Après ça, j'ai acheté une ___.
A+

Salut, Ali!

Ça va? Moi, ça va bien.

Hier, j'ai visité un parc safari avec mes parents et ma copine Sarah. Le parc s'appelle Monde Sauvage. C'était génial! Il y a beaucoup d'animaux: j'ai vu des éléphants, des rhinocéros, des zèbres, etc. J'ai pris beaucoup de photos!

Après ça, j'ai vu un film en 3D sur les animaux sous-marins. C'était trop long. À midi, j'ai mangé un hamburger et des frites au restaurant, et j'ai bu un coca. J'ai acheté une vidéo, et puis j'ai acheté une peluche pour toi... Non, c'est une blague! La peluche, c'est pour ma cousine. Le soir, j'ai regardé la vidéo.

À+

Marine

une blague – *joke*

	j'ai vu	j'ai mangé	j'ai bu	photos?
1	rhinocéros			

j'ai visité	un parc safari
tu as vu	quels animaux?
j'ai vu	des girafes / des autruches des rhinocéros / des zèbres des éléphants des hippopotames
j'ai pris	des photos
j'ai mangé	un hamburger / des frites
j'ai bu	un coca / une limonade
j'ai acheté	une casquette / une peluche
c'était	génial

5 b 🖊 *extra*! Imagine la visite d'un parc safari. Ton modèle: la lettre de Marine.

10B Le match de foot

- describe a football match
- prepare for a listening activity
- use *il* and *elle* with the past tense

Samedi dernier, Marine a vu le match Anderlecht contre Standard. Son cousin, Pierre, a regardé le match à la télé.

Samedi dernier, je suis allée à un match de foot. C'était Standard Liège contre Anderlecht, et Anderlecht a gagné 3 à 0.

L'équipe d'Anderlecht a bien joué. Forrestier a marqué deux buts. À la quarantième minute, Mérode a passé le ballon à Genet, qui a marqué un troisième but.

C'était un match passionnant et une victoire sensationnelle!

Marine

Il a marqué un but

Il a sauvé un but

J'ai regardé le match Standard Liège contre Anderlecht à la télé.

L'équipe d'Anderlecht a gagné 3 à 0, mais Anderlecht n'a pas bien joué. Van Den Borre d'Anderlecht a eu un carton rouge. Ranson, le gardien de but de Standard, a sauvé deux buts.

C'était un match très médiocre, et une catastrophe pour Standard.

Pierre

1 a 💿 Écoute et lis les deux descriptions. Puis recopie le nom de:
a quatre footballeurs d'Anderlecht   **b** un footballeur de Standard.

1 b 📖 Regarde les mots a–c, puis réponds aux questions.

> **a** une équipe   *team;*
>   gagner   *to win* ⟶ *Which team won: Anderlecht or Standard?*
>
> **b** marquer un but   *to score a goal* ⟶ *Which two players scored goals?*
> **c** bien jouer   *to play well* ⟶ *Who says Anderlecht **didn't** play well?*

1 c 📖 C'est quoi en français?

1 *against*	**5** *an exciting match*
2 *Anderlecht won*	**6** *(he) got a red card*
3 *the team*	**7** *the goalkeeper*
4 *(he) passed the ball to*	**8** *(he) saved two goals*

1 d 📖 Relis les textes. À ton avis, qui est fan de Standard Liège: Marine ou Pierre?

1 e 💬 Lis les phrases de Marine et de Pierre: A une phrase, B une phrase.

2 ✏️ Relis les textes. Recopie huit expressions avec un verbe au passé.

Exemple: **1 Marine a vu**

> ♻️ **Grammaire:** *le passé avec* il *et* elle
>
> *j'ai* joué   *tu as* joué   *il/elle a* joué
> - Note how the **auxiliary verb** changes: *j'ai, tu as, il/elle a.*
> - The **past participle** (*joué, eu, vu,* etc.) doesn't change.
> - *Marine = elle   ⟶   Marine a joué*
>   *mon frère = il   ⟶   mon frère a vu*

3 a 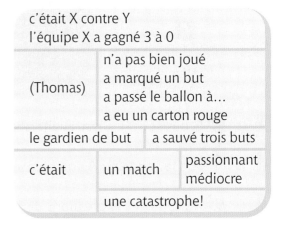 **Un match à la radio. Écoute et note la bonne réponse: *a* ou *b*.**

1 Le match était au stade de **a** Bruges **b** Charleroi.

2 Il y avait **a** 8 000 spectateurs **b** 10 000 spectateurs.

3 Le match a commencé **a** à 14h **b** à 15h.

4 **a** Deneuve **b** Van Damme a marqué le deuxième but.

5 À la mi-temps, le score était de **a** 1 à 1 **b** 2 à 0.

3 b *extra!* **Écoute et réponds aux questions.**

6 Quelle équipe a bien joué pendant la *deuxième* partie du match?

7 Le footballeur Trichard a fait quoi?

8 Quelle équipe a gagné? Et quel était le score final?

4 **Tu es reporter. Décris un match de football pour une émission de radio. Tu peux inventer un match, ou tu peux décrire un vrai match.**

- *Look at Marine's and Pierre's reports on page 90. Change any details (teams, players, score, etc.).*
- *Write out what you are going to say. Practise it out loud, with your partner checking your pronunciation.*
- *Give your radio report in a lively and convincing voice!*

Stratégies!
Preparing for listening activities

Listening is easier if you know what you're listening for!

- Read the questions carefully *before* the recording is played.
- Say the numbers you expect to hear so that you know what they'll sound like.

c'était X contre Y l'équipe X a gagné 3 à 0		
(Thomas)	n'a pas bien joué	
	a marqué un but	
	a passé le ballon à…	
	a eu un carton rouge	
le gardien de but	a sauvé trois buts	
c'était	un match	passionnant médiocre
	une catastrophe!	

5 a 📖 **Lis le texte, et recopie:**

1 sept pays européens

2 cinq adjectifs de nationalité

Exemples: **1 France, …**
           2 zimbabwéen, …

5 b 📖 *Explain in English:*

1 *the importance of Switzerland for young African players in Europe*

2 *the impact of the Africa Cup on European clubs.*

5 c **Si possible, écris le nom de footballeurs africains qui jouent dans ton pays!**

Les footballeurs africains en Europe

Il y a beaucoup de footballeurs africains dans les championnats d'élite de France, d'Allemagne, du Portugal, de Belgique, d'Angleterre et d'Italie. La Suisse est souvent une sorte de passage vers les grands championnats européens. Le joueur zimbabwéen, Benjani Mwaruwari, a joué en Suisse avant de jouer en France. Le footballeur congolais Shabani Nonda a aussi joué en Suisse. En 1997–8, il était le meilleur buteur de la ligue suisse – et pendant la saison 2002–3, il était le meilleur buteur de la ligue française!

Les footballeurs africains retournent en Afrique pour la Coupe d'Afrique: ils jouent dans leur équipe nationale. En 2004, par exemple, la ligue anglaise a perdu 17 joueurs africains – et la ligue française a perdu 53 footballeurs!

Shabani Nonda

vers – *towards*
le meilleur buteur – *best striker*
la coupe – *cup*
a perdu – *lost*

10C La visite chez un copain

- describe a visit to a friend
- say what 'we' did
- use time markers

D Nous avons regardé un match de foot à la télé.

A Hier, je suis allé(e) chez un copain.

B D'abord, nous avons bavardé.

C Puis nous avons fait un gâteau au chocolat.

E Puis nous avons bu un coca.

F Après ça, nous avons lu des magazines et des BD.

G Le soir, nous avons commandé une pizza.

1 a 💿 Écoute (1–7). C'est quelle phrase (A–G)?

1 b 💬 Lis les phrases: A une phrase, B une phrase.

1 c ✏️ Recopie les expressions de temps en français et en anglais.

Exemple: **1** hier – *yesterday*

Grammaire: *le passé avec* nous

j' **ai** joué	nous **avons** joué
tu **as** joué	
il/elle **a** joué	

- Note the auxiliary verb forms: j'**ai**, tu **as**, il/elle **a**, nous **avons**.
- The past participle (*bavardé, fait, lu*, etc.) doesn't change.

Remember this special verb:

je **suis** *allé* (male)/*je* **suis** *allée* (female) I went

---

Stratégies! *Time markers*

Describing a visit is easier if you use time markers like *hier*, *après ça* and *le soir* to say:

1 where you went yesterday
2 then what you did
3 what you did after that
4 what you did in the evening.

2 a ✏️ Recopie et complète les phrases.

Exemple: **1 Hier nous** *avons* **joué au badminton.**

1 Hier, nous ___ joué au badminton.
2 Puis ___ avons bavardé.
3 Mon frère ___ fait ses devoirs.
4 Puis il a ___ un magazine.
5 Mardi dernier, je ___ allé chez une copine.
6 ___ avons fait un gâteau au chocolat.
7 La mère de ma copine ___ commandé une pizza.
8 Le soir, nous ___ écouté de la musique.

2 b ✏️ extra! Écris en français.

1 *Yesterday, I went to my friend Lisa's house.*
2 *We watched a film on TV.*
3 *Then we read some comics.*
4 *In the evening, Lisa ordered a pizza.*

3 💿 Écoute les dialogues (1–5).

Note **a** l'activité **b** quand

extra! **c** où **d** avec qui

Exemple: **1 a** vélo; **b** samedi

(extra! **c** campagne; **d** deux amis)

4 💬 **La chaîne: A dit une phrase, B répète la phrase et ajoute une phrase, etc.**

Exemple: **A** Hier, nous avons fait du vélo.
B Hier, nous avons fait du vélo et nous avons regardé un film.
A Hier, nous avons fait du vélo et nous avons regardé un film
et nous avons...

5 a ♻️ 🖊️ **Recyclage de vocabulaire. À deux: recopiez et complétez
les phrases avec les quatre verbes.** ▶

Exemple: **Nous avons mangé un sandwich au jambon, une glace à la menthe, ...**

> du vélo
> un sandwich au jambon
> un magazine   un jus d'orange
> les courses   une lettre   du judo
> une glace à la menthe
> une BD   la vaisselle   du lait
> de la natation   des bonbons
> les devoirs   un livre
> un grand crème   des biscuits

Nous avons mangé...

Nous avons fait...

Nous avons bu...

Nous avons lu...

5 b 🖊️ **extra! Écris huit phrases avec
nous avons + participes passés différents.**

Exemples: **1** Nous avons surfé sur Internet.

Proposition: «Les jeunes d'aujourd'hui sont accros à la télé et aux jeux électroniques.»

accros à/aux – *addicted to*

Vrai ou faux?

Je pense que c'est ridicule. Hier, par exemple, je suis allé chez un ami. Nous avons fait du vélo. Il a fait beau, et nous avons pris des photos. Nous n'avons pas joué aux jeux électroniques!

Seydou

6 a 📖 **Lis les textes.**

1 Seydou, Louise et Aïcha sont d'accord avec
la proposition: oui ou non?

2 Ton opinion: qui est le plus actif/la plus active:
Seydou, Louise ou Aïcha? Pourquoi?

Exemple: **Je pense que c'est... parce qu'il/elle a...**

Ça dépend. Ma copine Inès regarde souvent la télé, c'est vrai. Mais moi, je préfère lire des livres. La semaine dernière, j'ai lu deux gros livres. Et Inès et moi, nous avons joué au ping-pong, et nous avons aussi fait une pizza.

Louise

6 b 🖊️ **Écris une réponse au magazine.**

Exemple:

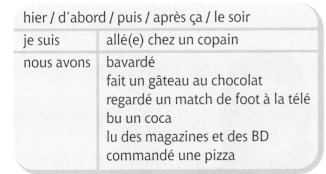

Je pense que c'est ridicule/vrai.
Hier, par exemple, j'ai...
Samedi, mes copains et moi,
nous...

Hier, nous avons regardé la télé pendant trois heures, et nous n'avons pas beaucoup bavardé. Nous avons commandé une pizza, et nous avons mangé la pizza devant la télé. Mais avant-hier, nous avons fait du patin à glace, et samedi, nous avons fait une marche de 10km!

Aïcha

hier / d'abord / puis / après ça / le soir	
je suis	allé(e) chez un copain
nous avons	bavardé
	fait un gâteau au chocolat
	regardé un match de foot à la télé
	bu un coca
	lu des magazines et des BD
	commandé une pizza

10D Le bus pour le stade

- ask for the right bus
- understand instructions with *ne ... pas*

Aujourd'hui, Anderlecht joue contre Sporting Charleroi. Marine et sa copine Sarah arrivent à la gare de Charleroi.

> Ne prenez pas le 81. Prenez le 16 – c'est plus rapide.

> Non. Descendez à l'hôtel de ville, et prenez le 22 pour le stade.

> Merci, monsieur.

> De rien.

> Pardon, monsieur. C'est quel bus pour le stade de football? C'est le 81?

> Le 16 va au stade?

1 a 💿 Écoute et lis. C'est vrai ou faux?

1 Marine et Sarah sont à un arrêt de bus à Charleroi.
2 Marine veut aller au stade de football.
3 Le bus numéro 16 va au stade.

1 b 📖 Écris les mots en français et en anglais.

Exemple: prenez – *take*

> prenez c'est quel bus pour...?
> de rien descendez
> ne prenez pas plus rapide

1 c 💿 Réécoute le dialogue, puis joue le dialogue avec ton/ta partenaire.

> pardon, monsieur
> c'est quel bus pour (le stade)?
> c'est le 81?
> ne prenez pas le 81
> prenez le 16: c'est plus rapide
> le 16 va (au stade) / (à la poste)?
> descendez à l'hôtel de ville
> merci, monsieur
> de rien

Grammaire: giving instructions to more than one person

- Use the *vous* form of the verb:
  *pren**ez** le bus* take the bus
- *Ne* in front of the verb and *pas* after the verb make the instruction negative (i.e. 'don't...'):
  ***ne** prenez **pas** le 11*
  don't take the number 11

2 b 🗣 extra! Invente deux dialogues similaires.

2 a ✏️ Écris les dialogues A et B. Change les mots en rouge.

– Pardon, monsieur. C'est quel bus pour la gare? C'est le 4?
– Non, ne prenez pas le 4. Prenez le 18: c'est plus rapide. Descendez à la piscine et prenez le 22 pour la gare.
– Merci, monsieur.
– De rien.

A	B
madame le théâtre/9?	monsieur la patinoire/12?
✗ 14 à la poste 78/le théâtre	✗ 26 au parc 3/à la patinoire
madame	monsieur

> Hourra! Anderlecht a gagné 2 à 1!

Le parc safari / The safari park

Le parc safari	The safari park
j'ai visité	*I visited*
un parc safari	*a safari park*
tu as vu quels animaux?	*what animals did you see?*
j'ai vu...	*I saw...*
des girafes	*some giraffes*
des autruches	*some ostriches*
des rhinocéros	*some rhinos*
des éléphants	*some elephants*
des hippopotames	*some hippos*
des zèbres	*some zebras*
j'ai pris des photos	*I took some photos*
j'ai mangé...	*I ate...*
un hamburger	*a hamburger*
des frites	*some chips*
j'ai bu...	*I drank...*
un coca	*a coke*
une limonade	*a lemonade*
j'ai acheté...	*I bought...*
une casquette	*a cap*
une peluche	*a cuddly toy*
c'était génial	*it was great*

Le match de foot / The football match

Le match de foot	The football match
c'était X contre Y	*it was X against Y*
l'équipe...	*the team...*
a gagné 3 à 0	*won 3–0*
Thomas...	*Thomas...*
n'a pas bien joué	*didn't play well*
a marqué un but	*scored a goal*
a passé le ballon à...	*passed the ball to...*
a eu un carton rouge	*got a red card*
le gardien de but	*the goal keeper*
a sauvé trois buts	*saved three goals*
c'était un match passionnant	*it was an exciting match*
médiocre	*mediocre*
une catastrophe	*a catastrophe*

Chez mon copain / At my friend's house

Chez mon copain	At my friend's house
hier	*yesterday*
d'abord	*to begin with*
puis	*then*
après ça	*after that*
le soir	*in the evening*
je suis allé(e)...	*I went...*
chez un copain	*to a friend's house*
nous...	*we...*
avons bavardé	*chatted*
avons fait un gâteau au chocolat	*made a chocolate cake*
avons regardé un match de foot à la télé	*watched a football match on TV*
avons bu un coca	*drank a coke*
avons lu des BD et des magazines	*read comics and magazines*
avons commandé une pizza	*ordered a pizza*

Le bus pour le stade / The bus to the stadium

Le bus pour le stade	The bus to the stadium
pardon, monsieur	*excuse me* (to man)
pardon, madame	*excuse me* (to woman)
c'est quel bus pour le stade?	*which bus is it for the stadium?*
c'est le 81?	*is it the 81?*
ne prenez pas le 81	*don't take the 81*
prenez le 16	*take the 16*
c'est plus rapide	*it's faster*
le 16 va à la poste?	*does the 16 go to the post office?*
descendez à l'hôtel de ville	*get off at the town hall*
merci	*thank you*
de rien	*don't mention it*

Cross-topic words

hier – *yesterday*
d'abord – *to begin with*

Grammaire:

- le passé:

  j' **ai** joué/vu
  tu **as** joué/vu
  il/elle **a** joué/vu
  nous **avons** joué/vu

  Exception: je **suis** allé (*male*)
  je **suis** allée (*female*)

- instructions (plural):
  pren**ez** le bus *take the bus*
  ne prenez **pas** le 11 *don't take the number 11*

Stratégies!

★ predicting from the spelling how new words will be pronounced

★ preparing for listening activities by studying the instructions *before* the recording begins

★ using time markers (e.g. *hier, puis, après ça, le soir*) to describe a sequence of activities

11 Une visite à Bayeux

11A Un pique-nique

- suggest what food to take on a picnic
- say what you eat and drink
- use *ou* (or)

On prend du lait?

Et on prend de l'eau minérale?

Oui, bonne idée, j'aime ça.

Non, je n'ai pas envie.

Ali et sa famille vont visiter la ville de Bayeux. Ils préparent un pique-nique...

A

du lait

B

des poires f

C

de la salade

D

des pêches f

E

du pain

F

de l'eau minérale f

G

du beurre

H

de la confiture

I

du sucre

1 a 💿 Écoute (1–5). Note les deux choses (A–I) mentionnées dans chaque dialogue.

Exemple: **1** A (du lait) + F (de l'eau minérale)

1 b 💬 Joue des dialogues avec ton/ta partenaire.

A On prend du lait?

on – 1 *they, people* 2 *we*

B Oui, bonne idée, j'aime ça.   *ou*   Non, je n'ai pas envie!

Grammaire: *du, de la , de l', des* (some)

	masc. sing*	fem. sing*	*if starting with vowel/h	all plurals
some	*du*	*de la*	*de l'*	*des*
On prend...	*du* lait?	*de la* confiture?	*de l'*eau?	*des* pêches?
Shall we take...	some milk?	some jam?	some water?	some peaches?

---

2 a Stratégies! *Working out the gender*

- Which words in 1a are masculine? Which are feminine? Discuss with a partner.

  Examples:

1 *Du lait*: *du* means 'some' with masculine words, so *lait* must be masculine – *le lait* milk.

2 *Des poires*: *des* means 'some' with all plural words: it gives no clue about gender. But the *f* shows that *poire* is feminine.

2 b 🖊 Recopie les mots de l'exercice 1a dans trois listes.

masc. sing.	fém. sing.	masc. et fém. pluriel
le lait *milk*	la...	les...

2 c 🖊 *extra!* Écris six questions.
On prend *du/de la/de l'/des...?*

Exemple: **1 On prend des biscuits?**

1 biscuits *pl*   **3** jambon *m*   **5** ail *m*
2 limonade *f*   **4** poisson *m*   **6** chips *pl*

3 a 💿 Écoute et lis les textes. Puis regarde les images (A–F). C'est qui, Ali ou Marine?

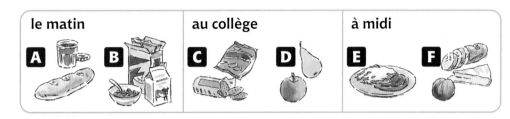

le matin   **A**   **B**   au collège   **C**   **D**   à midi   **E**   **F**

Tu manges quoi le matin et à midi? Tu bois quoi?

Le matin, normalement, je mange du pain avec du beurre et de la confiture. Je bois du lait ou du thé. Au collège, je mange une pomme ou une poire. À midi, je prends de la viande avec du riz ou des pommes de terre, et si j'ai envie, je prends un dessert.
Ali

Le matin, je prends des céréales avec du lait. Je bois du chocolat chaud. Au collège, je mange parfois des biscuits ou des chips. À midi, je mange du pain avec du fromage, ou de la salade. Si j'ai envie, je mange aussi une pêche. Je bois du jus d'orange.
Marine

3 b 🖊 Trouve les phrases avec *ou* dans les deux textes. Écris les phrases en français et en anglais.

Exemple: **Je bois du lait ou du thé.**
           I drink some milk or some tea.

4 a 💿 *Listen to four presentations. Which speaker:*

a *speaks too fast?*   **c** *has a boring voice?*
b *says too little?*   **d** *stumbles too much?*

4 b 🖊 Tu manges quoi le matin et à midi? Tu bois quoi? Écris un paragraphe.

● Adapte les phrases de l'exercice 3a.
  (Des problèmes? Consulte la page 29.)
● Si possible, écris des phrases avec *ou*.

4 c 💬 Prépare ta présentation (suggestions: ◀◀ p. 29).
Puis donne ta présentation!

Stratégies! *Using the word* **ou** *(or)*

Alternatives can make sentences more interesting:
*Je mange une pomme **ou** une poire.*
I eat an apple **or** a pear

on prend... / je mange...	
du	pain / lait / beurre / sucre
de la	confiture / salade
de l'	eau minérale
des	poires / pêches
bonne idée / non, je n'ai pas envie	
le matin,	je mange (parfois)...
au collège,	ou je mange...
à midi,	je bois (aussi)...

11B Au musée de Bayeux

- ask for tickets at a museum
- learn and act out a longer dialogue
- use *il faut*

Dans ce musée à Bayeux, il y a une BD de 70 mètres de long, créée en 1070: la tapisserie de Bayeux.

1 a 💿 Écoute et lis. Quelles images sont correctes: a ou b?

1a **ouvert 9h à 19h** 1b **ouvert 9h à 17h**

2a **6,80€** 2b **6,50€**

Mme Amrani:	Bonjour, monsieur. L'entrée, c'est combien, s'il vous plaît?
L'employé:	C'est six euros cinquante pour un adulte.
Mme Amrani:	Et pour un enfant?
L'employé:	Deux euros quarante pour un enfant.
Mme Amrani:	Alors, deux adultes et un enfant. Voilà.
L'employé:	Merci, madame.
Mme Amrani:	Le musée ferme à quelle heure?
L'employé:	À dix-neuf heures, madame.
Mme Amrani:	Merci, monsieur.
L'employé:	De rien.

1 b 💬 Joue les petits dialogues (1–6).

Exemple: A Le musée ferme à quelle heure?
B À quatorze heures trente.

1 `14:30` **2** `15:00` **3** `16:15`

4 `17:45` **5** `18:00` **6** `19:30`

bonjour, monsieur / madame
l'entrée, c'est combien, s'il vous plaît?
c'est (six) euros (vingt)
 pour un adulte / pour un enfant
alors, un(e) adulte et un(e) enfant
le musée ferme à quelle heure?
à (quinze) heures (trente)

merci	de rien

1 c 💬 Joue le dialogue de Mme Amrani et l'employé.

2 a 💿 Écoute (1–4). C'est le dialogue A, B, C ou D?

A
entrée/combien?
4,30€ adulte/2,60€
 enfant
Voilà.
ferme?
17h00
Merci, madame.

B
entrée?
3,20€/1,80€
Voilà.
ferme?
18h30
Merci, monsieur.

C
entrée?
5,60€/4,10€
Voilà.
ferme?
18h15
Merci, madame.

D
entrée?
6,70€/3,90€
Voilà.
ferme?
17h45
Merci, monsieur.

2 b 💬 Joue les dialogues A–D avec ton/ta partenaire. Ton modèle: l'exercice 1a.

2 c ✏️ Écris deux dialogues. Remplace les chiffres par des mots.

Exemples: 3,20€ = trois euros vingt; 17h00 = dix-sept heures.

les chiffres *f – figures*
les mots *m – words*

3 a 🎧 Écoute et lis. C'est quoi en français?

1 *you have to wait*
2 *over there*
3 *at the cash desk*
4 *you have to leave your bag*
5 *here*

3 b 🎧 Écoute les dialogues <u>incomplets</u>. Dis les derniers mots à ton/ta prof!

3 c 💬 Joue les trois dialogues.

Grammaire:

● ***il faut + l'infinitif*** **(it is necessary to/you have to)**
Il faut is followed by the infinitive – just as after *je peux*, *je veux*, *je dois* (◀◀ pp. 63 et 67).
*il faut pay**er*** you have to pay
*il faut laiss**er*** *votre sac* you have to leave your bag
Il faut is a set phrase: there are no forms with *je*, *tu*, etc.

● ***attendre*** **to wait**
The infinitive of regular verbs ends in *-er* (e.g. *jou**er***).
Note that some verbs have an infinitive ending in *-re*:
*il faut atten**dre*** you have to wait

4 ✏️ Recopie et complète les phrases.

> attendre   laisser   parler   payer
> rouler   tourner

Exemple: **Il faut laisser votre sac à la réception.**

1 Il faut ___ votre sac à la réception.
2 Vous attendez le guide? Il faut ___ là-bas.
3 Pour les toilettes, il faut ___ à gauche.
4 Dans un supermarché, il faut ___ à la caisse.
5 En France, il faut ___ à droite.
6 Au Québec, il faut ___ français.

5 🎧 Écoute (1–4) et note:

a combien d'adultes et d'enfants?
b le musée ferme à quelle heure?
c *extra!* une instruction avec *il faut*

Exemple: **1 a 2 adultes, 2 enfants; b 18h;**
extra! c il faut attendre là-bas.

il y a une visite guidée?
oui, il faut attendre le guide là-bas
je peux acheter des cartes postales?
oui, il faut payer à la caisse
il faut laisser votre sac ici

6 a *Stratégies! Learning a longer dialogue.*

● Read the first seven lines of the dialogue on page 100, then try to say them off by heart.
● Now do the same with the whole dialogue.
● Practise the speech bubbles at the top of this page. Then try the dialogue from page 100, adding in any two of the *il faut* instructions.

6 b ✏️ *Writing helps most people remember better. Copy out the dialogue in exercise 1 but:*

● *change any parts you can change (discuss with your partner what these changes could be);*
● *add two of the three instructions from the top of this page.*

11C L'histoire de France

- *ils* and *elles* form of present tense verbs
- read about events in French history
- find parallels between French and English

A

B

1 a 💿 Écoute et lis les textes (1–4).
Les images A et B illustrent quels *deux* textes?

L'histoire de France en huit épisodes: épisodes 1–4

1 Les Romains (124 avant Jésus-Christ)
Les Romains arrivent en France.
- Il y a des amphithéâtres, des aqueducs…
- Les familles riches habitent dans des villas.

2 Les Vikings (800–1066)
Les Vikings attaquent la France.
- En 911, ils occupent la Normandie.
- Guillaume le Conquérant, duc de Normandie, attaque l'Angleterre en 1066.

3 Les Anglais (1300–1453)
- Les Anglais occupent le sud et l'ouest de la France. Il y a cent ans de guerre entre la France et l'Angleterre!
- En 1453: les Anglais quittent la France.

quitter – *to leave*
la guerre – *war*

4 Louis XIV (1643–1715)
- Louis XIV (Louis Quatorze) naît en 1638.
- Louis aime la musique et il aime danser.
- Ses architectes construisent une résidence magnifique: c'est le palais de Versailles.
- Il se marie deux fois: avec Marie-Thérèse (1660) et avec Madame de Maintenon (1683).
- Louis est intelligent mais arrogant. Il persécute les Protestants en France.
- Ses guerres en Europe ruinent la France.
- Louis meurt en 1715 à 77 ans.

naît – *is born*
meurt – *dies*

1 b 📖 *Answer in English.*
1. *What sort of buildings did the Romans build?*
2. *In which part of France did the Vikings live?*
3. *What happened in 1453?*
4. *List any three facts about Louis XIV.*

1 c Stratégies! *French gu- often = English w-*
- Find two examples of a French word beginning with *gu-* where the English word begins with *w-*.

1 d 💿 extra! Écoute les dates. Note *une* erreur pour chaque épisode.
Exemple: **1 1͟34 av. J.-C.**

2 📖 Recopie huit phrases avec un verbe *-ent*. Écris les phrases en français et en anglais.
Exemple: **1 Les Romains arrivent.** *The Romans arrive.*

♻️ **Grammaire: *ils/elles* form of the verb**

The verb ending after *ils/elles* (they) is usually -*ent*: *elles arriv**ent**, ils attaqu**ent***.

- You pronounce the -*ent* ending like the -*e* ending, so *il quitte* and *ils quittent* sound the same.
- Plural nouns (e.g. *les Vikings, mes parents*) take the same endings as *ils/elles*.

◀

L'histoire de France en huit épisodes: épisodes 5–8

5 La Révolution française (1789)

Le 14 juillet 1789, c'est la Révolution!

- Les Parisiens attaquent la prison de la Bastille. 40 000 personnes passent à la guillotine.
- La Révolution transforme la France en République.

6 Napoléon (1792–1815)

Napoléon établit l'Empire.

- Les armées françaises occupent l'Espagne, l'Italie, l'Allemagne du Nord, la Hollande, la Belgique, etc.
- Les armées françaises marchent à droite. Conséquence? On roule à droite en Europe!

7 Hostilités franco-allemandes (1870–1945)

- Une guerre en 1870.
- La première guerre mondiale 1914–18.
- La deuxième guerre mondiale 1939–45.

allemand – *German*
la guerre mondiale – *world war*

8 L'Union européenne (1957–aujourd'hui)

- Après la guerre: la reconstruction de la France.
- En 1957, la France, l'Allemagne, l'Italie, la Belgique, la Hollande et le Luxembourg créent la Communauté européenne. Aujourd'hui, c'est l'Union européenne.

aujourd'hui – *today*

3 a Écoute et lis. Trouve les paires: épisodes historiques (5–8) et images (C–F).

3 b Réécoute et lis les épisodes 5–8. Réponds *en anglais*.

1 La Révolution française commence à quelle date?
2 Une conséquence (aujourd'hui) dans les pays occupés par Napoléon?
3 En 1870, c'est la guerre entre quels deux pays?
4 Quels pays créent la Communauté européenne en 1957?

3 c Trouve et recopie quinze mots similaires en français et en anglais.

Exemple: histoire – *history*

4 extra! Écoute et note des détails sur le développement de l'Union européenne.

Exemple: *three new members in 1973, ...*

5 extra! Adapte le texte sur Louis XIV (◄◄ p. 102): décris le roi Henri VIII d'Angleterre.

Exemple: ~~Louis XIV~~ naît ~~en 1638~~ .
→ Henri VIII naît en 1491.

Henry VIII d'Angleterre: 1491–1547
aime musique
palais de Hampton Court
six fois
intelligent, arrogant
persécute les Catholiques

11D Un e-mail d'Ali

- say what someone else did
- revise past tense with *il* and *elle*

> Génial! Un e-mail d'Ali.

Salut, Marine!

Hier, j'ai fait une excursion. J'ai visité le musée de Bayeux, et j'ai vu la tapisserie: c'était super!

J'ai acheté une vidéo.

À midi, j'ai fait un pique-nique dans un parc. Le soir, j'ai regardé la vidéo.

A+

Ali

> Hier, **Ali a** fait une excursion. **Il a** visité le musée de Bayeux et **il a** vu la tapisserie: c'était super!
>
> **Il a** acheté une vidéo.
>
> À midi, **il a** fait un pique-nique dans un parc. Le soir, **il a** regardé la vidéo.

1 a 🔘 Écoute et lis. Ali a fait les activités A–F: oui ou non?

 **A**  **B** **C**  **D**  **E**  **F**

1 b 🔘 Écoute (1–5). Il/Elle a fait *deux* activités (A–F). Lesquelles?

lesquelles? – which ones?

Exemple: **1 C + D**

♻ Grammaire: *il/elle* in the past tense

- *J'ai…* changes to *il a…* or *elle a…*
- But there's no change in *joué, acheté, fait, vu,* etc.
  j'ai mangé I ate → *il/elle a* mangé he/she ate
  j'ai fait I did → ***Marine a** fait* Marine did

2 a ✏ Écris huit phrases.

Exemple: **Hier, elle a eu maths.**

Hier, À midi, Le soir,	elle a il a	eu visité joué surfé vu fait mangé acheté	un musée un film un T-shirt maths au restaurant au foot du vélo sur Internet

2 b 💬 Tu es le père/la mère de Marine.

Pose cinq questions sur Ali. (Regarde l'e-mail d'Ali!)

Exemples: **A** Ali a eu maths?   **B** Non.
          A Il a visité un musée?   **B** Oui.

> hier / à midi / le soir
>
> il a
> elle a
>
> visité le musée
> acheté une vidéo
> regardé la vidéo
> vu la tapisserie
> fait un pique-nique / une excursion

3 ✏ Complète le texte et décris le week-end de Marine.

Exemple: Samedi, Marine *a acheté* un pull en ville.
Puis *elle…*

> Samedi, (acheter) un pull en ville. Puis, (manger) un hamburger. L'après-midi, (jouer) au tennis avec Élise, et puis (faire) du vélo.
>
> Dimanche, (inviter) des amies. Le soir, (écouter) de la musique.

Un pique-nique	*A picnic*
on prend...	*shall we take...*
du pain?	*some bread?*
du lait?	*some milk?*
du beurre?	*some butter?*
du sucre?	*some sugar?*
de la confiture?	*some jam?*
de la salade?	*some salad?*
de l'eau minérale?	*some mineral water?*
des poires?	*some pears?*
des pêches?	*some peaches?*
bonne idée	*good idea*
je n'ai pas envie	*I don't feel like it*
le matin	*in the morning*
au collège	*at school*
à midi	*at midday*
je mange (parfois)	*I (sometimes) eat*
ou je mange	*or I eat*
je bois (aussi)	*I (also) drink*

Au musée	*At the museum*
bonjour, monsieur	*good morning/good afternoon, sir*
bonjour, madame	*good morning/good afternoon, madam*
l'entrée, c'est combien, s'il vous plaît?	*how much is it to go in, please?*
c'est six euros vingt	*it's 6 euros 20*
pour un adulte	*for an adult*
pour un enfant	*for a child*

alors, un(e) adulte et un(e) enfant	*well then, one adult and one child*
le musée ferme à quelle heure?	*what time does the museum close?*
à quinze heures dix	*at 15.10*
merci	*thank you*
de rien	*don't mention it*
il y a une visite guidée?	*is there a guided tour?*
je peux acheter des cartes postales?	*can I buy some post cards?*
il faut...	*you have to...*
payer à la caisse	*pay at the cash-desk*
laisser votre sac	*leave your bag*
attendre le guide	*wait for the guide*
là-bas	*over there*
ici	*here*

Un e-mail d'Ali	*An email from Ali*
hier	*yesterday*
le soir	*in the evening*
à midi	*at midday*
il...	*he...*
a visité le musée	*visited the museum*
a acheté une vidéo	*bought a video*
a regardé la vidéo	*watched the video*
elle...	*she...*
a vu la tapisserie	*saw the tapestry*
a fait un pique-nique	*had a picnic*
a fait une excursion	*went on a trip*

Grammaire:

● some:

masc. sing*	fem. sing*	*if starting with vowel/h	all plurals
du lait	**de la** salade	**de l'**eau	**des** pêches

● *il faut + infinitif* (you have to): *il faut payer*   you have to pay

The infinitive of regular verbs ends in -er but some infinitives end in -re (e.g. *attendre* to wait).

● ♻ The verb ending after *ils/elles* (they) is usually -ent: *elles arriv**ent**, ils attaqu**ent**.

● The past tense with he/she: **il a** *mangé*   he ate, **elle a** *bu*   she drank.

Stratégies!

★ working out the gender from grammatical clues

★ making sentences more interesting by using *ou* (or)

★ practising and learning a longer dialogue

★ French *gu-* often = English *w-*: *Guillaume* – **W**illiam, *guerre* – **w**ar

Cross-topic words

ici – *here*
là-bas – *there*

12 L'anniversaire de Marine

12A Préparations

- say which presents you like
- say why you like or dislike them
- predict how new words are said

> Oui, c'est un cadeau original. Et j'aime aussi cette écharpe.

> Regarde. Tu aimes ce réveil?

Samedi, c'est l'anniversaire de Marine. Ses amies sont en ville: ils achètent des cadeaux d'anniversaire.

> Tu aimes... ?

> J'aime...

A

B *ce livre*

C *ce réveil*

D *ce poster*

F *cette gourde*

1 a 🔘 Écoute (1–6).
Note les *deux* lettres (A–F).

Exemple: **1 C + D**

D *cette écharpe*

E *cette trousse*

1 b 💬 Discute et compare avec ton/ta partenaire.

    A   Tu aimes cette écharpe?

    B   Oui, j'aime bien.   Non, pas beaucoup.

                 Bof...

G *ces boucles d'oreille*

H *ces gants*

2 a ✏️ **Regarde les images 1–8. Écris ta liste de préférences. (Position 1 = ton cadeau préféré, 8 = ton dernier choix!)**

Exemple:

> Ma liste de préférences
> J'aime   1 ce réveil
>   2 c___ ___

> **Grammaire: *ce*, *cette* (this), *ces* (these)**
>
> | masculine nouns | feminine nouns | all plural nouns |
> |---|---|---|
> | ***ce*** *livre*   this book | ***cette*** *écharpe*   this scarf | ***ces*** *gants*   these gloves |

1   *CD m*

2   *casquette f*

3   *trousse f*

4   *bottines pl*

2 b ✏️ **Écris les questions (1–8).**

Exemple: **1 Tu aimes <u>ce</u> CD?**

5   *réveil m*

6   *ceinture f*

7   *boucles d'oreille pl*

8   *T-shirt m*

3 a ⚲ Les opinions se prononcent comment?

> **C'est un cadeau amusant!**

> **C'est un cadeau pratique!**

> **C'est un cadeau original!**

> **Je n'aime pas la couleur!**

Stratégies! *Predicting the pronunciation of new words*

Here are two useful phrases for discussing how words are pronounced:
– *"Amusant": on ne prononce pas le* **t**.
 You don't pronounce the **t**.

– *"Original":* **a** *comme 'la'.*   Original: **a** as in *la*.

3 b 💿 Écoute et vérifie.

4 a 💿 Écoute les dialogues A et B. Puis joue et adapte les dialogues: discute des cadeaux (A–H) à la page 106.

A – Tu aimes ce livre?
 – Oui, j'aime bien.   Ben, … – *Well, …*
 – Pourquoi?
 – Ben… c'est un cadeau original. Et toi?
 – Moi, je n'aime pas ce livre.

B – Tu aimes cette écharpe?
 – Non, pas beaucoup.
 – Pourquoi?
 – Ben… je n'aime pas la couleur. Et toi?
 – Moi, j'aime cette écharpe. C'est un cadeau pratique.

4 b ✏️ Écris deux dialogues adaptés.

5 📖 extra! *Read the article.*

a *What is it about?*
b *Summarise Axel's, Océane's and Laurent's opinions.*
c *Whose opinion do you most agree with?*

tu aimes	ce	poster / livre / réveil
j'aime	cette	écharpe / trousse / gourde
je n'aime pas	ces	boucles d'oreille / gants
oui, j'aime bien / bof… / non, pas beaucoup		
pourquoi?	ben…	c'est un cadeau	amusant / pratique / original
		je n'aime pas la couleur	

Des cadeaux stéréotypés pour garçons et filles?

> Je déteste les magasins avec des articles bleus pour les garçons et des articles roses pour les filles! Des CD, des posters… voici de bonnes idées pour les garçons *et* les filles, non?

Laurent

> À mon avis, il faut attaquer les rôles stéréotypés! Il faut acheter des soldats et des voitures pour les petites filles et des peluches pour les garçons. Pourquoi pas?

Axel

> À mon avis, les filles et les garçons sont différents!
> Pour mes copines, j'achète une peluche ou un parfum. Pour mes copains, j'achète un magazine sur les voitures, un ballon de foot ou un poster.

Océane

> Des cadeaux sexistes – ou réalistes?

6 💿 Écoute et note la bonne réponse, *a* ou *b*.

1 Pour sa sœur, Sylvain achète   **a** un livre   **b** une vidéo.
2 Son père   **a** aime la pêche et le vélo   **b** ne va pas à la pêche.
3 À sa mère il offre   **a** du parfum, des gants ou des boucles d'oreille   **b** un gâteau.
4 Son petit frère   **a** joue avec ses petites voitures   **b** ne joue pas avec ses petites voitures.

> le garçon – *boy*
> la fille – *girl*

12B La soirée de Marine

- exchange contact details
- deduce the meaning of new words
- say phone numbers and email addresses

Salut, Marine!
Bon anniversaire!

1 a 🎵 **Écoute et lis le dialogue. Puis explique les mots en rouge à ton/ta partenaire.**

Stratégies! *Working out the meaning of words from the context*

Knowing the situation (i.e. Élise wants Nathan's contact details) helps you to deduce what many of the new words must be.

A
| Élise: | Nathan, c'est quoi ton adresse? |
| Nathan: | Mon adresse, c'est 45, rue Piroé, Lille. |

B
| Élise: | Ça s'écrit comment? |
| Nathan: | P – I – R – O – E accent aigu. |

C
| Élise: | Et le code postal? |
| Nathan: | Le code postal, c'est 59800 Lille. |

D
| Élise: | Ton numéro de téléphone? |
| Nathan: | Mon numéro de téléphone, c'est le 03-20-22-17-72. |

E
| Élise: | Et ton numéro de portable? |
| Nathan: | C'est le 06-68-32-07-51. |

F
| Élise: | Et ton adresse e-mail? |
| Nathan: | C'est nat.lille@retinet.fr |

Élise, une copine de Marine, bavarde avec Nathan, un cousin de Marine.

en français:
@ = on dit "arobas"
.fr = on dit "point F R"

> **Grammaire:**
> *mon, ton* + feminine
>
> To avoid two vowel sounds coming together, use *mon/ton* (not *ma/ta*) with feminine nouns that begin with a vowel: **mon** *adresse (f)*, **mon** *amie (f)*.

1 b 🎵 **Écoute deux dialogues similaires. Note l'ordre des questions (A–F).**

extra! **Note aussi d'autres détails.**

Exemple: 1 A, … (*extra!* adresse: 32, rue Gustave…)

1 c 💬 **À deux: répétez les deux numéros de téléphone de Nathan.**

| Les numéros de téléphone: | 05 | – | 20 | – | 32 | – | 18 | – | 73 |
| on dit: | zéro, cinq | | vingt | | trente-deux | | dix-huit | | soixante-treize |

1 d 💬 **Joue le dialogue d'Élise et de Nathan.**

Attention! Prononciation française pour *adresse, code postal, téléphone*, etc.

2 💿 **Écoute les dialogues (1–4). Note le numéro de téléphone.**

3 a ✏️ **Recopie et complète le dialogue.**

> c'est   code   Mon   numéro   quoi   ton

Jonas: Halima, c'est ___ ¹ ton numéro de téléphone?
Halima: Mon numéro de téléphone, ___ ² le 01-63-45-91-07.
Jonas: Et ton ___ ³ de portable?
Halima: C'est le 06-71-05-06-80.
Jonas: Halima, c'est quoi ___ ⁴ adresse e-mail?
Halima: Je n'ai pas d'adresse e-mail.
Jonas: Et ton adresse?
Halima: ___ ⁵ adresse, c'est 12, rue Bosquet, Paris.
Jonas: Et le ___ ⁶ postal?
Halima: 75007 Paris.

3 b 🗨️ **Joue et adapte le dialogue de l'exercice 1a.**

3 c 🗨️ *extra!* **Ajoute deux ou trois questions.**

Exemples: **Tu as un album préféré? Tu as fait du vélo hier?**

– C'est quoi, ton numéro de portable?
– Je n'ai pas de portable!
– Et ton numéro à la maison?
– Nous n'avons pas de téléphone!
– C'est quoi ton adresse?
– Je n'ai pas d'adresse!
– Tu m'aimes, Coralie?

4 💿 **Quand tu es en Grande-Bretagne, si tu téléphones en France, il faut faire le 00 33 + le numéro (sans le zéro!). Écoute (1–6). Note les numéros pour:**

1	la Belgique	4	le Sénégal
2	l'Allemagne	5	le Brésil
3	le Pakistan	6	l'Algérie

5 📖 **Read the text and answer the questions.**

1 *What is the text about?*
2 *Find two meanings of* il faut *in the glossary. What does the first* il faut *in the text mean?*
3 *Do French public phones operate mainly with cards or coins?*
4 *Where can you buy phone cards?*

6 a ✏️ **Write to a new French penfriend.**

● *Write four questions to ask his/her post code, email address, phone number and mobile number.*
● *Give your own contact details.*

6 b ✏️ *extra!* **Add six things about yourself.**

Exemple: **J'ai deux frères et une sœur.**

Le téléphone en France

Pour les téléphones publics, il faut normalement des cartes téléphoniques.

Il faut acheter ces cartes à l'aéroport, dans les agences France Télécom, à la poste, dans les bureaux de tabac et les kiosques avec le logo Télécarte.

c'est quoi,	ton adresse / ton adresse e-mail?
	ton numéro de téléphone?
	ton numéro de portable?
	le code postal?

ça s'écrit comment?
mon adresse, c'est... / le code postal, c'est...
mon numéro, c'est le zéro un, ...

je n'ai pas d'adresse e-mail

12C Bon anniversaire!

- recycle language from earlier units
- answer in longer sentences

A C'est bien, ton village?
Non, c'est nul. Il n'y a pas grand-chose pour les jeunes. Il n'y a pas de piscine, ...

B Tu veux faire du karting samedi?
Je ne peux pas, parce que je vais aller chez mes grands-parents, samedi.

C Ta cousine est sympa?
Oui, elle est amusante. Elle aime les animaux et les ordinateurs.

D Tu es allé à un parc safari?
Oui, samedi dernier, et j'ai vu des lions, des rhinocéros, des girafes... C'était super!

E Tu aimes les vêtements de marque?
Non, mais j'aime ce pull. C'est le top!

F Vous faites quoi le week-end?
Parfois nous allons en ville, ou parfois nous jouons aux cartes à la maison.

1 a 💿 Écoute et lis (1–6). Note les lettres (A–F) dans le bon ordre.

Stratégies! *Making a better impression*

Here are four tips for making your sentences longer – and not drying up at a party!

1 Extend yes/no answers: *Oui, et...* (Yes, and...), *Non, mais...* (No, but...).
2 Link sentences with: *et* (and), *mais* (but), *ou* (or), *parce que* (because).
3 Say what you think about any given topic: *c'est amusant, c'est nul*.
4 Use the past tense (e.g. *j'ai joué, je suis allé(e)*) or the future tense (e.g. *je vais aller*).

1 b 📖 Lis les dialogues A–F, et note les stratégies 1–4.

Exemple: A – stratégies 1 et 3

1 c 💿 Écoute les dialogues (1–5). Note les stratégies 1–4.

Exemple: 1 – stratégies 1 et 3

2 a ✏️ Prépare tes réponses aux questions A–F.

Consulte les *Sommaires* indiqués. Des réponses intéressantes, s'il te plaît!

A C'est bien, ton village?   ◄◄ p. 41

B Tu veux faire du karting samedi?   ◄◄ pp. 69 et 87

C Ta cousine est sympa?   ◄◄ p. 51

D Tu es allé à un parc safari?   ◄◄ p. 95

E Tu aimes les vêtements de marque?   ◄◄ p. 77

F Vous faites quoi le week-end?   ◄◄ p. 59

2 b 💬 Pose les questions (A–F) à ton/ta partenaire et réponds aux questions.
extra! Pose aussi d'autres questions.

Exemple: **extra!** Tu aimes la cuisine indienne et les plats épicés?   ◄◄ p. 33

3 🖉 **En août, tu vas passer une semaine chez Ali!
Écris une lettre: décris-toi! Voici des idées:**

extra! **Ajoute trois phrases!**

This is your chance to show off some of the language you've learnt this year!

> **Chers Monsieur et Madame Amrani, cher Ali,**
>
> **Je m'appelle Alex/Sophie. Je suis (assez/très) petit/petite et bavard/bavarde. J'aime beaucoup la politique et la musique mais je n'aime pas...**
>
> **J'habite à York. J'aime la ville/le village parce qu'il y a...**
>
> **Le week-end, en famille, nous faisons des excursions à la mer, ou nous...**
>
> **Samedi dernier, j'ai visité..., j'ai invité... et puis j'ai vu..., j'ai fait...**
>
> **Dimanche, je suis allé(e) chez mon copain.**
>
> **À bientôt!**

4 💿 **Écoute. Il y a quelle surprise pour Marine?**

Sommaire

Préparations	**Preparations**	**La soirée de Marine**	**Marine's party**
tu aimes... ?	*do you like... ?*	c'est quoi, ... ?	*what is... ?*
ce poster/ce livre	*this poster/this book*	ton adresse	*your address*
ce réveil	*this alarm clock*	le code postal	*the postcode*
cette écharpe	*this scarf*	ton adresse e-mail?	*your email address*
cette trousse	*this pencil case*	ton numéro de	*your phone/mobile*
cette gourde	*this water bottle*	téléphone/de portable	*number*
ces gants	*these gloves*	mon adresse, c'est...	*my address is...*
ces boucles d'oreille	*these earrings*	ça s'écrit comment?	*how do you spell it?*
oui, j'aime bien	*yes, I like it/them*	mon numéro, c'est le zéro	*my number is*
bof...	*pfff... (expressing indifference)*	un, ...	*01-...*
ben...	*well...*	je n'ai pas d'adresse e-mail	*I don't have an email address*
non, pas beaucoup	*no, not much*		
pourquoi?	*why?*		
c'est un cadeau amusant	*it's a fun present*		
c'est un cadeau pratique	*it's a useful present*		
c'est un cadeau original	*it's an original present*		
je n'aime pas la couleur	*I don't like the colour*		

Grammaire: *ce, cette* (this), *ces* (these)

ce *livre m*   this book   **cette** *trousse f*   this pencil-case   **ces** *gants pl*   these gloves

Cross-topic words

parfois – *sometimes*
quoi? – *what?*

Stratégies!

★ predicting how new words will be pronounced

★ deducing the meaning of new words from the context

★ not drying up: linking sentences and giving opinions

Unité 11 (Des problèmes? Consulte la page 105.)

1 a 📖 *Read Laetitia's text. Then answer in English: what does she eat and drink for breakfast and lunch?*

1 b ✏️ **Tu manges quoi le matin et à midi? Écris des phrases en français.**

Ton modèle: le texte de Laetitia.

> Le matin, je mange du pain avec du beurre et de la confiture. Je bois du lait ou du jus de fruits. À midi, je mange un sandwich au jambon ou au fromage, des chips et une pomme ou une pêche. Je bois de l'eau.
>
> Laetitia

2 a 💿 **Écoute les conversations (1–3) au musée, au château et à la piscine.**

Note:

a le tarif adulte   **c** on ferme à quelle heure?

b le tarif enfant   **d** une instruction avec *il faut...*

Exemple: **1 a** 4,80€; **b** 3,20€; **c** ...

2 b 💬 **Joue les dialogues 1 et 2.**

Exemple: **1** – **Bonjour, monsieur. L'entrée, c'est combien, s'il vous plaît?**

      – **C'est 8,50 euros pour un adulte et 4,80 euros pour un enfant.**

      – **Alors, deux adultes et...**

Musée de la Voile

1 adultes: 8,50€
enfants: 4,80€
le musée ferme: 17h45

visite guidée?
→ attendre/là-bas

Musée du Château

2 adultes: 2,60€
enfants: 1,30€
le musée ferme: 18h15

cartes postales?
→ payer/caisse

Unité 12 (Des problèmes? Consulte la page 111.)

3 a 💬 **Joue et adapte le dialogue.**

– Tu aimes ce réveil?
– Oui, j'aime bien.
– Pourquoi?
– Ben… c'est un cadeau pratique et j'aime la couleur. Et toi?
– Moi, je n'aime pas ce réveil.

3 b ✏️ **Écris quatre petits dialogues (1–4).**

Exemple: **1** – Tu aimes ce livre?
      – Oui, c'est un cadeau amusant.

1 livre? (m)
oui/amusant

2 écharpe? (f)
oui/original

3 trousse? (f)
oui/pratique

4 gants? (mpl) non/je
n'aime pas/couleur

4 a 💿 **Écoute (1–2) et note l'adresse (le numéro + la rue).**

4 b 💿 **Écoute et complète les quatre numéros de téléphone:**

1 04-64-32-__-__   **3** 01-60-91-__-__

2 01-07-12-__-__   **4** 02-74-17-__-__

Stratégies! *Revision*

Which six words from *Voilà 2* do you find most difficult to remember? Write each one on a separate piece of paper, and stick them up next to your bed.

Look at them every evening for a week – and you'll probably never forget them again!

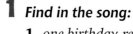 Joyeux anniversaire!

1
Sur la table,
des cadeaux,
un gâteau.
Des textos,
sur mon portable.
C'est mon anniversaire
et c'est super!
Joyeux anniversaire!
Bisous, bisous, bisous!

2
Mes parents,
mon petit frère,
ma sœur Claire,
mon hamster,
mes grands-parents,
Tout le monde est là pour moi!
Ça, c'est sympa!
Joyeux anniversaire!
Bisous, bisous, bisous!

3
Une pizza
chez Luigi,
des biscuits,
des jus de fruits,
des chocolats!
Il est midi et demi,
bon appétit!
Joyeux anniversaire!
Bisous, bisous, bisous!

4
Et demain,
une soirée!
Mes CD
préférés
et mes copains,
Paul, Tom, Lise et Juliette.
Oui, c'est la fête!
Joyeux anniversaire!
Bisous, bisous, bisous!

tout le monde est là – *everyone is here*
joyeux anniversaire! – *happy birthday!*
bon appétit! – *enjoy your meal!*

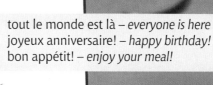

1 *Find in the song:*
  1 *one birthday-related object*
  2 *one birthday greeting*
  3 *four family members*
  4 *one pet*
  5 *three items of food*
  6 *one drink*

2 **C'est dans quelle partie de la chanson – 1, 2, 3 ou 4?**
  1 Ses grands-parents sont là pour son anniversaire.
  2 Demain, c'est la fête avec ses copains.
  3 On déjeune dans un restaurant italien.
  4 Super! Il y a des SMS.

3 **Vrai ou faux?**
  1 Il y a un gâteau sur la table.
  2 Sa sœur s'appelle Juliette.
  3 Il y a de la pizza pour le déjeuner.
  4 La fête d'anniversaire avec ses copains, c'est le week-end prochain.

4 *Choose your four favourite lines from the song, and learn them by heart.*

1 a 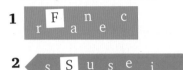 Test yourself on the first two sections of the *Sommaire* on page 15. (◄◄ pp. 8–11)

2 Write the countries in French – don't forget to add *le, la, l'* or *les*. (◄◄ pp. 8–11)

Example: **1** *la France*

1 r F a n c e
2 s S u s e i

3 D k a r n a e m

 4 A l e e n l g m a

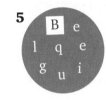 5 B e l q e g u i

6 P y a s- a B s

3 Write these sentences correctly. (◄◄ pp. 8–11)

Example: **1** *On parle quelle langue en Inde?*

1 quelle │ en Inde? │ parle │ langue │ On
2 anglais. │ parle │ On │ hindi │ et
3 une │ C'était │ britannique. │ colonie
4 la capitale │ Londres │ est │ pays? │ de quel
5 France. │ de la │ le sud │ est │ dans │ Nice
6 dans │ Liège │ est │ Belgique. │ l'est │ de la

4 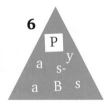 Test yourself on the third and fourth sections of the *Sommaire* on page 15. (◄◄ pp. 12–14)

5 Match up the sentence halves and write them in both French and English. (◄◄ pp. 12–13)

Example: **1** *Je ne comprends pas l'exercice.* I don't understand the exercise.

1 Je ne comprends
2 Pouvez-vous
3 J'ai
4 Je ne
5 Ça s'écrit
6 Réponds aux
7 Écris les phrases
8 Choisis un mot

répéter la phrase?
comprends pas la question.
comment?
questions.
dans le bon ordre.
pas l'exercice.
fini l'exercice.
pour chaque blanc.

6 Write full sentences. (◄◄ p. 14)

Example: **1** *Le Rhin est plus long que la Seine.*

1 le Rhin/long/la Seine
2 la France/grande/la Grande-Bretagne
3 le mont Everest/haut/le mont Blanc
4 la Belgique/petite/les Pays-Bas
5 la Tamise/longue/la Mersey
6 la tour Eiffel/haute/la tour de Blackpool

Le mont Blanc

1 📖 **Lis le texte. Vrai ou faux?** (◄◄ pp. 8–11)

1 Le roi habite à Bruxelles.

2 Le roi Albert n'a pas d'enfants.

3 La reine s'appelle Astrid.

4 La reine Fabiola était belge.

Now answer these questions in English.

5 *What languages does Queen Paola speak?*

6 *Why did Albert become king after his brother?*

2 ✏️ **Écris un article sur la famille royale de Monaco. Voici des notes pour t'aider:**

- le prince Rainier III / habite / Monte Carlo
- 3 enfants: Albert, Caroline, Stéphanie
- femme (la princesse Grace) / était / américaine

Idée! Fais des recherches sur la famille royale d'Espagne et écris un article.

Albert II, roi des Belges

Le roi Albert et sa femme, la reine Paola, habitent au château de Laeken, à Bruxelles, la capitale de la Belgique.

La reine Paola et le roi Albert

Ils ont trois enfants qui s'appellent Philippe, Astrid et Laurent. La reine Paola est italienne et elle parle français, italien, anglais et allemand.

Le roi Albert est le *frère* du roi précédent, le roi Baudoin Ier. Pourquoi? Parce que Baudoin et sa reine, Fabiola – qui était espagnole – n'ont pas eu d'enfants.

3 📖 **Quiz de logique!** (◄◄ pp. 12–14)

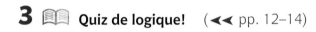

C'est qui? Écris les noms!

1 __?__ mesure 1 m 80.

2 __?__ mesure 1 m 75.

3 __?__ mesure 1 m 68.

4 __?__ mesure 1 m 59.

Grégoire

Joël

Raoul est plus petit que son cousin.

Joël est plus grand que Grégoire.

Le frère de Sabine mesure 1 m 75.

Le cousin de Grégoire est plus grand que Louis.

Grégoire est le frère de Sabine.

Raoul et Grégoire sont cousins.

Raoul

Louis

Stratégies!

pour les jeux de logique

- Pour chaque phrase, note les paires de noms dans le bon ordre:
- cousin de Raoul
- Raoul

- Note les autres informations aussi:
- cousin de Raoul = ??

1 📖 **Match the sentence halves and write out the full sentences.** (◄◄ pp. 16–17)

1 Lundi dernier, j'ai

2 Mardi après-midi, j'ai retrouvé

3 J'ai mangé un sandwich

4 J'ai envoyé un

5 Dimanche

6 Samedi matin, j'ai acheté

un CD en ville.

texto à mon cousin qui s'appelle Franck.

rangé ma chambre.   ma copine au centre sportif.

et une glace.   soir, j'ai surfé sur Internet à la maison.

2 📖 **Copy the grid and tick all the possible combinations.** (◄◄ pp. 18–19)

	une vidéo	des frites	des vêtements	la télé	des copains	mon vélo
j'ai réparé			✔	✔		✔
j'ai acheté						
j'ai retrouvé						
j'ai mangé						
j'ai invité						
j'ai regardé						

lundi 13

tennis, au centre sportif
texto à Julien

mercredi 15

réparé vélo avec Alexandre
le soir: une vidéo

3 🖊 **Write eight sentences in the past tense.**
(◄◄ pp. 18–19)

Example: *Lundi dernier, j'ai joué au tennis au centre sportif.*

mardi 14

télé, avec des copains
rangé chambre

jeudi 16

promené chien dans le parc
acheté vêtements, en ville

4 🖊 **Write six sentences.** (◄◄ p. 22)

Example: *Hier, nous avons écouté de la musique.*

aujourd'hui,	j'	avez	joué	ma	Internet
hier soir,	tu	as	envoyé	une	football
hier,	elle	avons	écouté	de la	musique
le week-end dernier,	nous	a	loué	sur	texto
	vous	ont	surfé	un	chambre
la semaine dernière,	ils	ai	rangé	au	vidéo

5 🖊 **Write two or three sentences in the past tense to go with this photo (le château de Chenonceau). Use some of these words:**
(◄◄ pp. 20–21)

dernier   visité   père   et
acheté   carte postale   génial

Le château de Chenonceau

1 🖊 **Écris six phrases au passé.**   (◄◄ pp. 16–19)

Exemple:

1 Samedi après-midi, *j'ai organisé* un pique-nique.

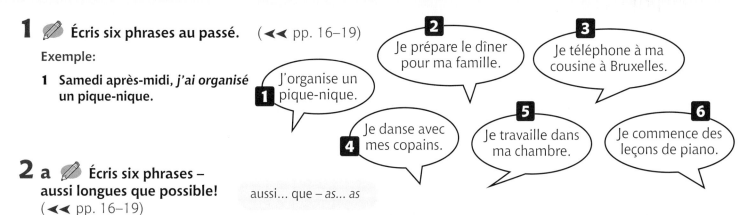

1 J'organise un pique-nique.

2 Je prépare le dîner pour ma famille.

3 Je téléphone à ma cousine à Bruxelles.

4 Je danse avec mes copains.

5 Je travaille dans ma chambre.

6 Je commence des leçons de piano.

2 a 🖊 **Écris six phrases – aussi longues que possible!** (◄◄ pp. 16–19)

aussi... que – *as... as*

Exemple: **Lundi dernier, j'ai loué une vidéo avec ma copine, Sarah, en ville à neuf heures et demie, et c'était super!** *(20 mots)*

1 lundi – vidéo   **2** mardi – vêtements   **3** mercredi – ping-pong

4 jeudi – chien   **5** vendredi – frites   **6** week-end – copains

Les scores

10–15 mots: 5 points

16–20 mots: 20 points

21+ mots: 50 points

2 b 📖 **Vérifie et corrige les phrases de ton/ta partenaire.**

3 🖊 **Écris les phrases.**   (◄◄ p. 22)

Exemple: **1 Claire a promené son chien.**

1 Claire – promené – chien

2 nous – loué – vidéo

3 ils – invité – copains

4 tu – acheté – vêtements?

5 mon frère – réparé – vélo

6 vous – envoyé – textos?

7 tu – rangé – chambre?

8 mes parents – regardé – télé

4 🖊 **Imagine une visite à la Grotte de Han, en Belgique. Écris une description intéressante.** (◄◄ pp. 20–21)

Exemple:
La semaine dernière, nous avons...

Mots utiles *Useful words*

cher *expensive*	payer *to pay*
le guide *guide*	manger *to eat*
admirer *to admire*	après ça *after that*

Visitez la Grotte de Han!

une série de grottes spectaculaires

À votre service: restaurants et magasins

Tarifs: **10,50€ adultes**
6€ enfants (de 3 à 12 ans)
visites guidées multilingues

1 ✏️ Write the sentences with the correct form of the verb.   (◄◄ pp. 26–27)

Example: 1 Nous aimons le fromage.

1 Nous aimez/ons le fromage.

2 Mon frère adores/e les plats épicés.

3 Mes parents mangez/ent souvent des œufs brouillés.

4 Tu prépares/ez le dîner ce soir?

5 Vous aimez/ent l'ail?

6 Maxime déteste/es les oignons crus.

7 Nous déjeunons/ez à midi et demi.

8 Ismaël et Didier adore/ent la cuisine indienne.

2 ✏️ Write a shopping list to go with each basket.   (◄◄ pp. 28–29)

Example:

> I deux boîtes de tomates...

1

2

3 a ✏️ Write the dialogue correctly.
(◄◄ pp. 30–31)

Example: Bonjour, monsieur. 100g...

3 b ✏️ extra! Invent your own dialogue based on the one in exercise 3a.

monsieur. Bonjour, de plaît. pâté, s'il 100g vous

ça? Et Voilà. avec

chips. Deux de paquets

tout? C'est

Oui, tout. C'est combien? c'est

quatre-vingts. euro Un

revoir. Merci. Au

4 📖 Find the matching pairs.
(◄◄ pp. 30–31)

Example: ajoute – add

> ajoute coupe
> lave mets pèle
> choisis corrige écris
> réponds trouve

> find wash
> add choose answer
> write correct peel
> put cut

5 📖 Choose the right words to make logical pairs.

1 miam-miam! → j'adore ça / berk!

2 la Grande-Bretagne → britannique / la France

3 tu → s'il te plaît / vous

4 je → tu / nous

Une solution originale au vandalisme

À l'âge de neuf ans, Jody pose de graves problèmes à ses parents et à sa ville en Grande-Bretagne.

C'est un vandale: il incendie des garages et des magasins, et il essaie de faire dérailler un train... La police est horrifiée par la liste d'incidents.

Un jour, la police a une idée géniale, et envoie Jody chez le docteur Smith. Examens et tests révèlent que Jody est allergique au chocolat! Et Jody *adore* le chocolat.

Solution: pas de chocolat pour Jody, ... et Jody devient moins agressif. Bientôt, il n'est plus un vandale.

incendie – *sets fire to*
essaie de – *tries to*
ne... plus – *not... any more*

1 a 📖 **Lis le texte et trouve les paires.** ▶

Exemple: **1** Le nom du vandale: Jody

1 Le nom du vandale: *en Grande-Bretagne*
2 Son âge: *le chocolat*   *c'est un vandale*
3 Où il habite:
4 Le problème: *pas de vandalisme*
5 La cause du problème: *neuf ans*   *Jody*
6 La solution:
7 La conséquence pour la ville: *pas de chocolat pour Jody*

1 b 📖 **Réponds en français.**

1 Jody pose des problèmes à qui?
2 Écris deux exemples de son vandalisme.
3 Qui propose la solution au problème?
4 Regarde la solution au problème. Quel est…
  a l'avantage pour la ville?
  b le désavantage pour Jody?

1 c 📖 **Tu trouves combien de mots français similaires à des mots anglais?**

12–15 mots: OK
15–18 mots: très bien!
18+ mots: super bien!!

Exemples: âge – *age*; grave – *grave, serious*

1 d 📖 *In three or four sentences, summarise Jody's story and explain your reaction to it.*

2 a ✏️ **Écris un dialogue pour la photo.** (◀◀ pp. 30–31)

Exemple:
Bonjour, madame. Un kilo de…

2 b ✏️ **Tu inventes combien de phrases pour la photo?**

Exemples:
1 Madame Dupont a 46 ans.
2 La ville est en France.

1 ✏️ **Write the French words for these places.** (◄◄ pp. 34–35)

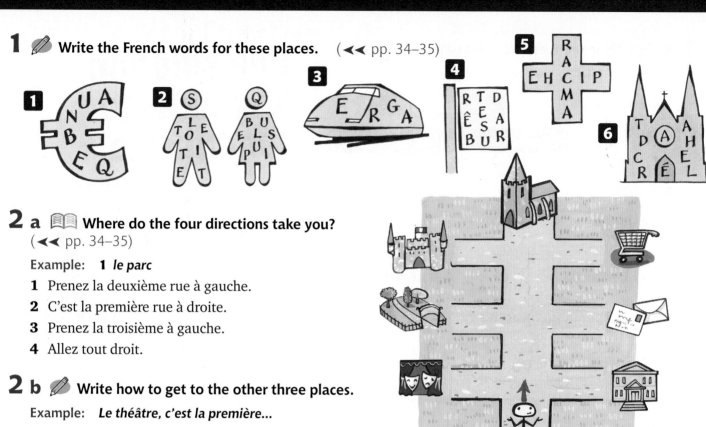

2 a 📖 **Where do the four directions take you?**
(◄◄ pp. 34–35)

Example: **1** *le parc*

1 Prenez la deuxième rue à gauche.
2 C'est la première rue à droite.
3 Prenez la troisième à gauche.
4 Allez tout droit.

2 b ✏️ **Write how to get to the other three places.**

Example: *Le théâtre, c'est la première...*

3 ✏️ **Read the dialogue. Then write two similar dialogues.** (◄◄ pp. 38–39)

A Pardon, madame. C'est où, le château?
B C'est sur la place du Château.
A C'est loin?
B Non. Prenez la première rue à droite,
et puis la deuxième rue à gauche.
A La première rue à droite, et puis la deuxième
à gauche?
B Oui. C'est en face de l'hôtel de ville.
A Merci beaucoup, madame. Au revoir.

4 ♻️ **Categories and letters of the alphabet.**
Find two, three or four words in these different
categories, all beginning with the same letter.

Example: **S**

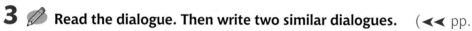
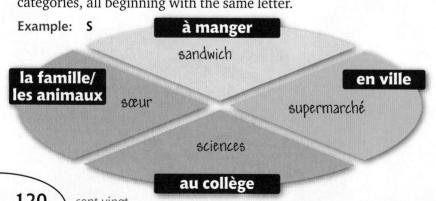

2 mots: bien – 10 points
3 mots: très bien – 40 points
4 mots: excellent – 100 points!

1 ✏️ **Recopie et complète le texte avec les mots *gauche* ou *droite*.** (◄◄ pp. 34–37)

L'hôtel de ville de Bruxelles est magnifique... et symétrique, non?

Non! C'est une illusion d'optique célèbre!

Attention! Regarde de plus près:

- L'aile ____, commencée en 1402, est plus longue que l'aile ____, qui date de 1444.
- La tour n'est pas au milieu: elle est un peu à ____.
- Il y a sept fenêtres à ____; mais il y a dix fenêtres à ____!
- En bas, il y a 11 arcs à ____ et six arcs à ____.
- Au premier étage, les fenêtres à ____ sont plus hautes que les fenêtres à ____.
- Les fenêtres à ____ sont rectangulaires.
- À ____, il y a une série de statues au-dessus des fenêtres; à ____, non!
- L'entrée n'est pas au milieu de la base de la tour: l'entrée est un peu à ____!

> célèbre – *famous*
> l'aile *f* – *wing*
> au milieu – *in the middle*
> un peu – *a bit*
> la fenêtre – *window*
> l'arc *m* – *arch*
> au-dessus de – *above*

---

2 a 📖 **Lis le texte. C'est quoi en français?** (◄◄ pp. 38–39)

1 *famous*
2 *... metres high*
3 *which dates from*
4 *ancient*
5 *at the top*
6 *the tower*

> **La piscine «Olympia»: avec toboggan!**

> Beaucoup de cafés et de magasins sur la Grand-Place!

> **La Maison du Chocolat**
> **(à 100m de l'Hôtel de Ville)**

Bruges – ville médiévale

- l'Église Notre-Dame (13e–15e siècles): la tour est haute de 122 mètres
- célèbre: l'Hôtel de Ville gothique (1376)
- l'Ancienne Pharmacie, qui date de 1650: grande collection d'ustensiles de pharmacie
- la tour du Beffroi. En haut: une vue exceptionnelle!
- amusant: le parc d'attraction avec dolfinarium – à Zeebruges

Célèbres: les canaux

2 b ✏️ **Tu fais du marketing pour la ville de Bruges, en Belgique. Écris une brochure enthousiaste!**

Exemple: **Visitez l'hôtel de ville célèbre, qui date de 1376.**

Admirez / Visitez	le / la / les...
Achetez / Mangez	du / de la / de l' / des...
Allez	au / à la / à l' / aux...

1 ✏️ **Rémi is like Mélanie. Copy the descriptions: write the adjectives in the correct form.** (◄◄ pp. 44–45)

Example: *Mélanie est actrice. Elle n'est pas très vieille. Elle...*

Mélanie est actrice.
1 Elle n'est pas très...
2 Elle est assez célèbre.
3 Je la trouve très amusante, et très belle aussi.
4 Elle est assez...
5 Mélanie n'est pas...

Rémi est acteur.
1 Il n'est pas très vieux.
2 Il est...
3 Je le trouve...
4 Il est assez sportif.
5 Rémi n'est pas marié.

2 📖 **Read the article. Are these sentences true or false?**
(◄◄ pp. 46–47)
1 La star préférée de Bruno est footballeur.
2 Pauleta est français.
3 Nicole Kidman est australienne.
4 Elle n'aime pas le chocolat.
5 L'anniversaire de Nicole Kidman est en février.
6 Dieudonné est la star préférée de Grégory.
7 Dieudonné est chanteur.
8 Il habite à la campagne.

Qui est ta star préférée?

Ma star préférée, c'est le footballeur Pauleta, parce qu'il a beaucoup de talent. Il est portugais mais il joue en France. Il est vraiment génial. **Bruno**

Ma star préférée, c'est l'actrice Nicole Kidman. Elle est australienne, très grande et je la trouve très belle. Elle adore le chocolat! Son anniversaire, c'est le 20 juin. Elle n'est pas mariée en ce moment – elle était mariée avec Tom Cruise jusqu'en 2001. **Tiana**

Ma star préférée, c'est Dieudonné. C'est un comique et je le trouve très, très amusant. Il est français – il vient de Paris. Il est noir, et assez grand. Il aime les voitures et la politique aussi. Il est marié et il habite à la campagne. **Grégory**

3 📖 **Rewrite the text with the correct words from the box.** (◄◄ pp. 48–49)

Example: **1 Salut! Je *m'appelle...***

Salut! Je ___¹ Martin et je travaille dans ___² café. Samedi ___³, je suis allé au café à neuf heures. À ___⁴, j'ai mangé une omelette et ___⁵ frites. J'ai travaillé jusqu'à ___⁶ heures. Puis, je ___⁷ allé à la piscine, et ___⁸, j'ai promené mon chien.

après ça
dernier
des
deux
m'appelle
midi
suis
un

4 ✏️ **These people are saying where they went yesterday. Write six sentences.** (◄◄ p. 50)

Example: **1 *Je suis allée à l'hôtel Royal.***

1 Catherine – hôtel Royal *m*
2 Victor – poste *f*
3 Patricia – restaurant *m*
4 Alice – collège *m*
5 Nicolas – studios *mpl*
6 Sophie – piscine *f*

allé / allée?
au / à la / à l' / aux?

Stratégies! *Les familles de mots*

Les familles de mots existent en anglais,
par exemple:

verbe	adjectif	nom
beautify	*beautiful*	*beauty*
marry	*married*	*marriage*

Les familles de mots existent en français aussi,
par exemple:

verbe	adjectif	nom
marier	marié	mariage *m*

1 📖 **Trouve un exemple pour chaque ❓**
Regarde dans le dictionnaire. ▶

Verbe	Adjectif	Nom
marier	marié	mariage *m*
❓	bavard	
	sportif	❓
vieillir	❓	❓
❓		interview *f*
	malade	❓
	jeune	❓
❓	❓	amusement *m*
photographier		❓

2 🖊 **Écris douze phrases sur Katy.**

Exemple: **Elle s'appelle Katy.**

elle s'appelle...
elle est...
elle a...
elle joue au...
elle aime le/la/les...
son...
sa...

Katy

anniversaire – le 2 avril
badminton
géographie
anglaise
3 frères
ordinateurs
2 cochons d'Inde

13 ans
Jamie Theakston
belle
frites

3 Stratégies! *Improving a text*

This text is very basic and abrupt! Make it flow better by:

● adding words such as: *très, assez, beaucoup, après ça, puis* and other time phrases;

● joining short sentences together with *et*.

Example: *Hier, je suis allé au collège **et** j'ai travaillé jusqu'à midi.*

> Je suis allé au collège. J'ai travaillé jusqu'à midi. J'ai mangé un sandwich. J'ai parlé avec mon copain. Il est sportif et amusant. Il aime les voitures.
>
> Après le collège, je suis allé au parc. J'ai promené mon chien. Il est intelligent. J'ai envoyé des textos. J'ai regardé un film à la télé.

1 📖 Read the weather phrases and identify the mystery symbols!
(Each symbol represents two or three letters.)   (◄◄ pp. 52–53)

Example: **1** 🔺 = *au* (en *au*tomne)

1 🔺   **2** 🌓   **3** ⭐   **4** ✳   **5** ■   **6** ●   **7** ♥   **8** ◄

> en 🔺tomne   il n🌓ge   il f⭐t b◄   il pl✳t   il f⭐t fr●d   il f⭐t m🔺v⭐s
> quel t■ps f⭐t-il?   🔺 pr♥t■ps   il y a parf●s du sol🌓l

2 ✏ Write out the sentences with the correct verbs.   (◄◄ pp. 54–55)

Example: **1** *Le week-end, nous sortons...*

1 Le week-end, nous ___ ensemble: nous allons au cinéma.
2 Nous ___ de la viande.
3 Nous ne ___ rien ensemble.
4 Nous ___ au ping-pong. Vous aussi?
5 Le soir, nous ___ souvent la télé.
6 Parfois nous ___ au centre commercial ou au bowling.

> allons
> regardons
> faisons
> sortons
> jouons
> mangeons

3 📖 Choose the right definition for each sentence.
Then write the sentence in English.   (◄◄ pp. 56–57)

Example: **1** sheep
>   **There are lots of animals, for example sheep.**

1 Il y a beaucoup d'animaux, par exemple des **moutons**.
2 13 heures, c'est l'**heure** de la sieste.
3 Il pleut et il y a parfois des **éclairs**.
4 En hiver, on mange des **marrons**.
5 Le samedi, je vais en **boîte** si j'ai le **temps**.   si – if

> **mouton** *m* 1 sheep 2 mutton
>
> **heure** *f* 1 hour 2 time
>
> **éclair** *m* 1 lightning 2 *(pastry)* éclair
>
> **marron** 1 *m* chestnut 2 *adj* brown
>
> **boîte** *f* 1 box 2 night-club
>
> **temps** *m* 1 weather 2 time

4 📖 Copy and complete the information on
Cameroon. (◄◄ p. 58)

> dans   de   est   et   jouent   la   le   parc

Le Cameroun

____¹ capitale du Cameroun s'appelle Yaoundé. C'est ____² le sud du
pays. Mais la plus grande ville du Cameroun ____³ le port de Douala.

Dans le nord du pays, près ____⁴ la ville de Maroua, il y a un parc
national. On peut visiter le ____⁵: il y a des animaux sauvages, par
exemple des girafes, des lions, des autruches ____⁶ 1700 éléphants.

____⁷ football est populaire au Cameroun. Beaucoup de footballeurs
camerounais ____⁸ dans des équipes françaises.

Stratégies! *Show off the French you know!*

Here's a sentence from unit 6 that you could adapt, using language you learnt in previous units:

Le samedi, nous mangeons dans la cuisine; le dimanche, nous mangeons dans la salle à manger.

Nous déjeunons à 13h le dimanche.

Le week-end, nous mangeons ensemble.

Ma mère aime les plats épicés, mais moi, je préfère les pizzas.

Nous ne mangeons jamais ensemble.

1 a ✏ **Écris quatre possibilités (a–d) pour chaque phrase.**

Exemple: **1 a Nous allons à la bibliothèque.**

1 Quand nous sortons, nous allons au/à la/à l'...   **a** ____   **b** ____   **c** ____   **d** ____

2 Nous sortons avec...   **a** ____   **b** ____   **c** ____   **d** ____

1 b ✏ **Change/Ajoute des détails.**   ◀

1 Nous regardons la télé.

2 Nous allons au centre commercial.

3 Nous faisons du vélo.

Stratégies!

● Here's your chance to show off! Change and/or extend the sentences in any way you like.

2 a 📖 *Read the text and explain the importance of these dates:*

1 1534	**3** 1604	**5** 1682
2 1535	**4** 1670	**6** 1802

Exemple: **1 *In 1534, the French explorer Jacques Cartier arrived in Canada.***

2 b 📖 **Trouve et écris les verbes français. (Attention: *deux* mots en français!)**

Exemple: **1** *(he) arrived* – est arrivé

1 *(he) arrived*   **4** *(it) started*

2 *(he) spent*   **5** *(they) went down*

3 *(they) founded*   **6** *(it) became*

2 c Stratégies! *Noting useful words*

● Note in French and English the four new words from the text which you think will be most useful to you in the future. (Use the *Glossaire* on pp. 149–159.)

Le français en Amérique du Nord

L'explorateur français Jacques Cartier est arrivé au Canada en 1534. Il a passé l'hiver de 1535 au Québec. Les Français ont fondé la ville de Québec en 1604. L'exploration française du centre et de l'ouest de l'Amérique du Nord a commencé en 1670. Les Français ont fondé la ville de Chicago, ils ont descendu le Mississippi et sont arrivés au Golfe du Mexique. En 1682, l'ouest de l'Amérique du Nord était une possession française – la "Nouvelle France"!

En 1802, les États-Unis ont acheté les territoires français à l'ouest du Mississippi. Le Canada est devenu une colonie britannique.

Les traces de la colonisation française? Des noms français en Louisiane (par exemple: la Nouvelle-Orléans) et le français au Québec.

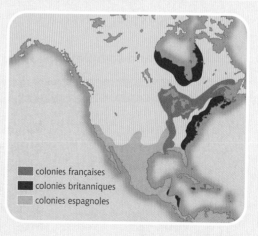

colonies françaises
colonies britanniques
colonies espagnoles

1 a ✏️ **Unjumble the sentences.** (◀◀ pp. 62–63)

Example: *Est-ce que je peux aller aux toilettes?*

1 toilettes? peux Est-ce que je aux aller
2 je Est-ce que ouvrir fenêtre? peux la
3 sûr. bien Oui,
4 de papier? je une avoir peux feuille Est-ce que
5 voir peux je Mme Dupont? aller Est-ce que
6 assieds- Non, toi!
7 peux je fenêtre? Est-ce que la fermer
8 toi! tais- Non,

1 b 📖 **Choose the right picture (A–H) for each sentence in exercise 1a.**

2 ✏️ **How many different questions can you write?** (◀◀ pp. 64–65)

Example: *Tu veux faire du vélo?*

à la piscine
la télé · regarder · au basket
en ville · aller · Tu veux... ? · jouer · du vélo
un film · faire · du kayak
à un jeu vidéo

3 ✏️ **Copy and complete the sentences with *faire* or *aller*.** (◀◀ pp. 66–67)

1 Samedi après-midi, je dois ___ chez mon grand-père.
2 Tu veux ___ du karting cet après-midi?
3 Ce matin, je dois ___ en ville avec ma mère.
4 Est-ce que tu veux ___ au cinéma avec moi ce soir?
5 Je ne peux pas venir: je dois ___ mes devoirs.
6 Je ne veux pas ___ les courses. C'est barbant!

4 📖 **Copy and complete the rhymes with *four* words from the box.** (◀◀ p. 68)

bien courses devoirs faire karting kayak lundi pas

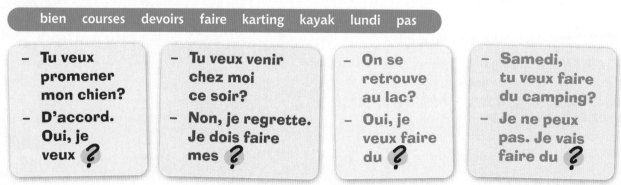

– Tu veux promener mon chien?
– D'accord. Oui, je veux ❓

– Tu veux venir chez moi ce soir?
– Non, je regrette. Je dois faire mes ❓

– On se retrouve au lac?
– Oui, je veux faire du ❓

– Samedi, tu veux faire du camping?
– Je ne peux pas. Je vais faire du ❓

1 📖 Trouve le mot mystère! C'est un monument à Bruxelles (anagramme!).

1 Note la deuxième lettre du mot français pour *yesterday*.

2 Note la cinquième lettre du mot français pour *today*.

3 Et la première lettre de l'expression française pour *last Tuesday*?

4 Note la cinquième lettre de l'expression française pour *this morning*.

5 Prends la quatrième lettre de l'expression française pour *this afternoon*.

6 Et la quatrième lettre de l'expression française pour *this evening*?

7 Prends la troisième lettre du mot français pour *tomorrow*.

2 📝 Tu trouves combien de possibilités pour 1–3?   (◀◀ pp. 64–65)

1

Tu veux aller
- en ville?
- au...?
- à la...?
- à l'hôtel de ville?
- aux studios?

2

Je veux faire
- du...
- de la...
- mes...
- les...

3

Je peux avoir
- un...?
- une...?

3 📝 Tu trouves un exemple pour combien de lettres de l'alphabet?

Exemple: amusant, le bic, c'était, ... le zèbre!

4 📝 Écris des phrases avec *je dois* + infinitif.   (◀◀ pp. 66–67)

Attention!
ton → mon, etc.

Exemple: Je dois faire mes devoirs.

1 Fais tes devoirs!

2 Ferme ton livre!

3 Promène le chien!

4 Mange ton poisson!

5 Va dans ta chambre!

5 📝 Écris une longue phrase pour chaque photo.   (◀◀ pp. 66–67)

Modèle: **A** Olivier veut... [*invente!*], mais il ne peut pas, parce qu'il doit... [*regarde la photo*].

A Olivier

B Claire

C Baptiste

D Delphine

1 ✎ **Write the dialogue with the correct words from the box.** (◄◄ pp. 80–81)

Example: *Qu'est-ce que tu <u>vas</u> faire...*

> à aller ça chez faire halles ma pendant prochaine vas

– Qu'est-ce que tu ___¹ faire ___² les vacances?
– ___³ dépend. Je vais peut-être ___⁴ de la voile en Normandie. Et toi?
– Je vais aller ___⁵ mon oncle et ___⁶ tante.
– Quand?
– La semaine ___⁷.
– Tu vas aller ___⁸ la plage?
– Peut-être. Et mercredi, je vais ___⁹ à Honfleur. Je vais aller aux ___¹⁰.

2 a ✎ **Missing vowels! Copy and complete the sentences.** (◄◄ pp. 82–83)

Example: **1** *Je vais faire de la voile.*

1 Je vais *fr d l vl.* **5** Je vais *fr d l ptr.*
2 Je vais *fr d ptn ` glc.* **6** Je vais *fr d th´^tr.*
3 Je vais *fr d l'scld.* **7** Je vais *fr d VTT.*
4 Je vais *fr d tr ` l'rc.* **8** Je vais *fr d chvl.*

2 b 📖 **Find the matching pairs: sentences 1–8 above and pictures A–H.**

Example: **1 D**

3 📖 **Write the sentences with the words in the correct order.** (◄◄ pp. 84–85)

Example: **1** *Le car va partir...*

1 va – Le – partir – 8h30 – car – à
2 arriver – Nous – 11h00 – vers – allons
3 film – Le – nous – allons – voir – un – matin
4 midi – allons – À – un – manger – dans – nous – café
5 patin – Après – nous – ça – glace – allons – faire – du – à
6 au – allons – Nous – vers – 18h30 – collège – rentrer

4 **Thinking skills: find the words or phrases in each box that go together, and explain why.** (◄◄ p. 86)

Example: **1** *ça + dépend* – because it's a phrase that means 'it depends'

> ça avec qui? facile quand?
> ma tante voir un film partir
> je vais le mauvais

> beau à midi au cinéma un
> mon oncle rentrer
> difficile dépend avec ma sœur aller

1 a ✏️ **Lis le texte et réponds aux questions.** (◄◄ pp. 82–83)

Exemple: **1 C'est pendant les vacances d'été, en juillet et août.**

1 C'est quand?
2 C'est pour qui?
3 On peut faire du vélo?
4 On peut jouer au tennis?
5 Les jeunes dînent où?
6 Les dortoirs sont comment?

1 b 📖 **Choisis le bon titre (1–6) pour chaque groupe d'activités au centre d'aventures (A–D).** le titre – *title*

Exemple: **Groupe d'activités A: titre…**

Sports   **Sciences/informatique**

Histoire   **Cirque**   **Musique**

Cuisine

1 c 📖 **Choisis quatre mots. Regarde dans le glossaire: écris les mots en français et en anglais.**

Exemple: **accueille –** *welcomes*

Le Centre Aventure Normandie

Pendant les vacances d'été (juillet–août), la base accueille des jeunes de 8 à 16 ans.
Les activités sont classées en quatre groupes.
Au programme:

A voile, kayak, sports de raquettes, VTT, escalade, tir à l'arc

B jonglage, équilibre, composition d'un petit spectacle

C microfusées, jouets animés, atelier photo, initiation à Internet

D guitare ou batterie, initiation aux techniques d'enregistrement

Les jeunes (au maximum 60) mangent dans une salle spacieuse, et dorment dans des dortoirs bien équipés (au nombre de 6).

2 ✏️ **Les élèves de 5ᵉᵐᵉ B (la classe d'Ali) vont faire une excursion mardi prochain. Regarde les images. Décris le programme.** (◄◄ pp. 84–85)

Exemple: **1 Mardi, les élèves de 5ᵉᵐᵉ B vont partir à…**
2 Ils vont arriver…

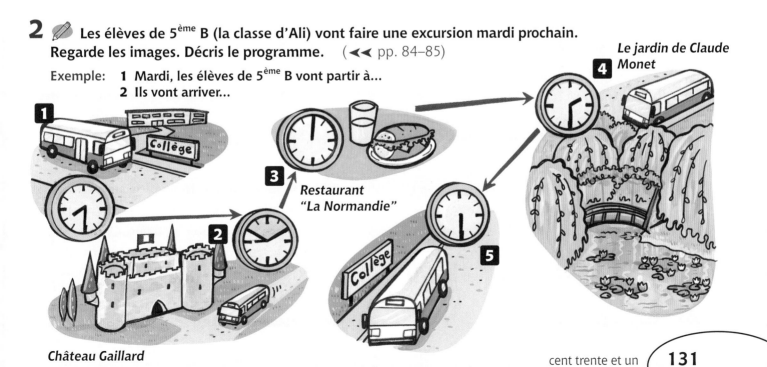

Le jardin de Claude Monet

Restaurant "La Normandie"

Château Gaillard

1 a 📖 **Read the advert. Then answer the questions about the safari park.** (◄◄ pp. 88–89)

1 Where is the park in relation to **a** Lyon **b** Marseille?

2 What warning are you given if you visit the park in your car?

3 What animals are there in the park?

4 What three facilities does the park offer?

5 What is the price for a 14-year-old?

6 Who gets free entry to the park?

1 b ✏️ **How full an A–Z of animals can you write in French? Look up the animals in a dictionary.**

Example: *antilopes, bisons, chats, ...*

2 a 📖 **Match the beginnings and ends of the sentences.** (◄◄ pp. 90–91)

Example: 1 *Samedi dernier, je suis allé au stade.*

1 Samedi dernier, je suis...   passionnant.
2 J'ai vu...   allé au stade.
3 Monaco a joué...   2 à 0.
4 C'était un match...   sauvé trois buts.
5 Un footballeur de Monaco...   contre Paris St Germain.
6 Le gardien de but a...   deux buts!
7 Mon héros, Zombra, a marqué...   un match de foot.
8 L'équipe de Monaco a gagné...   a eu un carton rouge.

2 b ✏️ **Now write five sentences about a football match you have seen (or invent one!). Use sentences from the *Sommaire*.** (◄◄ p. 95)

3 a ✏️ **Copy and complete the text with the right words from the box.** (◄◄ pp. 92–93)

> a chez contre était la lu on soir

Hier, je suis allée ___¹ un copain. On ___² bavardé, puis on a regardé un match de foot à ___³ télé. C'était Arsenal ___⁴ Leeds: c'___⁵ une catastrophe!
Après ça, ___⁶ a bu un coca, et on a ___⁷ des magazines et des BD. Le ___⁸, on a commandé une pizza.

Le parc safari de Peaugres

– à une heure 45 minutes au sud de Lyon
– à deux heures au nord de Marseille

La visite:

Faites la visite en voiture – mais fermez les fenêtres!

Nos animaux: zèbres, hippopotames, éléphants, tigres, lions, dromadaires, antilopes, autruches, hyènes, bisons, etc.

🐾 snack-bar: salades, sandwichs, glaces
🐾 aire de pique-niques
🐾 souvenirs: cartes postales, T-shirts, etc.

Tarifs:
Adultes (à partir de 13 ans) 16,00€
Enfants (3 à 12 ans) 10,50€
Enfants moins de 3 ans gratuit

3 b ✏️ *extra!* **Write four lines in French about what you did last weekend. Put gaps instead of some words (as in exercise 3a). Give your partner your text and see if he/she can fill the gaps!**

4 ✏️ **Separate out the words and write a dialogue at a bus stop.** (◄◄ p. 94)

Example: – *Pardon, madame. C'est...*

pardonmadamec'estquelbuspourlech âteau?c'estle22?nonneprenezpasle22 prenezle9c'estplusrapidele9vaauchât eau?ouidescendezàl'hôteldevillemerc imadamederien

Stratégies! *Deducing a grammar pattern*

By using your knowledge of how the past tense works, you can work out the reason for forms of the past tense which you meet for the first time.

1 a 📖 **Read the text and find the French for:** (◄◄ pp. 88–89)

1 my brother went   **2** my mother went

● Look at what you have written, and then explain how you use the verb *aller* (to go) in the past tense with 'he' and 'she'.

Example: In the past tense, most verbs start *il a...* or *elle a...* , but with *aller*, you use...

1 b 📖 **Find the French for:**

1 the weather was nice   **2** it was cold   **3** it was hot

● You learnt *il fait beau, il fait froid*, etc. in unit 6. Look at what you have written and explain the difference.

1 c 📖 **Now find the French for:**

1 they played   **2** they ate

● Look at what you have written, and use the pattern to write in French:

3 they listened to music (*boys*)

4 they won (*girls*)

> Mercredi dernier, mon frère est allé à la mer avec trois amis. Le matin, il a fait beau, mais l'après-midi, il a fait froid. Ils ont nagé dans la mer et puis ils ont joué au tennis sur la plage.
>
> Ma mère est allée en ville avec une copine. Il a fait chaud, et elles ont mangé une glace dans un café en ville.

2 ✏️ **Change les phrases: présent → passé.**   (◄◄ pp. 92–93)

Exemple: **1 Nous *avons regardé* la télé.**

1 Nous regardons la télé.

2 Le soir, nous dînons à 18h00.

3 Samedi, ma sœur joue au foot.

4 Elle marque des buts.

5 Je bavarde avec mon frère.

6 Après ça, je lis des magazines.

3 ✏️ **Décris ta visite chez une amie. Recopie les phrases et ajoute *deux détails* dans chaque phrase.**   (◄◄ pp. 92–93)

Exemple: **1 Hier *après-midi*, je suis allé(e) chez une amie *qui s'appelle Julie*.**
      ou
   1 Hier, je suis allé(e) à *vélo* chez une amie. *C'était amusant*.

1 Hier, je suis allé(e) chez une amie.

2 Nous avons joué.

3 Puis nous avons fait un gâteau.

4 Nous avons regardé la télé.

5 Puis nous avons bu un coca.

6 Nous avons lu des magazines.

7 Le soir, nous avons commandé une pizza.

Stratégies! *Giving more details*

You could for example:

● use time expressions like *d'abord*

● state your opinion with *c'était*

● use an adjective (e.g. *grand, intéressant*)

● give more detail (e.g. what sort of cake, magazine or pizza, what you watched on TV).

1 a 📖 Look at the pictures (A–C). Which item is missing in each text? (◀◀ pp. 98–99)

Example: A *du pain*

A À midi, je mange du jambon et un yaourt, et je bois un jus de fruits.

B À midi, je mange une tomate et je bois de la limonade. Je mange aussi du chocolat.

C À midi, je bois du lait. Je mange une orange, une pomme et des biscuits.

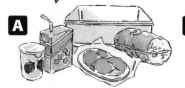 A

 B

 C

D

1 b ✏️ Imagine that D is your packed lunch. Write what you eat and drink at midday.

2 ✏️ Write the dialogue, supplying words for the numbers and pictures. (◀◀ pp. 100–101)

Example: *C'est sept euros...*

M. Briand:	Bonjour, mademoiselle. L'entrée, c'est combien, s'il vous plaît?
L'employée:	C'est **7** euros **75** pour un adulte
	et **4** euros **60** pour un .
M. Briand:	Alors, un ⬛ et un enfant. Je peux acheter des  ?
L'employée:	Oui, il faut payer à la .
M. Briand:	Le musée 🪟 à quelle heure?
L'employée:	À **20** heures. Et il faut laisser votre  ici, monsieur.

3 a 📖 Without looking back, put the following sentences in the correct historical order. (◀◀ pp. 102–103)

Example: E, ...

A La deuxième guerre mondiale.
B 25 pays dans l'Union européenne.
C Napoléon fait la guerre en Europe.
D Les Vikings arrivent en France.
E Les Romains arrivent en France.
F Les Anglais occupent l'ouest de la France.
G La Révolution commence le 14 juillet.
H Le roi Louis XIV habite à Versailles.
I La première guerre mondiale.

3 b 📖 Now check your answers on pages 102–103.

4 a ✏️ Write what Nicolas did last weekend. (◀◀ p. 104)

Example: *Samedi dernier, il a fait du vélo...*

Samedi dernier, **j'ai fait** du vélo. Le soir, **je suis allé** au cinéma en ville.

Dimanche, **j'ai écouté** de la musique et **j'ai envoyé** un texto à une copine. Puis **j'ai lu** des BD. Le soir, **j'ai invité** un ami.

Nicolas

4 b ✏️ Write four sentences about what *you* did last weekend. Exchange them with your partner: now write down what *he/she* did.

1 🖊 **Tu manges quoi, normalement, le soir? Et le week-end? Réponds en 6–8 phrases.** (◄◄ pp. 98–99)

Exemple:

> Le soir, je mange parfois du/de la/de l'/des... ou...
>
> Je bois du/de la/de l'/des... ou...
>
> Le week-end, nous mangeons devant la télé/à six heures/ensemble.
>
> Nous mangeons du/de la/de l'/des... ou...

2 a 📖 **Read the text about French colonies. Then answer the questions in English.** (◄◄ pp. 102–103)

1 *How big was the French empire in 1945 (in size and population)?*

2 *What events forced France to give independence to Vietnam in 1954?*

3 *Which were the first two French colonies in Africa to achieve independence?*

4 *Why did many French people find it especially hard to accept the idea of Algerian independence?*

5 *What did most French people in Algeria do when the country became independent?*

6 *Which is the largest French overseas territory today, and where is it?*

Les colonies françaises – et la décolonisation

En 1945, l'empire français est énorme: 10 millions de km², avec 100 millions d'habitants, principalement en Afrique et en Indochine (au Viêt Nam, par exemple).

En Indochine, la France refuse l'indépendance à ses colonies, et il y a neuf ans de guerre. Après la défaite décisive de l'armée française à Dien Bien Phû en 1954, la France doit accepter l'indépendance de trois pays: le Viêt Nam, le Laos et le Cambodge.

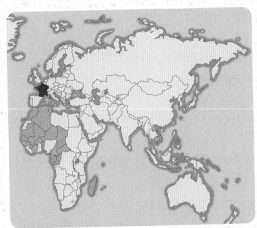

Les colonies françaises en Afrique et en Indochine

En Afrique, la France doit accepter l'indépendance de la Tunisie et du Maroc en 1956, et l'indépendance de toutes ses autres colonies africaines en 1960 – à l'exception de l'Algérie.

Pour beaucoup de Français, l'Algérie est un cas spécial. Le pays est plus près de la France que les autres colonies. Plus d'un million de Français habitent en Algérie. De 1954 à 1961, il y a une guerre violente, et les cas de brutalité et de torture se multiplient. Enfin, en 1962, la France accepte l'indépendance de l'Algérie. 800 000 Français quittent le pays...

Aujourd'hui, il n'y a plus de colonies, mais il y a des Départements et Régions d'Outre-Mer. Le département le plus grand, c'est la Guyane française, en Amérique du Sud.

> toutes *fpl – all*
> encore – *still*
> outre-mer – *overseas*

2 b 🖊 **Fais des recherches sur Internet sur la décolonisation de l'empire britannique. Puis écris 4–5 phrases en français.**

Exemples:
● indépendance de l'Inde: 1948
● indépendance du Ghana: 1957
● Gibraltar: territoire britannique

1 🖊 **What do you think of these ideas for presents (A–F)?** (◀◀ pp. 106–107)
Write six sentences with *j'aime/je n'aime pas* **+** *ce/cette/ces...*

Example: A   *Je n'aime pas* **cette** *chemise.*

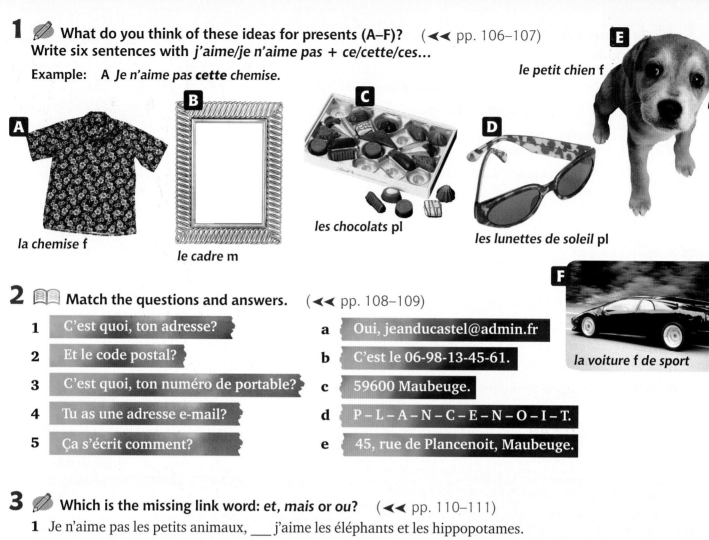

le petit chien f

la chemise f

le cadre m

les chocolats pl

les lunettes de soleil pl

la voiture f *de sport*

2 📖 **Match the questions and answers.** (◀◀ pp. 108–109)

1   C'est quoi, ton adresse?   a   Oui, jeanducastel@admin.fr

2   Et le code postal?   b   C'est le 06-98-13-45-61.

3   C'est quoi, ton numéro de portable?   c   59600 Maubeuge.

4   Tu as une adresse e-mail?   d   P – L – A – N – C – E – N – O – I – T.

5   Ça s'écrit comment?   e   45, rue de Plancenoit, Maubeuge.

3 🖊 **Which is the missing link word:** *et, mais* **or** *ou?* (◀◀ pp. 110–111)

1 Je n'aime pas les petits animaux, ___ j'aime les éléphants et les hippopotames.

2 Tu veux aller au cinéma vendredi ___ samedi? – Vendredi.

3 J'ai beaucoup de livres ___ j'ai beaucoup de CD.

4 Tu aimes ce réveil? – Non, pas beaucoup, ___ j'aime cette écharpe.

5 Qu'est-ce que tu vas faire le week-end prochain?

Ça dépend. Je vais peut-être aller chez ma tante, ___ je vais aller chez ma grand-mère.

6 Cet après-midi, je dois promener mon chien ___ laver la voiture. C'est trop!

4 a ♻ 📖 **One word in each bracket** *doesn't* **fit in the sentence. Which is it?**

Example: **1** *vélo*

1 Le week-end, je joue parfois au (**ping-pong/foot/vélo/basket**).

2 C'est bête! Le samedi, je dois faire (**la vaisselle/les courses/mes devoirs/les animaux**).

3 Dans le sud du pays, on cultive (**le coton/les voitures/le riz/les bananes**).

4 À mon avis, les vêtements de marque, c'est (**le top/trop cher/du vol/ensemble**).

5 Tu veux aller au (**centre commercial/pantalon/stade/café**) ?

4 b 🖊 **Write a sentence in French with two correct words and one incorrect word in brackets, as in exercise 4a. Can your partner identify the word that doesn't fit?**

1 Écris cinq phrases sur ta ville: donne ton opinion. (◄◄ pp. 106–107)

Exemple: **En ville, il y a _un_ parc. J'aime _ce_ parc.**

En ville, il y a ...	un château un stade des magasins des cafés un parc un centre sportif une bibliothèque des supermarchés des piscines un marché un bowling un centre commercial une patinoire

J'aime Je n'aime pas	ce... cette... ces...

2 J'aime les... Complète la phrase avec un mot français pour chaque lettre de l'alphabet! (Tu peux regarder dans le dictionnaire!)

Exemple: J'aime les animaux.   J'aime les westerns.
         J'aime les boucles d'oreille, ...   J'aime le xylophone.
                                          J'aime les yoyos.
                                          J'aime les zoos.

3 a *Read the three profiles. Who...*
1 *plays a musical instrument?*
2 *goes out on trips at weekends?*
3 *wants to travel?*
4 *likes doing a sport?*
5 *likes casual clothes?*
6 *wants to be famous?*

Nom et prénom: Leclerc, Édouard

Le week-end: Je surfe beaucoup sur Internet. Je vais en ville, je retrouve mes amis en ville.

Vêtements: J'aime les vêtements de marque.

Cadeaux préférés: Les jeux vidéo.

Sports: J'adore jouer au foot mais je ne marque jamais de buts!!

Je veux... être un acteur célèbre.

Nom et prénom: Ahmed, Khalid

Le week-end: J'écoute souvent de la musique. J'ai des cours de guitare.

Vêtements: J'aime les vêtements confortables et simples, les vêtements de sport.

Cadeaux préférés: Les vêtements, les chocolats, l'argent.

Sports: J'aime le basket à la télé, mais je ne joue pas au basket.

Je veux... visiter l'Amérique du Sud.

Nom et prénom: Savigny, Mathilde

Le week-end: Nous faisons des excursions en famille. J'invite souvent une copine et nous bavardons, nous discutons, etc.

Vêtements: J'aime les pantalons noirs et les chemises blanches.

Cadeaux préférés: Les vêtements, les livres, les accessoires.

Sports: Je joue au hockey au collège. Je déteste le hockey!

Je veux... deux hamsters et un DVD.

3 b Écris un profil similaire pour toi.

3 c *Which of the three teenagers is most similar to you? Explain what you have in common – and what is different!*

Grammaire

- Use these pages to check up on any grammar point you're not quite sure of.

- If you're still not clear about any point, ask your teacher.

Here's an example to show where you can find explanations of various parts of a French sentence:

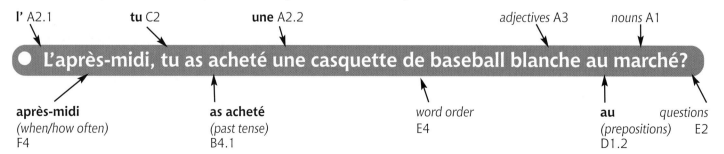

l' A2.1   tu C2   une A2.2   *adjectives* A3   *nouns* A1

● **L'après-midi, tu as acheté une casquette de baseball blanche au marché?**

après-midi   **as acheté**   word order   **au**   *questions*
(*when/how often*)   (*past tense*)   E4   (*prepositions*)   E2
F4   B4.1   D1.2

Glossary of terms

- **Adjectives** Les adjectifs
  ... are words that describe somebody or something:
  grand *big*, **vert** *green*

- **Determiners**
  ... come before nouns and limit them:
  les *the*, **un** *a*, **ma** *my*

- **The infinitive** L'infinitif
  ... is the 'name' of the verb, as listed in a dictionary:
  jouer *to play*, **aller** *to go*

- **Nouns** Les substantifs
  ... are words for somebody or something:
  frère *brother*, **musique** *music*

- **Prepositions** Les prépositions
  ... are words used with nouns to give information about when, how, where, etc.
  à *at, in, to*   **pour** *for*
  avec *with*   **dans** *in*

- **Pronouns** Les pronoms
  ... are short words used instead of a noun or name:
  je *I*, **tu** *you*, **il** *he*, **elle** *she*

- **Singular and plural** Singulier et pluriel
  Singular refers to just one thing or person:
  chat *cat*, **sœur** *sister*

  Plural refers to more than one thing or person:
  chats *cats*, **sœurs** *sisters*

- **Verbs** Les verbes
  Verbs express an action or a state:
  j'**habite** *I live*
  j'**ai** *I have*
  elle **aime** *she likes*

A Masculine and feminine, singular and plural

A1 *Les noms* Nouns

A1.1 Singular and plural nouns

- As in English, French nouns can be singular or plural. Most plural nouns end in *-s*:
  1 frère, 2 frères *1 brother, 2 brothers*

  Unlike in English, the added *-s* is usually not pronounced.

- Some French nouns take a different ending in the plural:
  1 animal, 2 animaux *1 animal, 2 animals*

A1.2 Masculine and feminine nouns

- One key difference between English and French grammar is that all French nouns fall into one of two categories. We call these categories **masculine** and **feminine**.
  For example: **pantalon, sucre, vélo, musée** are all masculine nouns.
  chemise, limonade, danse, gare are all feminine nouns.

- Some nouns have a masculine and a feminine form:
  le prof *the male teacher*   **la prof** *the female teacher*

- Other nouns have two different forms:
  un copain *a male friend*   **une copine** *a female friend*

A2 Determiners

A2.1 le, la, les *the*

- The word for 'the' depends on whether the noun is masculine or feminine, singular or plural.

masculine singular	feminine singular	masculine and feminine plural
le	la	les

  le chat *the cat*   la ville *the town*   les magasins *the shops*

  If singular nouns begin with a vowel or a silent *h*, **le** and **la** are shortened to **l'**: **l'animal** *the animal*

- **le**, **la** and **les** are sometimes used when we don't say 'the' in English:
  la capitale de **la** France *the capital of France*
  Je rentre à **la** maison. *I go home.*

- **le** is also used with expressions of time:
  le soir *in the evening*
  le week-end *at the weekend*
  le lundi *on Mondays*
  le lundi après-midi *on Monday afternoons*
  le lundi après-midi, je fais du judo.
  I do judo on Monday afternoons.

  (**lundi** *on one particular Monday*)

A2.2 un, une *a, an*

- The word for 'a' or 'an' depends on whether the noun is masculine or feminine.

masculine singular	feminine singular
un	une

  un village *a village*   une règle *a ruler*

- **un** or **une** is usually omitted with professions:
  Elle est prof au collège en ville.
  *She's **a** teacher at the school in town.*

Grammaire

A2.3 du, de la, de l', des *some*

- Like the words for 'the', the words for 'some' depend on whether the noun is masculine or feminine, singular or plural.

	masculine singular*	feminine singular*	masculine and femine plural
some	**du**	**de la**	**des**

if the singular noun starts with a vowel or silent h
de l'

> **du** lait *some milk*
> **de la** salade *some salad*
> **des** céréales *some cereal*
> **de l'**eau *some water*

- **du, de la, de l', des** are sometimes used when we don't say 'some' in English:
> Je voudrais des frites.
> *I'd like chips or I'd like some chips.*

A2.4 mon, ton, son, etc. my, your, his/her

- The word for 'my' depends on whether the noun it is used with is masculine or feminine, singular or plural.

masculine singular	feminine singular	masculine and feminine plural
mon	**ma**	**mes**

> **mon** frère **ma** sœur **mes** parents
> *my brother* *my sister* *my parents*

- The word for 'your' also depends on whether the noun it is used with is masculine or feminine, singular or plural.

masculine singular	feminine singular	masculine and feminine plural
ton	**ta**	**tes**

> **ton** frère **ta** sœur **tes** parents
> *your brother* *your sister* *your parents*

- The word for 'his' and 'her' is the same. It depends on whether the noun it is used with is masculine or feminine, singular or plural.

masculine singular	feminine singular	masculine and feminine plural
son	**sa**	**ses**

> **son** frère **sa** sœur **ses** parents
> *his brother,* *his sister,* *his parents,*
> *her brother* *her sister* *her parents*

> Ma copine s'appelle Anne. **Ses** parents sont très stricts.
> *My (girl)friend is called Anne.* **Her** *parents are very strict.*

> J'ai un frère. **Son** chien s'appelle Ajax.
> *I have a brother.* **His** *dog is called Ajax.*

A2.5 ce, cette *this*, ces *these*

- The words for 'this' and 'these' depend on whether the noun that follows is masculine or feminine, singular or plural.

	masculine singular	feminine singular		masculine and femine plural
this	**ce**	**cette**	*these*	**ces**

> **ce** livre **cette** écharpe **ces** gants
> *this book* *this scarf* *these gloves*

- Use **cet** with a masculine noun that starts with a vowel or a silent h:
> **cet** après-midi *this afternoon*

A2.6 Summary of determiners

	masculine singular	feminine singular	masculine and feminine plural
the	**le**	**la**	**les**
a	**un**	**une**	*(not applicable)*
some	**du**	**de la**	**des**
my	**mon**	**ma**	**mes**
your	**ton**	**ta**	**tes**
his, her	**son**	**sa**	**ses**
this, these	**ce**	**cette**	**ces**

A3 *Les adjectifs* Adjectives

A3.1 Masculine/feminine, singular/plural adjectives

- Adjectives are words that describe nouns. The basic rules in French are:
  - add an **-e** to the adjective if the noun it describes is feminine singular
  - add an **-s** to the adjective if the noun it describes is masculine plural
  - add **-es** to the adjective if the noun it describes is feminine plural

	masculine	feminine
singular	mon peti**t** frère	ma petit**e** sœur
plural	mes peti**ts** frères	mes petit**es** sœurs

- Adjectives that end in -e anyway don't take a second -e in the feminine:
> (masc. sing.) un pull **rouge** *a red pullover*
> (fem. sing.) une chemise **rouge** *a red shirt*

- But adjectives that end in -é <u>do</u> take a second -e in the feminine:
> (masc. sing.) il est **marié** *he is married*
> (fem. sing.) elle est **mariée** *she is married*

- Here are some special cases:

	masculine singular	feminine singular
white	blanc	blan**che**
sporty	sportif	sport**ive**
old	vieux	**vieille**
good-looking	beau	b**elle**
boring	ennuyeux	ennuy**euse**
long	long	lon**gue**
brown	marron	marron
nice	sympa	sympa

une table **blanche** *a white table*
elle est **sportive** *she is sporty*
une ceinture **marron** *a brown belt*
ma sœur est **sympa** *my sister is nice*

- Most adjectives ending in **-al** change to **-aux** in the masculine plural:

   des poissons **tropicaux** *tropical fish*

- Where an adjective describes a group including masculine and feminine, use the masculine form of the adjective:
   Les élèves sont **bruyants.**
   The pupils (boys <u>and</u> girls) are noisy.

A3.2 The position of adjectives

- **petit** (small), **grand** (big), **vieux** (old) and **beau** (beautiful) come before the noun, as in English:
   un **petit** village *a small village*
   une **grande** ville *a big town*

   un **vieux** village *an old village*
   une **belle** ville *a beautiful town*

- Other adjectives come <u>after</u> the noun they describe:
   un pull **large** *a baggy pullover*
   une ville **importante** *an important town*

A3.3 No capitals for adjectives of nationality

Adjectives of nationality begin with small letters:
   Thomas est **anglais.** *Thomas is English.*
   Sarah est **écossaise.** *Sarah is Scottish.*

A3.4 Comparing adjectives

- Use **plus** + adjective + **que**...
   Français est **plus** intéressant **que** maths.
   French is more interesting than maths.
   La Seine est **plus** longue **que** la Tamise.
   The Seine is longer than the Thames.

- Remember to add *e* for feminine and *s* for plural, as usual.

B1 The present tense of regular verbs

- French verbs take different endings according to <u>who</u> is doing the action.

The regular pattern is:

verb: **regarder** *to watch*

je	-e	je	regard**e**	*I watch, I'm watching*
tu	-es	tu*	regard**es**	*you watch, you're watching*
il	-e	il	regard**e**	*he watches, he's watching*
elle		elle	regard**e**	*she watches, she's watching*
on		on	regard**e**	*we/they watch, are watching*
nous	-ons	nous	regard**ons**	*we watch, we're watching*
vous	-ez	vous*	regard**ez**	*you watch, you're watching*
ils	-ent	ils	regard**ent**	*they (boys) watch, they're watching*
elles		elles	regard**ent**	*they (girls) watch, they're watching*

* For use of the pronouns (tu / vous, on, il / elle, etc.) see Section C below.

- *regard**e**, regard**es**, regard**ent*** are all pronounced the same.

- Other verbs that follow this pattern include:

j'adore *I love*	j'habite *I live*
j'aime *I like*	j'invite *I invite*
j'arrive *I arrive*	je joue *I play*
je bavarde *I chat*	je lave *I wash*
je chante *I sing*	je loue *I hire*
je commence *I begin*	je mange *I eat*
je déjeune *I have lunch*	je parle *I talk*
je déteste *I hate*	je quitte *I leave*
je dîne *I have my evening meal*	je range *I tidy*
	je reste *I stay*
je donne *I give*	je surfe *I surf*
j'écoute *I listen (to)*	je travaille *I work*
je ferme *I close*	je trouve *I find*
je gagne *I win*	je visite *I visit*

Tu aimes le tennis? – Oui, j'aime le tennis.
Do you like tennis? – Yes, I like tennis.
Vous habitez à Paris? – Non, nous habitons à Boulogne.
Do you live in Paris? – No, we live in Boulogne.
Les cours commencent à 9h00. *Lessons start at 9 o'clock.*

- Singular nouns take the same endings as *il / elle*:
   Ma mère travaille. *My mother works.*

- Plural nouns take the same endings as *ils / elles*:
   Les Vikings arrivent. *The Vikings arrive.*

Grammaire

B2 Reflexive verbs

- Reflexive verbs have an extra part between the pronoun and the verb:

je **me** lève *I get up*	je **m'**appelle *I am called*
tu **te** lèves *you get up*	tu **t'**appelles *you are called*

B3 The present tense of irregular verbs

- The following verbs don't follow the regular verb pattern described in Section B1 above.

B3.1 avoir to have

j'	**ai**	*I have*	nous	**avons**	*we have*
tu	**as**	*you have*	vous	**avez**	*you have*
il	**a**	*he has*	ils	**ont**	*they have*
elle	**a**	*she has*	elles	**ont**	*they have*

Tu as un animal? Oui, j'ai un hamster.
Do you have an animal? Yes, I have a hamster.

- In French, you use the verb **avoir** to say how old people are:

  J'**ai** onze ans. *(I have 11 years =) I'm 11 years old.*

- You also use **avoir** with most verbs in the past tense. See Section B4 below.

B3.2 être to be

je	**suis**	*I am*	nous	**sommes**	*we are*
tu	**es**	*you are*	vous	**êtes**	*you are*
il	**est**	*he is*	ils	**sont**	*they are*
elle	**est**	*she is*	elles	**sont**	*they are*

Je suis française. *I am French.*
Ils sont fatigués. *They're tired.*

- For saying how old you are, see the verb **avoir** (to have) in Section B3.1 above.

B3.3 aller to go

je	**vais**	*I go, I'm going*	nous	**allons**	*we go, we're going*
tu	**vas**	*you go, you're going*	vous	**allez**	*you go, you're going*
il	**va**	*he goes, he's going*	ils	**vont**	*they go, they're going*
elle	**va**	*she goes, she's going*	elles	**vont**	*they go, they're going*

Je vais en France en juin. *I'm going to France in June.*
Nous allons en ville. *We go to town.*

- This verb is often followed by **à**, **au**, **à la** (see Section D1.2).

- Use **aller** and the infinitive to say what people are going to do in the future (see Section B7).

- The past tense is: **je suis allé** *I went (male)*, **je suis allée** *I went (female)* (see Section B4.3).

B3.4 faire to do

je	**fais**	*I do, I'm doing*	nous	**faisons**	*we do, we're doing*
tu	**fais**	*you do, you're doing*	vous	**faites**	*you do, you're doing*
il	**fait**	*he does, he's doing*	ils	**font**	*they do, they're doing*
elle	**fait**	*she does, she's doing*	elles	**font**	*they do, they're doing*

- This verb has a range of meanings, depending on the noun it is used with:

  faire du cheval to **go** horse riding
  faire du tir à l'arc to **do** archery
  faire la sieste to **have** a midday rest
  faire un gâteau to **make** a cake
  faire des recherches to **carry out** research

Je fais de la natation. *I go swimming.*
Mes copains font du judo. *My friends do judo.*

- **Faire** is also used in expressions with weather:

  il fait froid *it's cold*
  il fait mauvais *the weather's bad*

B3.5 Some other irregular verbs

attendre	**to wait**	
j'	**attends**	*I wait for*
tu	**attends**	*you wait for*
il/elle	**attend**	*he/she waits for*
nous	**attendons**	*we wait for*
vous	**attendez**	*you wait for*
ils/elles	**attendent**	*they wait for*

Nous attendons le bus.
We are waiting for the bus.

devoir	**must**	
je	**dois**	*I must*
tu	**dois**	*you must*
il/elle	**doit**	*he/she must*
nous	**devons**	*we must*
vous	**devez**	*you must*
ils/elles	**doivent**	*they must*

Mon frère doit faire la vaisselle.
My brother must do the washing up.

finir *to finish*	
je **finis**	I finish
tu **finis**	you finish
il/elle **finit**	he/she finishes
nous **finissons**	we finish
vous **finissez**	you finish
ils/elles **finissent**	they finish

Tu finis à quelle heure?
What time do you finish?

pouvoir *can*	
je **peux**	I can
tu **peux**	you can
il/elle **peut**	he/she can
nous **pouvons**	we can
vous **pouvez**	you can
ils/elles **peuvent**	they can

Est-ce que je peux ouvrir la fenêtre?
Can I open the window?

prendre *to take*	
je **prends**	I take
tu **prends**	you take
il/elle **prend**	he/she takes
nous **prenons**	we take
vous **prenez**	you take
ils/elles **prennent**	they take

Prenez le 81.
Take the number 81 bus.

sortir *to go out*	
je **sors**	I go out
tu **sors**	you go out
il/elle **sort**	he/she goes out
nous **sortons**	we go out
vous **sortez**	you go out
ils/elles **sortent**	they go out

Nous sortons souvent en famille.
We often go out as a family.

vouloir *to want to*	
je **veux**	I want to
tu **veux**	you want to
il/elle **veut**	he / she wants to
nous **voulons**	we want to
vous **voulez**	you want to
ils/elles **veulent**	they want to

Tu veux faire du karting?
Do you want to go go-karting?

B4 *Le passé* The perfect tense/past tense

- The perfect tense consists of <u>two</u> parts:

	1	2	
	auxiliary verb	past participle	
j'	**ai**	joué	au rugby *I played rugby*
elle	**a**	regardé	la télé *she watched TV*
je	**suis**	allé(e)	en ville *I went to town*

- The first part, the *auxiliary verb*, is usually **avoir** (j'ai, tu as, il a, etc.), but it can be **être** (je suis, tu es, il est, etc.).

- The second part, the *past participle*, often ends in -**é**: the -**é** is pronounced.

B4.1 The past tense of regular verbs

- Examples of regular verbs are listed in Section B1 above.

- The auxiliary verb is **avoir** (j'ai, tu as, il/elle a, nous avons, etc. – see Section B3.1).

- The past participle is formed by replacing the verb ending with -**é**.

present → ~~j~~'ai jou~~e~~ é → j'ai joué
je joue
I play   past
                                               j'ai joué
                                               I played

Hier, nous **avons** visit**é** un château.
Yesterday we visited a castle.

À midi, j'**ai** mang**é** un hamburger.
At midday I ate a hamburger.

Mon père **a** achet**é** une chemise.
My dad bought a shirt.

B4.2 The past tense of irregular verbs

- The auxiliary verb is **avoir** (j'ai, tu as, il/elle a, nous avons, etc. – see Section B3.1).

- The past participle is unpredictable and has to be learnt.

<u>verb</u>	<u>past tense</u>	
avoir *to have*	j'ai **eu** *I had*	Le matin, j'ai eu maths. *In the morning I had maths.*
boire *to drink*	j'ai **bu** *I drank*	J'ai bu un coca. *I drank a coke.*
faire *to do*	j'ai **fait** *I did*	Puis j'ai fait mes devoirs. *Then I did my homework.*
lire *to read*	j'ai **lu** *I read*	Hier soir, j'ai lu. *Yesterday evening, I read.*
prendre *to take*	j'ai **pris** *I took*	J'ai pris des photos. *I took some photos.*
voir *to see*	j'ai **vu** *I saw*	J'ai vu un film. *I saw a film.*

B4.3 The past tense of verbs with auxiliary *je <u>suis</u>...*

- A few verbs have the auxiliary **je <u>suis</u>** (not j'<u>ai</u>). The most common is **je suis allé** (I went).
  Le week-end, je suis allé au théâtre.
  At the weekend, I went to the theatre.

- Unlike verbs that take **j'ai**, you add an -**e** to the past participle for females:
  (male) je suis allé
  (female) je suis allée

Grammaire

Lundi dernier, je suis all**é** en ville.
Last Monday, I went into town. (said by a male)
Lundi dernier, je suis all**ée** en ville.
Last Monday, I went into town. (said by a female)

B4.4 Special case: c'était

- **C'était** means 'it was' or 'it used to be':
  C'était une colonie française.
  It was/used to be a French colony.
  J'ai vu un film. C'était barbant.
  I saw a film. It was boring.

B5 Telling people what to do (the imperative)

B5.1 Speaking to someone of your own age

- To people with whom you would say **tu** (see Section C2 below), use the verb ending in -**e**:
  lave les fruits *wash the fruit*
  écoute les dialogues *listen to the dialogues*

- Some irregular verbs have an -**s** ending:
  mets les fruits dans un bol *put the fruit in a bowl*
  écris une lettre *write a letter*

B5.2 Speaking to more than one person, or to an adult not in your family

- To people with whom you would say **vous** (see Section C2 below), use the verb with the **vous** endings:
  (vous descendez *you get off*) **Descendez** à la gare.
  Get off at the station.
  (vous prenez *you take*) **Prenez** le bus. *Take the bus.*

B5.3 Telling people what **not** to do

- Use **ne** before the verb, **pas** after the verb:
  (**tu** form) **Ne** regarde **pas** le livre.
  Don't look at the book.
  (**vous** form) **Ne** prenez **pas** le 11.
  Don't take the number 11 bus.

B6 The infinitive

- The infinitive is the 'name' of the verb – the form you find in a dictionary. Unlike the forms used after *je, il,* etc. (*je fais, il fait,* etc.), the infinitive never changes.

- The infinitive of regular verbs ends in -**er**.
  The infinitive of other verbs ends in -**ir** or -**re**.
  aller *to go*
  faire *to do (shopping), go on (a trip), etc.*
  bavarder *to chat*
  avoir *to have*

- Use the infinitive after the following verbs:

j'aime, tu aimes, etc. *like*	J'aime **aller** en ville. *I like going into town.*	
je dois, tu dois, etc. *have to*	Tu dois **laver** la voiture. *You have to wash the car.*	
je peux, tu peux, etc. *can*	Je peux **fermer** la fenêtre? *Can I shut the window?*	
je veux, tu veux, etc. *want to*	Ma sœur veut **faire** du vélo. *My sister wants to cycle.*	

- Use **aller** and the infinitive to say what people are going to do in the future (see Section B7 below).

- Use the infinitive after **il faut** *(it is necessary to)*:
  Il faut **payer** à la caisse.
  It is necessary to (= you have to) pay at the till.

B7 The future

- Use **aller** and the infinitive to say what people are going to do in the future:
  Je **vais rester** chez moi. *I'm going to stay at home.*
  Tu **vas aller** en France? *Are you going to go to France?*
  Nous **allons partir** à 8h00. *We're going to leave at 8 am.*

C Pronouns

C1 je I

- **je** and **j'** both mean 'I'. Use **j'** if the word that follows begins with *h* or a vowel:
  Je regarde la télé. *I watch TV.*
  J'ai une souris. *I have a mouse.*

C2 tu, vous: two words for 'you'

- Use **tu** when you're talking to someone (one person) of your own age or someone in the family.

- Use **vous** when you're talking to an adult (one person) not in your family, e.g. your teacher.

- Use **vous**, also, when talking to more than one person – whatever their age, whether or not you know them well.

Tu as un bic, s'il te plaît, Marie?
Do you have a biro, please, Marie?
Vous avez un livre, s'il vous plaît, madame?
Do you have a book, please, Miss?
Vous travaillez, Karen et Michael?
Are you working, Karen and Michael?

C3 moi, toi me, you (after prepositions)

- avec **moi** *with me*   avec **toi** *with you*
  chez **moi** *at my house* chez **toi** *at your house*

C4 *il, elle* he, she

- **il** usually means 'he'; **elle** means 'she'.
  Matthieu habite à Lyon. **Il** *a 11 ans.*
  Matthieu lives in Lyon. He's 11 years old.
  J'ai une sœur. **Elle** *s'appelle Emma.*
  I have a sister. She's called Emma.

- **il** can mean 'it', referring to a masculine noun; **elle** can mean 'it', referring to a feminine noun:
  J'aime ma maison. **Elle** *est grande.*
  I like my house. **It** *is big.*

- **il** is also used in set expressions:
  - **il y a** *there is, there are*
    Il y a des cafés en ville. There are cafés in town.
    Mais il n'y a pas de cinéma. But there isn't a cinema.
  - **il faut** + infinitive (see Section B6 above) *it is necessary to, you have to*
    Il faut attendre le guide. You have to wait for the guide.
  - weather expressions
    il pleut *it rains, it is raining*
    il fait chaud *it's/the weather's hot*

C5 *on* we, they, people

- **on** takes the same part of the verb as *il/elle*.

- **on** can mean 'we', and can be used instead of *nous*:
  On *prend du lait?* = **Nous** *prenons du lait?*
  Shall we take some milk?

- **on** can also mean 'people generally' (in English, we often say 'they' or 'you'):
  En France **on** *roule à droite.*
  In France, people (you, they) drive on the right.
  On *parle français au Sénégal?*
  Do people (they) speak French in Senegal?

C6 *nous* we

- **nous** means 'we':
  Nous *allons au centre commercial.*
  We go to the shopping centre.

C7 *ils, elles* they

- There are two words for 'they':
  ils = *they* (all male, or mixed group of males and females)
  elles = *they* (female)

  Tes parents aiment la musique? – Oui, **ils** *aiment beaucoup la musique.*
  Do your parents like music? – Yes, they like music a lot.

D Prepositions

D1 *à: au, à la, aux*

D1.1 *à*

- **à** can mean:
  - **in** *J'habite* **à** *Paris. I live in Paris.*
  - **at** *J'arrive* **à** *une heure. I arrive at one o'clock.*
  - **to** *Je vais* **à** *Londres. I'm going to London* (for 'to' + *countries*, see Section D3 below)

- Some special expressions:
  - **à** *pied on foot,* **à** *vélo by bike*
  - *une glace* **à** *trois boules an ice cream with three scoops*
  - *l'équipe a gagné 3* **à** *0 the team won 3-0*

D1.2 *au, à la, à l', aux* to the, at the

- **à** + **le** <u>always</u> combine to form the one word **au**.
  à + **les** <u>always</u> combine to form the one word **aux**.
  à + **la** and **à** + **l'** are fine.

with masculine nouns	with feminine nouns
je vais **au** collège	tu vas **à la** mer?
I go to school	*do you go to the sea?*

if the singular noun begins with a vowel or silent *h*
je suis allé **à l'**hôpital *I went to hospital*

with all plural nouns
il va **aux** halles *he's going to the covered market*

- **au** is also used
  - with flavours and fillings:
    un sandwich **au** *jambon a ham sandwich*
  - with sports:
    Je joue **au** *basket. I play basketball.*

D2 *de: du, de la, des*

D2.1 *de*

- **de** can mean 'of'. Shorten **de** to **d'** before *h* or a vowel:
  la chambre **de** *ma sœur (the room of my sister =) my sister's room*
  le prof **d'**histoire *(the teacher of history =) the history teacher*

- **de** is used with <u>quantities</u> of food:
  un paquet **de** *chips a packet of crisps*
  un kilo **d'**oranges *a kilo of oranges*

(But when you say 'some', use **du / de la / des** – see Section A2.3 above.)

Grammaire

- **de** is sometimes part of an expression with different meanings:

près de *near*	J'habite **près de** Calais. *I live near Calais.*
beaucoup de *lots of*	J'ai **beaucoup de** CD. *I have lots of CDs.*
de... à ... *from... to...*	**de** 10h00 **à** 18h00 *from 10 am to 6 pm*

D2.2 du, de la, de l', des of the

- **de** + **le** <u>always</u> combine to form the one word **du**.
  de + **les** <u>always</u> combine to form the one word **des**.
  de + **la** and **de** + **l'** are fine.

  Use this pattern:

- to express 'of the', and after **près** (near the) and **en face** (opposite the):

with masculine nouns	with feminine nouns
près **du** cinéma *near the cinema*	en face **de la** gare *opposite the station*

if the singular noun begins with a vowel or silent *h*
près **de l'**arrêt de bus *near the bus stop*

with all plural nouns
la capitale **des** États-Unis *the capital of the USA*

- with **jouer** + musical instruments:
  Je joue **du** piano. *I play the piano.*
  Je joue **de la** guitare. *I play the guitar.*

- with activities and the verb **faire**:
  Je vais faire **du** tir à l'arc. *I'm going to do archery.*
  Tu fais **de l'**escalade? *Do you go rock-climbing?*

D3 Prepositions with countries

- The same French preposition means both 'in' and 'to' a country.

	masculine singular	feminine singular	all plural countries
in *or* to + country	**au** Brésil	**en** France	**aux** États-Unis

J'habite en Grande-Bretagne.
I live in Great Britain.
En été, je vais aller au Pakistan.
In the summer, I'm going to go to Pakistan.

D4 More prepositions

after	**après**	Après ça, je suis allée. *After that, I went.*
at	**à** + precise time	J'arrive au collège à 8h40. *I arrive at school at 8.40.*
	vers + vague time	Nous allons rentrer vers 20h00. *We'll return at about 8 pm.*
	le + weekend	Je fais mes devoirs le week-end. *I do my homework at the weekend.*
	chez (at ...'s house)	On se retrouve chez moi? *Shall we meet at my house?*
by	**à** + bike	Je vais au collège à vélo. *I go to school by bike.*
	en + other transport	Tu vas en bus ou en auto? *Are you going by bus or by car?*
during	**pendant**	Je travaille pendant les vacances. *I'm working during the holidays.*
for	**pour**	C'est super pour les jeunes. *It's great for young people.*
in	**à** + named town	J'habite à Birmingham. *I live in Birmingham.*
	dans + club	Je joue dans l'orchestre. *I play in the orchestra.*
	dans + direction	C'est dans le nord. *It's in the north.*
	en + lesson, class	Nous avons bavardé en anglais.
	en + month	en août *in August*
	en, au + season	en hiver, été, automne *in winter, summer, autumn* au printemps *in spring*
	no prep. + part of day	Le soir, nous avons bavardé. *In the evening, we chatted.*
in front of	**devant**	On se retrouve devant le cinéma? *Shall we meet in front of the cinema?*
near	**près de** (see D2.2)	C'est près du parc. *It's near the park.*
on	**sur**	Je surfe sur Internet. *I surf (on) the internet.*
	à + pied	Je vais au collège à pied. *I go to school on foot.*
opposite	**en face de** (see D2.2)	C'est en face de l'église. *It's opposite the church.*
to	**à** + named town	Je vais à Nice. *I'm going to Nice.*
	en + ville	Le week-end, je vais en ville. *At the weekend, I go to town.*
	en + country	En juillet, je vais en Espagne. *In July, I'm going to Spain.*
	chez + people	Il va chez sa tante. *He's going to his aunt's.*
	'to the' –	see D1.2 above
with	**avec** + person	Je suis allé avec mes copains. *I went with my friends.*
	par + letter	Ça commence par "c". *It begins with 'c'.*

E Shaping and linking sentences

E1 Negative sentences

- The basic rule is: to make a sentence negative, put **ne** before the verb and **pas** after it:

  Il fait froid.   Il **ne** fait **pas** froid.
  It's cold.   *It isn't cold.*

- Shorten **ne** to **n'** if the word that follows begins with *h* or a vowel:

  J'aime le fromage.   Je **n'**aime **pas** le fromage.
  I like cheese.   *I don't like cheese.*

- In negative sentences, **un** and **une** are replaced with **de**:

  J'ai un frère; je n'ai pas **de** sœur.
  I have a brother; I don't have a sister.

- Note these two special negatives:

  ne... rien = *nothing*   Nous **ne** faisons **rien**.
  We don't do anything.
  ne... jamais = *never*   Nous **ne** regardons **jamais** la télé.
  We never watch TV.

E2 Questions

- You can ask questions simply by making your voice go higher at the end of the sentence:

  Tu joues au tennis. *You play tennis.*
  Tu joues au tennis? *Do you play tennis?*

- You can start the question with **est-ce que**:

  Je peux faire du kayak. *I can go kayaking.*
  Est-ce que je peux faire du kayak? *Can I go kayaking?*

- Or you can invert the subject and the verb:

  As-tu un bic? *Do you have a pen?*

- Many questions contain special question words:

combien *how much*	C'est combien? *How much is it?*
comment *how*	Ça s'écrit comment? *How do you spell it?*
comment *what*	Comment t'appelles-tu? *What are you called*
où *where*	Où habites-tu? *Where do you live?*
pourquoi *why*	J'aime l'histoire. Pourquoi? Parce que c'est facile. *I like history. Why? Because it's easy.*
quand *when*	C'est quand, ton anniversaire? *When's your birthday?*
quel (m) *which, what*	Une glace? Oui. Quel parfum? *An ice cream? Yes. Which flavour?* Tu as quel âge? *(what age have you? =) How old are you?*
quelle (f) *which, what*	C'est quelle photo? *Which photo is it?* À quelle heure? *At what time?* Tu déjeunes à quelle heure? *What time do you have lunch?*
qu'est-ce que *what*	Qu'est-ce que tu aimes? *What do you like?*
qui *who*	Tu joues au tennis avec qui? *Who do you play tennis with?*
quoi *what*	Ta couleur préférée, c'est quoi? *What's your favourite colour?*

E3 Linking sentences

- Use the following words to link shorter sentences together to make longer ones:

et *and*	Je suis anglaise et j'habite à York. *I'm English and I live in York.*
et puis *and then*	Nous dînons et puis nous sortons. *We have our evening meal and then we go out.*
mais *but*	J'aime le jambon mais je déteste le fromage. *I like ham but I hate cheese.*
ou *or*	Je vais à la piscine ou je vais à la patinoire. *I go to the swimming pool or I go to the ice rink.*
parce que *because*	J'aime la géographie parce que c'est intéressant. *I like geography because it's interesting.*

E4 Word order

- Descriptions (adjectives or phrases) usually come <u>after</u> the noun in French.

- Adjectives usually come after the noun they describe:
  les chemises **blanches** *white shirts*

  (**grand**, **petit**, **vieux** and **beau** are exceptions:
  une **petite** maison *a small house*)

- Expressions with **de / d'**:
  un jus d'orange *an orange juice*
  la chambre de mes parents *my parents' room*

- Expressions with **à / au**:
  un pantalon à pattes d'éléphant *flared trousers*

- Names of places
  la place Saint-Pierre *St Peter's square*

Grammaire

F Numbers, time, frequency

F1 Numbers

1 un	11 onze	20 vingt
2 deux	12 douze	30 trente
3 trois	13 treize	40 quarante
4 quatre	14 quatorze	50 cinquante
5 cinq	15 quinze	60 soixante
6 six	16 seize	70 soixante-dix
7 sept	17 dix-sept	80 quatre-vingts
8 huit	18 dix-huit	90 quatre-vingt-dix
9 neuf	19 dix-neuf	100 cent
10 dix	20 vingt	1000 mille

21 vingt **et** un	25 vingt-cinq
31 trente **et** un	35 trente-cinq
41 quarante **et** un	45 quarante-cinq
51 cinquante **et** un	55 cinquante-cinq
61 soixante **et** un	65 soixante-cinq
71 soixante **et** onze	75 soixante-quinze
81 quatre-vingt-un	85 quatre-vingt-cinq
91 quatre-vingt-onze	95 quatre-vingt-quinze
101 cent un	105 cent cinq

- *quatre-vingts* on its own has an *-s* on the end. Linked with other numbers, it hasn't: *quatre-vingt-un, quatre-vingt-deux*, etc.

- Ordinal numbers are as follows:

    $1^{st} = 1^{er}$ premier *m*,
    1ère première *f*
    $2^{nd} = 2^{ème}$ le / la deuxième
    $3^{rd} = 3^{ème}$ le / la troisième
    $4^{th} = 4^{ème}$ le / la quatrième
    (note the *e* in *quatre* is dropped)
    $5^{th} = 5^{ème}$ le / la cinquième

    C'est la première rue à gauche. *It's the first road on the left.*
    Mon premier jour à l'école. *My first day at school.*

F2 Days and dates

- Use the usual numbers in dates (and no word for 'of'):
    Mon anniversaire, c'est le treize avril.
    My birthday is on the thirteenth of April.

- Exception: use **le premier** for the first of the month:
    le premier mai *the first of May*

- Days and months don't have capitals in French.

F3 Time

- Write the 24-hour clock with **heures** separating the minutes from the hours:
    il est dix heures quinze *it's ten fifteen*
    à treize heures quarante *at thirteen-forty*

    The abbreviation is written 10h15, 13h40, etc.

- The 12-hour clock is written as follows:
    il est deux heures cinq *it's five past two*
    il est deux heures et quart *it's a quarter past two*
    il est deux heures vingt *it's twenty past two*
    il est deux heures vingt-cinq *it's twenty-five past two*
    il est deux heures et demie *it's half-past two*
    il est trois heures moins vingt-cinq *it's twenty-five to three*
    il est trois heures moins vingt *it's twenty to three*
    il est trois heures moins le quart *it's a quarter to three*
    il est trois heures moins dix *it's ten to three*
    il est trois heures *it's three o'clock*

- Note: il est midi *it's midday*, il est minuit *it's midnight*

F4 When and how often

- There is no word for 'in' the evening, 'on' Saturday, or 'at' the weekend:

le soir *in the evening*	Le soir, je regarde la télé. *In the evening, I watch TV.*
le week-end *at the weekend*	Je vais en ville le week-end. *I go to town at the weekend.*
le samedi après-midi *on Saturday afternoons*	

- Use the following words to say how often you do an activity:

parfois *sometimes*	Je vais parfois au parc. *I sometimes go to the park.*
souvent *often*	Nous allons souvent à la mer. *We often go to the sea.*
toujours *always*	Je déjeune toujours à midi. *I always have lunch at midday.*

Réponse: le mystère de la porte ouverte (p. 86)

Regarde la position des anoraks sur la première image. L'anorak jaune est *sur* l'anorak rouge. Sandrine porte l'anorak rouge. Sabine porte l'anorak jaune.
→ Sabine est rentrée la dernière.

Glossaire français–anglais

Stratégies! *Using the glossary*

Words are in alphabetical order. To find a word, look up its first letter, then find it according to the alphabetical order of its second and third letters: e.g. **école** comes before **été** because **éc-** comes before **ét-**.

A

à 1 *to* à manger *to eat,* 3 à 0 *(score) 3-0*
2 *at, in + place* à Paris *in Paris,* à 100m de *100m from,* à mon avis *in my opinion*
3 *at + time* à trois heures *at three o'clock,* à quelle heure? *at what time?*
4 *on* à droite *on the right,* à la télé *on TV,*
à bientôt *hear from you soon!*
à demain *see you tomorrow*
à l'exception de *with the exception of*
à partir de 13 ans *from the age of 13*
à pied *on foot*
à ton tour *it's your turn*
à votre service *at your service*
à cause de *because of*
a *has*
il a 12 ans *he's 12 years old*
A+ (= à plus tard) *see you later*
abbaye *f abbey*
abominable *m or f awful*
abricot *m apricot*
absorber *to absorb*
accent aigu *m acute accent (e.g. é)*
accepter *to accept*
accès *m* (à) *access (to)*
accessoires *mpl accessories*
accro *m or f* (à) *addicted to*
accueillir *to welcome*
acheter *to buy*
Acropole *f Acropolis*
acteur *m actor*
actif *m,* **active** *f active*
activité *f activity*
actrice *f actress*
adaptation *f adaptation*
adapter *to adapt*
additionnel *m,* **additionelle** *f additional, extra*
adjectif *m adjective*
admiration *f admiration*
admirer *to admire*
admis *m,* **admise** *f allowed, admitted*
adorer *to love, adore*
adresse *f address*
adulte *m or f adult*
aéroport *m airport*
africain *m,* **africaine** *f African*
Afrique *f Africa*
âge *m age*
quel âge as-tu? *how old are you?*
agence *f agency*
agent *m agent*
agriculteur *m farmer*
agriculture *f agriculture*
ai *have* j'ai *I have*
aider *to help*
aide-moi! *help me!*
aigu: accent aigu *acute accent (e.g. é)*
ail *m garlic*
aile *f* 1 *wing* 2 *side of a building*
aimer *to like, love* je t'aime *I love you*
aire *f* de pique-niques *picnic area*
ajouté *m,* **ajoutée** *f added*
ajouter *to add*
alarmer: s'alarmer *to get alarmed*

alerte! *alert!*
Algérie *f Algeria*
allé: je suis allé *m I went;* **je suis allée** *f I went (past tense of* aller)
Allemagne *f Germany*
allemand *m,* **allemande** *f German*
aller *to go*
aller aux toilettes *to go to the toilet*
je peux aller voir...? *can I go and see...?*
allergique (à) *allergic (to)*
alliés *mpl allies*
alors 1 *well then* 2 *so*
américain *m,* **américaine** *f American*
Amérique *f America*
ami *m,* **amie** *f friend*
amphithéâtre *m amphitheatre*
amusant *m,* **amusante** *f fun, amusing*
amusement *m fun*
an *m year*
jour de l'an *New Year's Day*
ancien *m,* **ancienne** *f* 1 *ancient, old*
plus ancien que *older than*
2 *former*
anglais *m,* **anglaise** *f English*
Angola *f Angola*
animal *m animal*
animaux *mpl animals*
animaux sous-marins *underwater animals*
animiste *m or f animist*
année *f year*
anniversaire *m birthday*
annoncer (que) *to announce (that)*
antilope *f antelope*
août *August*
en août *in August*
appeler *to call, name*
comment t'appelles-tu? *what's your name?*
qui s'appelle *who is called*
approche: s'approcher de *to approach*
après *after, afterwards*
après-midi *m afternoon*
aquatique *m or f aquatic*
aqueduc *m aqueduct*
arabe *m or f Arab*
arachide *f ground-nut (= peanut)*
arc *m arch*
architecte *m or f architect*
arène *f arena*
argent *m* 1 *money* 2 *silver*
Argentine *f Argentina*
armée *f army*
arobas *m @*
arrêt *m* de bus *bus stop*
arriver *to arrive*
arrogant *m,* **arrogante** *f arrogant*
article *m article*
artiste *m or f artist*
as *have*
assez 1 *quite* assez bien *quite good*
2 assez de *enough*
assieds-toi *sit down*
atelier *m workshop*
Athènes *Athens*
Atlantique *f Atlantic ocean*
attaquant *m striker (in football)*
attaquer *to attack*

attendre *to wait*
attention! *be careful! watch out!*
attention à *watch out with/for*
au (see p. 145)
1 *to the* au sud de Lyon *to the south of Lyon,* du 01/10 au 30/04 *from 1st Oct to 30th April*
2 *at the* je mange au collège *I eat at school*
3 *in* au Mexique *in Mexico,* au passé *in the past,* au revoir *good-bye*
aubergine *f aubergine (vegetable)*
aujourd'hui *today*
aussi *also, too*
aussi... que *as... as*
australien *m,* **australienne** *f Australian*
auto *f car* en auto *by car*
automne *m autumn*
autre *other*
l'autre *the other one*
autrichien *m,* **autrichienne** *f Austrian*
autruche *f ostrich*
aux (see p. 145) *to the, at the, in*
réponds aux questions *answer the questions*
auxiliaire: verbe *m* **auxiliaire** *auxiliary verb*
avais: j'avais 12 ans *I was 12 years old*
avancer *to advance*
avant *before*
avant de jouer *before playing*
avant Jésus-Christ *BC*
avant-hier *the day before yesterday*
avec *with* avec qui? *with whom?*
aventure *f adventure*
avez, avons *have*
avis: à mon avis *in my opinion*
avoir (see p. 142) *to have*
avril *April*

B

baguette *f baguette, French stick (of bread)*
ballon *m ball*
banane *f* 1 *banana* 2 *bum-bag*
bande *f* **dessinée** *comic strip*
banque *f bank*
barbant *boring*
barrière *f* **magnétique** *magnetic barrier*
bas: en bas *downstairs*
base *f base*
basket *m basketball*
baskets *fpl trainers*
bataille *f battle*
bâtiment *m building*
batterie *f drums*
bavard *m,* **bavarde** *f chatty, talkative*
bavarder *to chat*
BD *f* (= bande *f* dessinée) *comic strip*
beau (pl: beaux) *m,* **belle** *f beautiful, good-looking*
il fait beau *the weather's nice*
beau-père *m step-father*
beaucoup (de) *lots of, many*
j'aime beaucoup... *I like... a lot*

Glossaire français–anglais

bébé *m* baby
bec *m* **Bunsen** Bunsen burner
beffroi *m* belfrey, tower
belge *m or f* Belgian
Belgique *f* Belgium
belle *f* beautiful
belle-mère *f* step-mother
ben... well...
beurk! yuk!
Berne Bern (capital of Switzerland)
bête *m or f* stupid
beurre *m* butter
bibliothèque *f* library
bic *m* biro
bien 1 well tu as bien joué *you played well*
2 *good, fine, OK* très bien *very good*, ça
va bien *I'm fine*
bien sûr *of course*
bientôt soon
à bientôt! *hear from you soon!*
bière *f* beer
bilingue *m or f* bilingual
billet *m* **aller-retour** return ticket
biscuit *m* biscuit
bises: grosses bises love and kisses (at end
of letter)
bison *m* bison
bisous *mpl* love and kisses (at end of letter)
blague *f* joke
blanc *m* blank, gap
blanc *m*, **blanche** *f* white
blazer *m* blazer
blé *m* wheat
bleu *m*, **bleue** *f* blue
blond *m*, **blonde** *f* 1 blond
2 bière blonde *lager beer*
bloquer to block
blouson *m* jacket
bof! expression meaning: so-so
boire to drink
boisson *f* drink
boit: il boit he drinks
boîte *f* 1 tin, can 2 box
3 disco je vais en boîte *I go to the disco*
bol *m* bowl
Bolivie *f* Bolivia
bon *m*, **bonne** *f* good, right, OK
bon, ils sont chers *true, they're expensive*
bonne anniversaire *happy birthday*
bonne chance! *good luck!*
bonbons *mpl* sweets
bonjour hello
bottines *fpl* boots
boucherie *f* butcher's shop
boucles *fpl* **d'oreille** earrings
boule *f* scoop of ice cream
bouteille *f* bottle
bowling *m* bowling alley
bravo! well done!
Brésil *m* Brazil
britannique *m or f* British
brochure *f* brochure, pamphlet
brun *m*, **brune** *f* brown
brutal *m*, **brutale** *f* brutal
brutalité *f* brutality
Bruxelles Brussels
bu: j'ai bu I drank (past tense of boire)
bureau *m* office
bureau de tabac *tobacconist's shop*
bus *m* bus
but *m* goal
buteur *m* (football) striker

C

ça that
ça dépend *it depends*
ça fait *that comes to (price)*
ça s'écrit comment? *how do you spell it?*
ça va *I'm OK*
ça va? *are you OK?*
cabine *f* **de téléphone public** public
phone box
cacao *m* cocoa
cadeau (pl: cadeaux) *m* present
cadre *m* frame (e.g. for photos)
café *m* 1 café 2 coffee
cagoule *f* balaclava, hood
cahier *m* exercise book
caisse *f* till, cash desk
camarade *m or f* friend
Cambodge *m* Cambodia (Kampuchea)
Cameroun *m* Cameroon
campagne *f* 1 countryside
2 campaign
Canada *m* Canada
canadien *m*, **canadienne** *f* Canadian
canaux *mpl* canals
canne *f* **à sucre** sugar cane
cantine *f* canteen
capitale *f* capital city
car *m* coach
caractère *m* character
carbone *m* carbon
carnaval *m* carnival
carotte *f* carrot
carrière *f* career
carrousel *m* carousel, roundabout
carte *f* 1 map
2 postcard 3 card
jouer aux cartes *to play cards*
carton *m* **rouge** red card (football)
cas *m* case
casque *m* helmet
casquette *f* cap
casse-tête *f* puzzle, brain-teaser
cassis *f* blackcurrant
catastrophe *f* catastrophe
catégorie *f* category
cathédrale *f* cathedral
catholique *m or f* (Roman) Catholic
cause *f* cause, reason
à cause de *because of*
ce *m*, **cette** *f* (see p. 140) this
ce sont deux mots *it's two words*
ce qui n'est pas bon *which isn't good*
ceinture *f* belt
célèbre *m or f* famous
cent hundred
pour cent *per cent*
centime *m* cent (100 cents = 1 euro)
centre *m* centre, middle
centre d'activités *activity centre*
centre commercial *shopping centre*
centre sportif *sports centre*
céréales *fpl* (breakfast) cereal
c'est it's, is it?
c'est ça *that's right*
c'est combien? *how much is it?*
c'est quel bus? *which bus is it?*
c'est quoi en français? *what's that in
French?*
c'est tout? *is that all?*
cet (see p. 140) this cet après-midi *this
afternoon*
c'était it was
cette *f* (see p. 140) this
chacun ses goûts 'each to his/her own'
chaleur *f* heat
chambre *f* bedroom

championnat *m* **d'élite** elite championship
chance *f* luck
j'ai de la chance *I'm lucky*
changer to change
chanson *f* song
chanter to sing
chanteur *m*, **chanteuse** *f* singer
chaque *m or f* each
charge: qui se charge de la promotion
who is in charge of promoting (e.g. a CD)
chat *m* cat
château *m* castle
chaud hot il fait chaud *the weather's hot*
chaussures *fpl* shoes
chemise *f* shirt
chenille *f* caterpillar
cher *m*, **chère** *f* 1 dear 2 expensive
chercher to look for
cheval *m* horse
chez at the house of
je vais chez ma tante *I'm going to my
aunt's*
chien *m* dog
Chine *f* China
chips *fpl* crisps
choc *m* shock
chocolat *m* chocolate
chocolaterie *f* chocolate shop
choisir to choose
choix *m* (de) choice (of)
chose *f* thing
chrétien *m*, **chrétienne** *f* Christian
**chronologique: dans l'ordre
chronologique** in chronological order
cinéma *m* cinema
cinq five
cinquante fifty
cinquième fifth
circuit *m* **électrique** electric circuit
circulaire *m or f* circular, round
cirque *m* circus
citron *m* lemon
classé *m*, **classée** *f* classed, classified
clés: mots clés key words
climat *m* climate
club *m* club
club des jeunes *youth club*
coach *m* (football) coach, trainer
coca *m* coke
cocher to tick
cochon *m* **d'Inde** guinea pig
cocon *m* cocoon
code *m* **postal** post code
collection *f* collection
collège *m* school
colonie *f* colony
colonisation *f* colonisation
combien (de) how many
c'est combien *how much is it?*
combinaison *f* (driver's) suit, outfit
comédien *m* comedian
comique *m or f* funny
commande *f* 1 order
2 control prend la commande de *take the
control(s) of*
commander to order
comme 1 as
2 like pas comme les autres! *not like the
others!*
commencer to start
comment how
comment t'appelles-tu? *what's your name?*
commerce *m* **extérieur** overseas trade
communauté *f* community
comparaison *f* comparison
comparer to compare

Glossaire français–anglais

compléter *to complete*
composition f d'un spectacle *making up a show*
comprendre *to understand*
  je ne comprends pas *I don't understand*
compris: je n'ai pas compris *I didn't understand (past tense of comprendre)*
confiture f *jam*
confortable *m or f* *comfortable*
confusion f *confusion*
congolais *m*, **congolaise f** *congolese*
conséquence f *consequence*
consonne f *consonant (sound other than a vowel)*
construisent *build*
construit *builds*
consulter *to consult, look at*
contact: je suis en contact *I'm in contact*
conteneur m *container*
contexte m *context*
continuation f *continuation*
contraire m *opposite*
contrat m *contract*
contre *against*
contrôle m *test, exam*
contrôler *to control*
conversation f *conversation*
cool *m or f* *cool, fashionable*
coordonnées fpl *contact details*
copain m, **copine f** *friend, pal*
  petit copain *boyfriend*
Copenhague *Copenhagen (capital of Denmark)*
copine f *(female) friend*
corps m 1 *body* 2 *corpse*
correct m, **correcte f** *correct, right*
corres *m or f* *pen-friend*
correspond à quelle phrase? *goes with which sentence?*
correspondant m, **correspondante f** *pen-friend*
corriger *to correct*
Corse f *Corsica*
cosmopolitain m, **cosmopolitaine f** *cosmopolitan*
costume m *costume*
côte f *coast*
coton m *cotton*
couleur f *colour*
coupe f *(sports) cup*
courageux m, **courageuse f** *courageous*
courgette f *courgette*
cours m *lesson*
cours: faire des cours *to take lessons*
courses: faire les courses *to do the weekly shopping*
cousin m, **cousine f** *cousin*
couteau m *knife*
cravate f *tie*
crayon m *pencil*
créer *to create*
crème f *cream*
  un grand crème *white coffee*
  à la crème *in a cream sauce*
créole m *creole (French mixed with local languages)*
crier *to shout*
critique *m or f* *critical*
croisés: mots m croisés *crossword*
croque-monsieur m *ham and cheese on toast*
cruel m, **cruelle f** *cruel*
crus: oignons crus mpl *raw onions*
cuir m *leather*
cuisine f 1 *kitchen*
  2 *cooking* cuisine indienne *Indian food*

cuivre m *copper*
cultiver *to grow*
cyclone m *cyclone*

D

d'abord *first of all, to begin with*
d'accord *OK*
  je suis d'accord *I agree*
Danemark m *Denmark*
dangereux m, **dangereuse f** *dangerous*
dans *in*
danse f *dance*
danser *to dance*
dater de *to date from*
d'autres *other*
de (see p. 145) 1 *of* la prof de maths *the maths teacher*
  2 *some*
  3 *from* de 10h à 18h *from 10 am to 6 pm*
  de rien *don't mention it*
dé m *dice*
débarquement m *disembarkation*
  les plages du débarquement *D-Day beaches*
débarquer *to disembark*
débat m *debate*
décider (de) *to decide (to)*
décisif m, **décisive f** *decisive*
décolonisation f *decolonisation*
décoration f *decoration*
découper *to cut*
décrire *to describe*
  décris! *describe*
défaite f *defeat*
défenseur m *defender (in football)*
définition f *definition*
déjeuner *to have lunch*
déjeuner m *midday meal*
délicieux m, **délicieuse f** *delicious*
demain *tomorrow*
demander *to ask*
demie f *half*
  à neuf heures et demie *at 9.30*
demi-frère m *half-brother*
dépend: ça dépend *it depends*
déplier *to unfold*
déposé m, **déposée f** *laid*
dernier m, **dernière f** *last*
des (see p. 146) 1 *some* on prends des œufs? *shall we take some eggs?*
  2 *of the* une des phrases *one of the sentences*
désastre m *disaster*
descendre 1 *to go down*
  2 *get off* descendez à la gare *get off at the station*
descendu: ils ont descendu le fleuve *they went down the river (past tense of descendre)*
description f *description*
désolé: je suis désolé m, **désolée f** *I am sorry*
dessert m 1 *dessert*
  2 *(verb)* serves
dessin m 1 *drawing*
  2 *(school subject)* art
destination f *destination*
détail m *detail*
détective m (de langues) *(language) detective*
détester *to hate*
deux *two*
deuxième *m or f* *second*
devant *in front of*
développement m *development*
devenir *to become*
deviner *to guess*

devoirs mpl *homework*
dialecte m *dialect*
dialogue m *dialogue, conversation*
dictionnaire m *dictionary*
différence f *difference*
différent m, **différente f** *different*
difficile *m or f* *difficult*
diffuser un flash *to give a news flash*
dimanche *Sunday*
dîner m 1 *evening meal*
  2 *(verb)* to have one's evening meal
dire *to say*
discussion f *discussion*
discuter *to discuss*
disent que *say that*
distribuer *to distribute, hand out*
distributeur m *distributor*
dit *says*
dix *ten*
dois: je dois *I must, have to*
  elle doit *she has to*
dolfinarium m *dolphinarium*
dominer *to dominate*
donc *so*
donner *to give*
dormir *to sleep*
dortoir m *dormitory*
Douvres *Dover*
drapeau m *flag*
droit: tout droit *straight on*
droite: à droite *on the right*
dromadaire m *dromedary*
du (see p. 146) 1 *some* du café *some coffee*
  2 *of*
  3 *from* du 02/05 au 30/09 *from 2nd May to 30th Sept*
  près du stade *near the stadium*
dynamique *m or f* *dynamic*

E

eau f minérale *mineral water*
échanger *to exchange*
écharpe f *scarf*
éclair m *flash of lightning*
école f *school*
écouter *to listen (to)*
écrire *to write*
  ça s'écrit comment? *how do you spell it?*
  écris-moi *write to me*
  je t'écris *I am writing to you*
Édimbourg *Edinburgh*
éducation f physique *physical education*
effets mpl spéciaux *special effects*
église f *church*
Elbe f *Elba*
élément m *element*
éléphant m *elephant*
élève *m or f* *pupil*
elle *she*
elles *they (females)*
e-mail m *email*
émotions fpl *emotions*
empereur m *emperor*
empire m *empire*
employé m, **employée f** *employee*
en 1 *in, to* en ville *in or to town*
  2 *in* en 1815 *in 1815*, en mai *in May*, en anglais *in English*, en silence *in silence, silently*
  3 *by* en train *by train*
  en face de *opposite*
  en ce moment *at this moment*
  en famille *as a family*
  en vacances *on holiday*
  en plus *more*
  en bas *downstairs*

cent cinquante et un **151**

Glossaire français–anglais

encore 1 *still* 2 *more*
encouragé *m*, **encouragée** *f* *encouraged*
enfant *m or f* *child*
enfin *at last*
enlève: j'enlève *I take off*
ennuyeux *m*, **ennuyeuse** *f* *boring*
énorme *m or f* *enormous*
ensemble *together*
enthousiaste *m or f* *enthusiastic*
entourer *to circle*
entre *between*
entrée *f* 1 *entrance* 2 *entrance fee*
entreprise *f* *enterprise, company, business*
envie: j'ai envie *I'd like to*
envoyer *to send*
   elles envoient *they send*
épisode *f* *episode*
équateur *m* *equator*
équilibre *m* *balance*
équipe *f* *team*
équipé: bien équipé *well equipped*
équivalent *m* *equivalent, word that means the same*
erreur *f* *error, mistake*
es: tu es *you are*
escalade: faire de l'escalade *to go rock climbing*
Espagne *f* *Spain*
espagnol *m*, **espagnole** *f* *Spanish*
essayer *to try*
   il essaie (de) *he tries (to)*
   je n'ai jamais essayé ça *I've never tried it*
essentiel *m*, **essentielle** *f* *essential, crucial*
est *east*
est: elle est *she is, it is,*
   c'est *it's*
est-ce que = *expression to introduce a question*
   est-ce qu'il y a...? *is there...?*
   est-ce que je peux...? *may I...?*
estuaire *m* *estuary*
et *and*
   et toi? *what about you?*
   et avec ça? *would you like anything else?*
établir *to establish*
étage *m* *floor, storey*
étaient *were*
était *was* c'était *it was*
état *m* *state*
États-Unis *mpl* *USA*
été *m* *summer*
   en été *in summer*
été: a été *was* a été inventé *was invented*
êtes: vous êtes *you are*
étranger *m* *foreigner, stranger*
être (see p. 142) *to be*
étudier *to study*
eu: j'ai eu *I had* (past tense of avoir)
euro *m* *euro (French currency)*
Europe *f* *Europe*
européen *m*, **européenne** *f* *European*
eux *them* avec eux *with them*
exactement *exactly*
exagéré *m*, **exagérée** *f* *exaggerated*
exception *f* *exception*
   à l'exception de *with the exception of*
exceptionel *m*, **exceptionnelle** *f* *exceptional*
excursion *f* *excursion, trip*
exemple *m* *example*
   par exemple *for example*
exercice *m* *exercise*
exil *m* *exile*
exister *to exist*
   il existe *there exist*

expédition *f* *expedition*
expliquer *to explain*
explorateur *m* *explorer*
exploration *f* *exploration*
exposé *m*, **exposée** *f* (à) *exposed (to)*
expression *f* *expression, phrase*
extraordinaire *m or f* *extraordinary*

F

facile *m or f* *easy*
faire (see p. 142) 1 *to do, to make*
   je fais du shopping *I do some shopping*
   j'ai fait mes devoirs *I did my homework*
   vous faites quoi? *what do you do?*
   faire du progrès *to make progress*
   on fait la sieste *people have a midday rest*
   il faut faire le 00 33 *you have to dial 00 33*
   faire dérailler un train *to derail a train*
   faire des recherches *to carry out research*
   faire la guerre *to wage war*
   2 *go + activity* je fais du vélo *I go cycling,*
   j'ai fait de la natation *I went swimming*
   3 *(weather)* il fait beau *it's nice*
fait *m*, **faite** *f* *made*
fait: j'ai fait *I did (past tense of faire)*
   je n'ai jamais fait ça *I've never done that*
famille *f* *family* en famille *as a family*
fan *m* *fan*
fantastique *m or f* *fantastic, great*
fascinant *m*, **fascinante** *f* *fascinating*
fast food *m* *fast food (restaurant)*
fatigant *m*, **fatigante** *f* *tiring*
fatigué *m*, **fatiguée** *f* *tired*
fauché *m*, **fauchée** *f* *skint, out of money*
faut: il faut 1 *you have to* il faut attendre *you have to wait*
   2 *you need* il faut une carte *you need a card*
faux *m*, **fausse** *f* *false, wrong*
   vrai ou faux? *true or false?*
féminin *m*, **féminine** *f* *feminine*
femme *f* 1 *woman* 2 *wife*
fenêtre *f* *window*
fer *m* *iron*
fermé *m*, **fermée** *f* *closed*
fermer *to close*
fête *f* *celebration, party, festival*
feu *m* *fire*
feuille *f* de papier *sheet of paper*
février *February*
fiction: de fiction *from fiction*
fille *f* *girl*
fin *f* *end*
final *m*, **finale** *f* *final*
finir *to finish*
flamand *m*, **flamande** *f* *Flemish*
fleur *f* *flower*
fleuve *m* *river*
flexibilité *f* *flexibility*
fois: trois fois *three times*
folklorique *m or f* *folk, full of folklore*
fonder *to found*
foot, football *m* *football*
footballeur *m* *football player*
force *f* 1 *strength*
   2 *fpl* forces, soldiers
forêt *f* *forest*
format: en format réduit *in reduced format*
forme *f* *form*
   à la forme négative *in the negative*
Formule *f* 1 *Formula 1*
foudre *f* *lightning*
fraise *f* *strawberry*
français *m*, **française** *f* *French*
France *f* *France*

franco-allemand *between France and Germany*
frère *m* *brother*
frites *fpl* *chips*
froid *m*, **froide** *f* *cold*
   il fait froid *the weather's cold*
fromage *m* *cheese*
frontière *f* *frontier, border*
fruits *mpl* *fruit*
   fruits de mer *sea food*
futur *m* *future*

G

gagner *to win*
gants *mpl* *gloves*
garçon *m* *boy*
gardien *m* de but *goalkeeper*
gare *f* *station*
gâteau *m* *cake*
gauche: à gauche *on the left*
gaufre *f* *waffle*
gaz *m* *gas*
géant *m*, **géante** *f* *giant*
Genève *Geneva*
génial *m*, **géniale** *f* *great*
géo, géographie *f* *geography*
géographique *m or f* *geographical*
gerbille *f* *gerbil*
Ghana *m* *Ghana*
girafe *f* *giraffe*
glace *f* 1 *ice cream* 2 *ice*
glossaire *m* *glossary*
golfe *m* *gulf*
   le Golfe du Mexique *Gulf of Mexico*
gorille *m* *gorilla*
gourde *f* *water bottle (for bike)*
gothique *m or f* *Gothic*
gousse *f* d'ail *clove of garlic*
goût *m* *taste*
   la semaine du goût *a week celebrating food*
goûter *to taste*
   je n'ai jamais goûté ça *I have never tasted that*
grâce à *thanks to*
grammaire *f* *grammar*
gramme *m* *gramme*
grand *m*, **grande** *f* *big*
   les grandes vacances *the summer holidays*
   un grand crème *white coffee*
grand-chose: pas grand-chose *not a lot*
Grande-Bretagne *f* *Great Britain*
grand-mère *f* *grandmother*
grand-père *m* *grandfather*
grand-place *f* *main square*
grands-parents *mpl* *grandparents*
graphique *m* *graph*
gratuit *m*, **gratuite** *f* *free*
grave *m or f* *serious, grave*
grille *f* *grid, table*
gros *m*, **grosse** *f* 1 *fat* 2 *thick*
   3 *big* grosses bises *love and kisses (at end of letter)*
grotte *f* *cave, grotto*
groupe *m* *group*
guerre *f* *war*
   la deuxième guerre mondiale *2nd World War*
   faire la guerre *to wage war*
guide *m* *guide*
guidée: visite guidée *guided visit*
Guillaume *William*
   Guillaume le Conquérant *William the Conqueror*
guillotine *f* *guillotine*

guitare *f* guitar
Guyane *f* (French) Guyana (in South America)

H

habitant *m* inhabitant
habiter to live
halles *mpl* covered market
handball *m* handball
haut *m*, **haute** *f* high
héros *m* hero
heure *f* 1 hour à huit heures at 8 o'clock 2 time à quelle heure? at what time?
hier yesterday
hi-fi *f* stereo system
hindi *m* Hindi
hippopotame *m* hippopotamus
histoire *f* 1 history 2 story
historique *m or f* historical
hiver *m* winter
hockey *m* hockey
hollandais *m*, **hollandaise** *f* Dutch
homme *m* man
hôpital *m* hospital
horrible *m or f* horrible
horrifié *m*, **horrifiée** *f* horrified
hostilités *fpl* hostilities
hôtel *m* hotel
hôtel de ville town hall
humilié *m*, **humiliée** *f* humiliated
hyène *f* hyena

I

ici here
idéal *m*, **idéale** *f* ideal
idée *f* idea
identifier to identify
identique *m or f* identical, the same
identité *f* identity
il 1 he
2 it
3 il y a there is, there are il n'y a pas de there isn't, there aren't
il y a du soleil it's sunny
il faisait très chaud it was very hot
île *f* island
illusion *f* **d'optique** optical illusion
illustrer to illustrate
ils they (males)
image *f* picture, image
imaginer to imagine
imiter to imitate, copy
immobile *m or f* immobile, unmoving
important *m*, **importante** *f* important
impossible *m or f* impossible
incendie *m* fire
incendier to set fire to
incomplet *m*, **incomplète** *f* incomplete
Inde *f* India
indépendance *f* independence
indien *m*, **indienne** *f* Indian
indiqué *m*, **indiquée** *f* indicated, shown
indiquer to indicate, show
individuel *m*, **individuelle** *f* individual
Indochine *f* Indochina (Vietnam, Laos, Cambodia)
industriel *m* industrialist
infinitif *m* (see p. 144) infinitive
influencé (par) influenced by
informatique *f* ICT
infos, informations *fpl* information, news
instruction *f* instruction
instrument *m* **de musique** musical instrument
intense intense

interactif: un jeu interactif an interactive game
intéressant *m*, **intéressante** *f* interesting
interview *f* interview
interviewer to interview
intrus: trouve l'intrus find the odd-one-out
inventer to invent
invisible *m or f* invisible
invitation *f* invitation
invité *m*, **invitée** *f* guest
invité: j'ai invité I invited (past tense of inviter)
irlandais *m*, **irlandaise** *f* Irish
irrégulier *m*, **irrégulière** *f* irregular
irrésistible *m or f* irresistible
irriter to irritate
isolé *m*, **isolée** *f* isolated
Italie *f* Italy
italien *m*, **italienne** *f* Italian

J

j' I j'ai I have
jaloux *m*, **jalouse** *f* jealous
jamais never
je n'ai jamais fait ça I've never done that
jambon *m* ham
janvier January
jardin *m* garden
jaune *m or f* yellow
je I
jean *m* jeans
jette le dé throws the dice
je les jette à l'eau I throw them into the water
jeu (pl: jeux) *m* game, puzzle
jeux d'arcades arcade games
jeux de logique logic games
jeux vidéo computer games
jeudi Thursday
jeune *m or f* young
les jeunes *mpl* young people
jonglage *m* juggling
jouer 1 to play je joue du piano I play the piano, j'ai joué au foot I played football, elle joue aux jeux vidéo she plays computer games
2 to act out
jouet *m* **animé** animated toy
joueur *m* player
jour *m* day
journaliste *m or f* journalist
joyeux *m*, **joyeuse** *f* happy
judo *m* judo
juillet July
juin June
jupe *f* skirt
jus *m* **d'orange** orange juice
jusqu'à up until, up to
jusqu'en 2010 until 2010
juste just
justifier to justify

K

karting: faire du karting to go go-karting
kayak: faire du kayak to go kayaking
Kenya *m* Kenya
kilo *m* kilo
kilomètre *m* kilometre
kiosque *m* kiosk
kiwi *m* kiwi (fruit)

L

là there là-bas over there
la *f* 1 the (see p. 139)
2 her, it je la trouve belle I find her good-looking
je la découpe I cut it

labyrinthe *m* labyrinth, maze
lac *m* lake
laisser to leave
qui a laissé la porte ouverte? who left the door open?
lait *m* milk
lampe *f* lamp
langue *f* language
Laos *m* Laos
large *m or f* wide, large
laver to wash
je me lave les mains I wash my hands
le *m* 1 the (see p. 139)
2 him, it je le trouve beau I find him good-looking
3 on le vendredi on Fridays, le 30 mars on the 30th March
le week-end at the weekend
leçon *f* lesson
léger *m*, **légère** *f* light (weight)
légumes *mpl* vegetables
les (see p. 139) *mpl or fpl* the
lettre *f* letter
lever to raise, put up
lève la main put up your hand
l'alerte est levée the alert is over
lézard *m* lizard
libération *f* liberation (e.g. from the Nazis)
liberté *f* liberty, freedom
lieu *m* **de naissance** place of birth
ligne *f* line
ligue *f* league
limonade *f* lemonade
liquide *m* liquid
lire to read lis! read!
liste *f* list
litre *m* litre
livre *m* book
logique *f* logic
logo *m* logo
loin (de) far (from)
Londres London
long *m*, **longue** *f* long
plus long que longer than
loto *m* bingo
louer to rent, hire
loyal *m*, **loyale** *f* loyal
lu: j'ai lu I read (past tense of lire)
lui him
lundi Monday
lunettes *fpl* **de soleil** sunglasses
Luxembourg *m* Luxemburg

M

ma *f* (see p. 140) my
madame *f* 1 Mrs 2 Madam
mademoiselle *f* Miss
magasin *m* shop
magazine *f* magazine
magnifique *m or f* magnificent
mai May en mai in May
main *f* hand
mais but
maïs *m* corn, maize
maison *f* 1 house
2 home à la maison at home, (to) home
majorité *f* majority
malade *m or f* ill, sick
Mali *m* Mali
maman *f* mum
Mamie *f* granny
manger to eat
m'appelle: je m'appelle I am called
marché *m* market
marche: faire de la marche to go walking

Glossaire français–anglais

marcher to march
mardi Tuesday
mariage m marriage
marié m, **mariée** f married
marier: il se marie he marries
Maroc m Morocco
marocain m, marocaine f Moroccan
marquer to score
marron 1 m or f brown
    2 m sweet chestnut
mars March
masculin m, **masculine** f masculine
match m **de foot** football match
matin m morning
mauvais m, **mauvaise** f bad
me: me voici here I am
médecin m doctor
médiéval m, **médiévale** f medieval
médiocre m or f mediocre
meilleur m, **meilleur** f better
    le meilleur m, la meilleure f the best
mélodie f melody
même m or f same
menthe f mint
mentionner to mention
mer f sea
merci thank you, thanks
mercredi Wednesday
mercure m mercury
mère f mother
mes (see p. 140) mpl or fpl my
mesurer to measure
métallique m or f metallic
météo f weather office, weather forecast
mètre m metre
mets put (from mettre)
meurt dies (from mourir)
Mexique m Mexico
miam-miam! yum-yum!
microfusée f micro-rocket
midi midday à midi at midday
mil m millet (a cereal)
milieu m middle
militaire m or f military
mille thousand
mimer to mime
ministre m: premier ministre prime
    minister
minorité f minority
minuscule m or f tiny
mi-temps f half-time
modèle m model, example
moi me
    chez moi at my house
moins less
    à huit heures moins le quart at a quarter
    to eight
    moins de 3 ans under 3 years old
    moins de fewer
mois m month
moment m moment
    en ce moment at this moment
mon m (see p. 140) my
monarchie f monarchy
monde m world
    tout le monde everybody
mondial: guerre f **mondiale** world war
monnaie f currency
monsieur m 1 Mr 2 Sir
montagne f mountain
montrer to show
monument m monument
morceau m piece
mot m word

moule f mussel
mouton m sheep
mouvement m movement
Moyen Âge m Middle Ages
Mozambique m Mozambique
multilingue m or f multilingual
multiplier to multiply, become widespread
musée m museum
musique f music
musulman m, **musulmane** f Muslim
mystère m mystery

N

nager to swim
naissance: date de naissance date of birth
naît is born (from naître)
nasal m, **nasale** f nasal
natation: faire de la natation to go
    swimming
nation f nation
national m, **nationale** f national
nationalité f nationality
naturellement naturally, of course
ne ... pas (expresses a negative)
    je n'aime pas I don't like
    ne prenez pas le 11 don't take the number
    11
né: il est né he was born
nécessaire m or f necessary
néerlandais m, **néerlandaise** f Dutch
négatif m, **négative** f negative
neige f snow
    il neige it's snowing, it snows
Nil m Nile
noir m, **noire** f black
nom m 1 noun
    2 name nom de famille surname, family
    name
nombre m number
non no
nord m north
noter to note
Notre-Dame our lady (often: name of
    church)
nous we nous avons we have
nouveau m, **nouvelle** f new
Nouvelle-Zélande f New Zealand
nuit f night la nuit at night
nul m, **nulle** f bad, rubbish, awful
numéro m number

O

objet m object
obstacle m obstacle
occupation f occupation
occupé m, **occupée** f **(par)** occupied (by)
occuper to occupy
Océan m **Indien** Indian Ocean
octobre October
œilletons mpl black spots ('eyes') on
    potatoes
œuf m egg
    œufs brouillés scrambled eggs
officiel m, **officielle** f official
offre: il offre he gives
oh là là! oh dear!
oignons mpl (crus) (raw) onions
omelette f omelette
on 1 they, people on parle quelle langue?
    what language do people speak?
    2 we on se retrouve où? where shall we
    meet?

oncle m uncle
ont have (from avoir)
onze eleven
opinion f opinion
opter (pour) to opt (for)
optimiste m or f optimistic
option f option, choice, alternative
orage m storm
orange f orange
ordinateur m computer
ordre m order
organiser to organise
original (pl: originaux) m, **originale** f
    original
origine: d'origine étrangère of foreign
    descent
ou or vrai ou faux? true or false?
où where
ouest west à l'ouest in the west
ouf! phew! (sigh of relief)
oui yes
ouvert m, **ouverte** f open
ouvrir to open
oxygène m oxygen

P

page f page
paie pays (from payer)
pain m bread
paire f **(de)** pair (of)
Pakistan m Pakistan
palais m palace
panda m panda
pantalon m trousers
    pantalon à pattes d'éléphant flared
    trousers
panthère f panther
papa m Dad
paparazzi mpl paparazzi (pestering
    journalists and photographers)
papillon m butterfly
paquet m packet
par by
    par exemple for example
paradis m paradise
paragraphe m paragraph
parc m park
    parc d'attractions theme park
parce que because
    parce qu'il y a... because there is...
pardon excuse me
parents mpl parents
parfois sometimes
parfum m perfume
parking m car park
parler to talk
part leaves, departs
partenaire m or f partner
participe m passé past participle
partie f part
partir to leave
pas not pas moi not me
passage m passage, transition
passager m passenger, traveller
passé m the past
    au passé in the past
passer 1 to pass ils passent à la guillotine
    they are sent to the guillotine
    2 to spend tu as passé un bon week-end?
    did you have a good weekend?
passe-temps m hobby, pastime
passionnant m, **passionnante** f exciting
pâté m paté
pâtes fpl pasta
patin: faire du patin à glace to go ice-
    skating

patinoire *f* *skating rink*
payer *to pay*
pays *m* *country*
Pays-Bas *mpl* *Holland, Netherlands*
peau *f* *skin*
pêche *f* 1 *peach*
  2 *fishing* aller à la pêche *to go fishing*
pèle! *peel!*
peluche *f* *cuddly toy*
pendant *during*
pense: je pense que *I think that*
pensent que *think that*
perdu: il a perdu *he has lost (past tense of* perdre)
père *m* *father*
période *f* 1 *period* 2 *half of a football match*
permis *m*, **permise** *f* *allowed, permitted*
Pérou *m* *Peru*
perruche *f* *budgie*
persécuter *to persecute*
personnage *m* *(important) person, personality*
personnalité *f* *personality*
personne *f* *person*
  les personnes *people*
personnellement *personally*
perte *f* **de temps** *waste of time*
pèse *weighs*
pessimiste *m or f* *pessimistic*
petit *m*, **petite** *f* *small, little*
peu: un peu *a bit*
peut: on peut *you can (from* pouvoir)
peut-être *perhaps, maybe*
peux: je ne peux pas *I can't (from* pouvoir),
  tu peux…? *can you…?*
pharmacie *f* *chemist's*
photographier *to photograph*
phrase *f* *sentence*
pilote *m* *driver*
ping-pong *m* *table-tennis*
pipette *f* *pipette*
pique-nique *m* *picnic*
piscine *f* *swimming pool*
pistolet *m* 1 *pistol*
  2 *(in Belgium) bread roll*
pittoresque *m or f* *picturesque, lovely*
pizza *f* *pizza*
place *f* 1 *place* à sa place *in his place*
  2 *(town) square*
plage *f* *beach*
plaisir: pour faire plaisir à ma mère *to please my mum*
planète *f* *planet*
plats *mpl* **épicés** *spicy dishes*
pleut: il pleut *it rains, it's raining*
plier *to fold*
plomb *m* *lead*
pluriel *m* *plural*
plus 1 *more* plus petit que *smaller than*,
  plus d'un million *more than a million*
  2 *most* le plus intéressant *the most interesting*
poème *m* *poem*
poète *m* *poet*
point *m* *point*
  point F R *.fr (in email address)*
poire *f* *pear*
poisson *m* *fish*
politique *f* *politics*
Pologne *f* *Poland*
pomme *f* *apple*
pomme *f* **de terre** *potato*
populaire *popular*
population *f* *population*

port *m* *port, harbour*
  port de plaisance *marina*
portable *m* *mobile phone*
porte *f* *door*
porter *to wear*
portugais *m*, **portugaise** *f* *Portuguese*
Portugal *m* *Portugal*
poser 1 pose des questions (sur) *ask questions (about)* ça pose de graves problèmes *that raises serious problems*
  2 poser (pour) *to pose (for)*
position *f* *position*
possède *has, contains*
possession *f* *possession*
possibilité *f* *possibility*
possible *m or f* *possible*
poster *m* *poster*
poterie: faire de la poterie *to do pottery*
pour *for*
pour cent *per cent*
pour faire *in order to make*
pourquoi? *why?*
pouvez-vous…? *can you…?*
pralines *fpl* *chocolates*
pratique *m or f* *useful*
précédent *m*, **précédente** *f* *preceding*
préféré *m*, **préférée** *f* *favourite*
préférence *f* *preference*
préférer *to prefer*
  tu préfères…? *do you prefer…?*
premier *m*, **première** *f* *first*
  le premier ministre *the prime minister*
prendre *to take*
  prends des notes *take some notes*
prenez *take (from* prendre)
prénom *m* *first name*
préparation *f* *preparation*
préparer *to prepare*
près de (see p. 146) *close to, near*
  près d'ici *near here*
  de plus près *closer*
présent *m* *present (tense)*
présentation *f* *presentation, short talk*
président *m* *president*
preuve *f* *proof*
primate *m* *primate*
princesse *f* *princess*
principal *m*, **principale** *f* *main, principal*
principalement *principally, mainly*
printemps *m* *spring*
pris: j'ai pris *I took (past tense of* prendre)
prisonnier *m* *prisoner*
prix *m* 1 *price* 2 *prize*
probablement *probably*
problème *m* *problem*
procession *f* *procession*
prochain *m*, **prochaine** *f* *next*
producteur *m* *producer*
produit *produces*
prof *m or f* *teacher*
professeur *m or f* 1 *teacher*
  2 *professor*
profession *f* *profession. job*
profil *m* *profile*
promener *to walk (an animal)*
promotion *f* *publicity*
prononcer *to pronounce*
prononciation *f* *pronunciation*
proposer *to suggest, propose*
proposition *f* *proposition*
protester *to protest*
provisions *fpl* *provisions, food*
public *m* *the public*
puis *then*
pull *m* *pullover*
punch *m* **aux fruits** *fruit punch*
pur *m*, **pure** *f* *pure*

Q

qualité *f* *quality*
quand *when*
quantité *f* *quantity*
quarante *forty*
quart *m* *quarter*
  onze heures moins le quart *a quarter to eleven*
quatorze *fourteen*
quatre *four*
quatre-vingts *eighty*
quatre-vingt-dix *ninety*
quatrième *fourth*
que: plus long que *longer than*
que faire? *what can I do?*
Québec *m* *Quebec*
quel *m*, **quelle** *f* *which? what?*
  quel âge as-tu? *how old are you?*
  à quelle heure? *at what time?*
  quel temps fait-il? *what's the weather like?*
  c'est quelle photo? *which photo is it?*
quelques *some*
qu'est-ce que…? *what…?*
  qu'est-ce que tu as fait le week-end dernier? *what did you do last weekend?*
question *f* *question*
qui 1 *who* qui s'appelle *who is called*
  2 *which*
quinze *fifteen*
quitter *to leave*
quiz *m* *quiz*
quoi *what*
  c'est quoi en français, "gold"? *what's 'gold' in French?*
  c'est quoi ton adresse? *what's your address?*
  eh bien, quoi? *so what?*

R

race *f* *race*
radio *f* *radio*
raï *m* *type of Algerian music*
raisonnable *m or f* *reasonable*
rallye *m* *(car-) rally*
rang *m* *rank*
ranger *to tidy*
rap *m* *rap*
raquette: sports de raquettes *racquet sports*
rare: les plus rares *the rarest*
ratatouille *f* *dish made with tomato, onion, aubergine, etc.*
réaliste *m or f* *realist*
recette *f* *recipe*
recherches *fpl* **(sur)** *research (about)*
recommencer *to recommence, begin again*
recopier *to copy*
recouvrir *to cover*
récréation *f* *(morning) break*
rectangulaire *m or f* *rectangular*
recyclage *m* *recycling*
réduire *reduce*
réduit: en format réduit *in reduced format*
réécouter *to listen again*
refuser *to refuse*
regarder *to watch, look at*
regrette: je regrette *I'm sorry*
régulier *m*, **régulière** *f* *regular*
reine *f* *queen*
relaxe-toi! *relax!*
religion *f* *religion*
relis *read again*
remplacer *to replace*
remplis les blancs *fill in the blanks*

Glossaire français–anglais

rendre visite à ma tante to visit my aunt
renforts *mpl* reinforcements
rentrée *f* return to school
rentrer to return
réparer to repair, mend
répartit: comment se répartit cette
 somme how this sum of money is shared
 out
répéter to repeat
répondre to answer
 réponds aux questions answer the
 questions
réponse *f* answer, response
reportage *m* (radio) report
république *f* republic
réserves *fpl* reserves
résidence *f* residence
résistant au feu fire resistant
résister à to resist
responsable *m* or *f* (de) responsible (for)
restaurant *m* restaurant
rester to stay
résultat *m* result, outcome
résumé *m* summary
retourner to return
retrouver 1 to find 2 to meet
 on se retrouve où? where shall we meet?
Réunion *f* Réunion (island in Indian Ocean)
réunir to reunite
réveil *m* alarm clock
révèlent que reveal that
révision *f* revision
révolution *f* revolution
Rhin *m* (river) Rhine
riche *m* or *f* rich
ridicule *m* or *f* ridiculous
rien nothing, not anything
 de rien don't mention it
rimer (avec) to rhyme (with)
ringard out of fashion
rivière *f* river
riz *m* rice
roi *m* king
rôle *m* role, part
Romains *mpl* Romans
rose *m* or *f* pink
rouge *m* or *f* red
rouler: on roule à droite they drive on the
 right
routine *f* routine
royal *m*, **royale** *f* royal
Royaume-Uni *m* United Kingdom
rue *f* street
rugby *m* rugby
ruiner to ruin
Russie *f* Russia
rythmique *m* or *f* rhythmical

S

sa *f* his, her (see p. 140)
sac *m* bag
safari: parc *m* **safari** safari park
sais: je sais I know
saison *f* season
salade *f* salad
salle *f* 1 hall, room 2 (cinema) screen
salut! hi! hello!
samedi Saturday
sandwich *m* sandwich
sans without
sauce *f* sauce
sauvage *m* or *f* wild
sauver to save
scénario *m* scenario, situation

sciences *fpl* science
score *m* score
seconde *f* second
secret *m* secret
Seine *f* the river which flows through Paris
seize sixteen
semaine *f* week
semelle *f* sole (of shoe)
Sénégal *m* Senegal
sens *m* de l'humour sense of humour
sensationnel *m*, **sensationnelle** *f*
 sensational
série *f* series
ses *mpl* or *fpl* (see p. 140) his, her
 ses amis his or her friends
sexiste *m* or *f* sexist
shopping *m* shopping
 je fais du shopping I go shopping
si if s'il pleut if it rains
siècle *m* century
sieste *f* siesta, midday rest
signé *m*, **signée** *f* signed
s'il te plaît please (to friend)
s'il vous plaît please (to adult)
silent *m*, **silente** *f* silent
similaire *m* or *f* (à) similar (to)
simple *m* or *f* simple
singulier *m*, **singulière** *f* singular
site *m* site site Web website
situation *f* situation
situé *m*, **située** *f* situated
skateboard *m* skateboard
ski *m* skiing
 le ski extrême high-speed skiing
snack-bar *m* snack bar
sœur *f* sister
soir *m* evening
soirée *f* party
soixante sixty
soixante-dix seventy
soldat *m* soldier
soleil *m* sun
 il y a du soleil it's sunny
solide *m* solid
solution *f* 1 solution (to problem)
 2 (chemical) solution
sommaire *m* summary
somme *f* sum of money
sommes: nous sommes we are (from être)
son *m* (see p. 140) his, her
son *m* sound
 un son nasal a nasal sound
sont are (from être)
sorte *f* (de) sort (of)
sortir to go out
soudain suddenly
souligner to underline
soupe *f* soup
sous-vêtements *mpl* under-clothes
souvenir *m* souvenir
souvent often
spacieux *m*, **spacieuse** *f* spacious
spécial (pl: spéciaux) *m*, **spéciale** *f* special
spécialité *f* speciality
spectacle *m* show
spectaculaire *m* or *f* spectacular
spectateur *m* spectator
sport *m* sport
sportif *m*, **sportive** *f* sporty
stade *m* stadium
star *f* (film, music) star
statue *f* statue
stéréotypé *m*, **stéréotypée** *f* stereotyped
stratégies *fpl* strategies, tips
strict *m*, **stricte** *f* strict

studios *mpl* studios
stupide *m* or *f* stupid
style *m* style
succès *m* success
sucre *m* sugar
 la canne à sucre sugar cane
sucré *m*, **sucrée** *f* sweet, sugary
sud *m* south
 au sud de to the south of
Suède *m* Sweden
suggestion *f* suggestion, tip
suis: je suis (see p. 142) I am
Suisse *f* Switzerland
super *m* or *f* great
supermarché *m* supermarket
supplément *m* supplement
sur 1 on sur Internet on the internet
 2 about
sûr: bien sûr of course
surf *m* surfing
surfer to surf
surhumain: une force surhumaine
 superhuman strength
surprise *f* surprise
syllabe *f* syllable
symbole *m* symbol
symétrique *m* or *f* symmetrical
sympa *m* or *f* nice
système *m* system

T

ta *f* (see p. 140) your
tabac *m* tobacco
 bureau *m* de tabac tobacconist's shop
tablette *f* **de chocolat** bar of chocolate
tais-toi! be quiet!
tajine *m* Moroccan meat dish
talent *m* talent
 il a du talent he's talented
Tamise *f* Thames
tante *f* aunt
tapisserie *f* tapestry
tard late
 deux jours plus tard two days later
tarif *m* price, cost
taxe *f* tax
technique *f* **d'enregistrement** art of
 recording
technologie *f* technology
télé *f* TV à la télé on TV
téléphone *f* telephone
téléphoner à to phone somebody
téléphonique: carte téléphonique phone
 card
température *f* temperature
temps *m* 1 time perte *f* de temps waste of
 time, mi-temps *f* half-time (football)
 2 weather quel temps fait-il? what's the
 weather like?
tenir to hold, to resist
tennis *m* tennis
tente *f* tent
terrain *m* pitch, (football) ground
terre *f* earth
terreur *f* terror
territoire *m* territory
tes *mpl* or *fpl* (see p. 140) your
tester (sur) to test (on)
teuf *f* party
texte *m* text
texto *m* text message
thé *m* tea
théâtre *m* theatre
 faire du théâtre to do drama
thème *m* theme, topic

tigre *m* tiger
tir *m* à l'arc archery
tissu *m* material
titre *m* title
toboggan *m* waterslide (at swimming pool)
toi *you* pour toi *for you*
toilettes publiques *fpl* public toilets
tomate *f* tomato
tombe *f* tomb
ton *m* (see p. 140) your
top: c'est le top! *it's brilliant*
torture *f* torture
tôt *early* trop tôt *too early*
total *m*, totale *f* total
toujours *always*
tour 1 *f* tower 2 *m* tour, trip
   à ton tour *your turn*
touriste *m or f* tourist
tourner *to turn, to turn over*
tout *m*, toute *f*, tous *mpl*, toute *fpl* all,
   every
   toutes les heures *every hour*
   tout droit *straight on*
   toute la famille *all the family*
   toute l'après-midi *all afternoon*
   tout ce qui… *everything which…*
trace *f* trace
traduis *translate*
train *m* train
tram *m* tram
trampoline *m* trampoline
tranche *f* (de) slice (of)
transformer (en) *to transform, change*
   (into)
travailler *to work*
traverser *to cross*
treize *thirteen*
trente *thirty*
très *very*
trois *three*
troisième *m or f* third
trop *too*
trousse *f* pencil case
trouver *to find*
T-shirt *m* T-shirt
tu *you*
tuer *to kill*
Tunisie *f* Tunisia

U
un *one*
un *m*, une *f* a, an
uniforme *m* uniform
union *f* européenne European Union (EU)
ustensiles *fpl* utensils
utile *m or f* useful
utiliser *to use*

V
va *goes* ça va? *are you OK?*
vacances *fpl* holiday en vacances *on*
   holiday
vais: je vais *I go (from aller)*
vaisselle: faire la vaisselle *to do the*
   washing up
vandale *m* vandal
vandalisme *m* vandalism
vanille *f* vanilla
variété *f* variety
Varsovie *Warsaw*
végétarien *m*, végétarienne *f* vegetarian
véhicule *m* vehicle
vélo *m* bike, bicycle
vendredi *Friday*
venir *to come*
Venise *Venice*
vent *m* wind
verbe *m* verb
   verbe auxiliaire *auxiliary verb*
   verbe irrégulier *irregular verb*
vérifier *to check*
vers 19h *around 7pm*
version *f* version
vert *m*, verte *f* green
Vésuve *(Mount) Vesuvius*
vêtements *mpl* clothes
   vêtements de marque *designer clothes*
veut: il, elle veut *he, she wants to*
veux: je veux faire du vélo *I'd like to go*
   cycling, je veux bien *I'd like to*
viande *f* meat
victoire *f* victory
vidéo *f* video
vieille *f* old
vieillir *to grow older*
vient de *comes from*
Viêt Nam *m* Vietnam
vieux *m*, vieille *f* old
villa *f* villa
village *m* village

ville *f* town
vingt *twenty*
violence *f* violence
violent *m*, violente *f* violent
violon *m* violin
visite *f* visit
   lui rendre visite *visit him/her*
visiter *to visit (place)*
voici *here is*
voilà *there you are*
voile: faire de la voile *to go sailing*
voir *to see*
voiture *f* car
   voiture de sport *sports car*
vol: c'est du vol! *it's a rip-off*
volcanique *m or f* volcanic
vont: ils vont *they go, they are going (from*
   aller)
votre *your*
voudrais: je voudrais *I'd like*
vous *you (1 to adult; 2 to more than one*
   person)
   je vous invite *I'll invite you*
voyage *m* journey
voyelle *f* vowel
vrai *m*, vraie *f* true
vraiment *really*
VTT: faire du VTT *to go mountain-biking*
vu 1 j'ai vu *I saw (past tense of voir)*
   2 vu *m*, vue *f* (par) seen (by)
vue *f* view

W
webcam *f* webcam
week-end *m* weekend
wolof *m* language spoken in Senegal

Y
y *there*
   on y va en bus? *are we going there by bus?*
yaourt *m* yoghurt
yoyo *m* yoyo

Z
zèbre *m* zebra
zéro *zero*
zimbabwéen *m*, zimbabwéenne *f*
   Zimbabwean
zoologue *m* zoologist
zut! *bother!*

Glossaire anglais–français

A
a, an *un* m, *une* f
after *après*
after that *après ça*
afternoon *l'après-midi* m
   in the afternoon *l'après-midi*
airport *l'aéroport* m
all: is that all? *c'est tout?*
also *aussi*
always *toujours*
am: I am *je suis* (see *être*, p. 142)
and *et*
April *avril*
are: you are *tu es* (see *être*, p. 142)
   there are *il y a*

arrive v *arriver*
ask v *demander*
at 1 at my friend's house *chez ma copine*,
   at my house *chez moi*
   2 at school *au collège*, at home *à la*
   maison
ate: I ate *j'ai mangé*
August *août*
aunt *la tante* f
awful: it's awful *c'est nul*

B
barbecue *le barbecue* m
basketball *le basket* m
   I play basketball *je joue au basket*

battle *la bataille* f
beach *la plage* f
because *parce que*
Belgium *la Belgique* f
best: the best *le meilleur* m, *la meilleure* f
between *entre*
big *grand* m, *grande* f
   bigger than *plus grand(e) que*
bike *le vélo* m by bike *à vélo*
birthday *l'anniversaire* m
black *noir* m, *noire* f
blue *bleu* m, *bleue* f
book *le livre* m
boring: it's boring *c'est barbant*
bottle (of) *la bouteille* f (de)
bowling alley *le bowling* m

Glossaire anglais–français

bought: I bought *j'ai acheté*
boy *le garçon* m
break 1 v *casser, briser*
  2 (school break) *la récréation* f
bridge *le pont* m
British *britannique* m or f
brother *le frère* m
brown *marron* m or f
bus *le bus* m by bus *en bus*
but *mais*
buy v *acheter*
by by car *en auto* by bike *à vélo*

C

café *le café* m
cake *le gâteau* m
camping: I go camping *je fais du camping*
campsite *le camping* m
can: can I...? *je peux...?*
car *l'auto* f, *la voiture* f
  by car *en auto*
cards: I play cards *je joue aux cartes*
castle *le château* m
cat *le chat* m
CD *le CD* m (pl: *les CD*)
centre: sports centre *le centre sportif* m
  shopping centre *le centre commercial* m
chat v *bavarder*
cheese *le fromage* m
child *enfant* m or f
  I'm an only child *je suis enfant unique*
chips *les frites* fpl
chocolate *le chocolat* m
choir *la chorale* f
church *l'église* f
clothes *les vêtements* mpl
coach *le car* m
coffee *le café* m
cold: the weather is cold *il fait froid*
come: I come *je viens*
computer *l'ordinateur* m
  computer games *les jeux vidéo*
cost: how much does it cost? *c'est combien?*
could: could you repeat? *pouvez-vous répéter?*
country *le pays* m
  in the country *à la campagne*
crisps *les chips* fpl

D

day *le jour* m
dear *cher* m, *chère* f
designer clothes *les vêtements* mpl *de marque*
dictionary *le dictionnaire* m
did: I did *j'ai fait*
difficult *difficile* m or f
do v *faire* (see p. 142) I do *je fais*
  I do my homework *je fais mes devoirs*
doesn't: it doesn't snow *il ne neige pas*
  he doesn't play *il ne joue pas (au...)*
dog *le chien* m
don't: I don't like *je n'aime pas*
drink v *boire* I drink *je bois*
drank: I drank *j'ai bu*
draw v *dessiner*
during *pendant*

E

each *chaque*
easy *facile* m or f
eat v *manger* we eat *nous mangeons*

eighty *quatre-vingts*
England *l'Angleterre* f
evening *le soir* m
  in the evening *le soir*
everybody *tout le monde*
exercise book *le cahier* m

F

family *la famille* f
famous *célèbre* m or f
fashionable *en mode*
father *le père* m
favourite *préféré* m, *préférée* f
February *février*
fifty *cinquante*
first *premier* m, *première* f
fish *le poisson* m
flavour: what flavour? *quel parfum?*
foggy: it's foggy *il fait du brouillard*
foot *le pied* m on foot *à pied*
football stadium *le stade de football* m
for *pour*
forty *quarante*
France *la France* f
French *français* m, *française* f
Friday *vendredi*
friend *copain* m, *copine* f; *ami* m, *amie* f
front: in front of *devant*
fun: it's fun *c'est amusant*

G

game *le jeu* m (pl: *jeux*)
gameboy *la console* f *de jeux*
garden *le jardin* m
girl *la fille* f
give: I give *je donne*
go v *aller* (see p. 142) I go *je vais*
  I go cycling *je fais du vélo*
  I go sailing *je fais de la voile*
going to: I'm going to buy *je vais acheter* (see p. 144)
good-bye *au revoir*
good-looking *beau* m, *belle* f
great *super, génial* m or f
green *vert* m, *verte* f
group *le groupe* m
gymnastics *la gymnastique* f

H

had: I had *j'ai eu*
half: at half past six *à six heures et demie*
ham *le jambon* m
happy *joyeux* m, *joyeuse* f
hard *difficile* m or f
have *avoir* (see p. 142) I have *j'ai*
he *il*
help v *aider*
here *ici*
high *haut* m, *haute* f
  higher than *plus haut(e) que*
hire v *louer*
hobby *le passe-temps* m
home 1 at home *à la maison*
  2 I come home *je rentre à la maison*
homework *les devoirs* mpl
honey *le miel* m
horse *le cheval* m (pl: *chevaux*)
horse-riding *l'équitation* f
  I go horse-riding *je fais du cheval*
hot: the weather is hot *il fait chaud*
house *la maison* f
  at my house *chez moi*

how 1 *comment*
  2 how many? *combien?*
  how much is it? *c'est combien?*
hundred *cent*

I

ice cream *la glace* f
ice rink *la patinoire* f
in 1 *dans*
  2 in London *à Londres*
  3 'in' = in fashion *en mode*
interesting *intéressant* m, *intéressante* f
Ireland *l'Irlande* f
  in Northern Ireland *en Irlande du Nord*
is *est* (see *être*, p. 142)
  it is *c'est* there is *il y a*
it's *c'est*

J

January *janvier*
journey *le voyage* m
juice *le jus* m
  an orange juice *un jus d'orange*
July *juillet*
June *juin*

K

kitchen *la cuisine* f

L

last: last weekend *le week-end dernier*
  last week *la semaine dernière*
left: on the left *à gauche*
lemon *le citron* m
less *moins*
lesson *le cours* m
library *la bibliothèque* f
like 1 v *aimer* I like *j'aime*
  2 I'd like *je voudrais*
  3 like a lion *comme un lion*
  4 what is it like? *c'est comment?*
lion *le lion* m
listen v *écouter*
live v *habiter*
London *Londres*
long *long* m, *longue* f
  longer than *plus long(ue) que*
lost: I've lost *j'ai perdu*
lot: a lot (of) *beaucoup (de)*
loud *bruyant* m, *bruyante* f
love v *adorer*
lunch: I have lunch *je déjeune*

M

map *la carte* f
March *mars*
market *le marché* m
marmalade *la marmelade* f *d'oranges*
married *marié* m, *mariée* f
May *mai*
meat *la viande* f
midday: at midday *à midi*
milk *le lait* m
mint *la menthe* f
Miss *Mademoiselle* f, (at school) *Madame*
Monday *lundi*
more *plus*
morning *le matin* m
  in the morning *le matin*
mother *la mère* f
motorbike *la moto* f
mountain *la montagne* f

much: how much is it? *c'est combien?*
museum *le musée* m
music *la musique* f
must: I must *je dois*
my *mon* m, *ma* f, *mes* pl

N
nature reserve *la réserve naturelle* f
near *près de*
next *prochain* m, *prochaine* f
next week *la semaine prochaine*
never *jamais*
nice 1 (friendly) *sympa*
2 (good-looking) *beau* m, *belle* f
3 the weather is nice *il fait beau*
ninety *quatre-vingt-dix*
no *non*

O
of *de*
of the *du* m, *de la* f
of course *bien sûr*
often *souvent*
OK *d'accord*
old *vieux* m, *vieille* f
how old are you? *quel âge as-tu?*
open 1 v *ouvrir*
2 *ouvert* m, *ouverte* f
or *ou*
other *autre*

P
packed lunch *le repas* m *froid*
packet (of) *le paquet* m (de)
park *le parc* m
pen 1 biro *le bic* m
2 fountain pen *le stylo* m
pencil *le crayon* m
perhaps *peut-être*
person *la personne* f
personally *personnellement*
pet *l'animal* m (plural: *animaux*)
phone: I phone *je téléphone*
play v *jouer*
I play tennis *je joue au tennis*
played: I played *j'ai joué*
please *s'il te plaît* (to friend)
s'il vous plaît (to adult)
porridge: some porridge *du porridge* m
post office *la poste* f
prepare v *préparer*
present *le cadeau* m
price *le prix* m
pupil *élève* m or f

Q
quite *assez*
quite hard *assez difficile*

R
rabbit *le lapin* m
railway station *la gare* f
rain: it's raining *il pleut*
read: v *lire* I read *je lis*
red *rouge* m or f
rich *riche* m or f
right: on the right *à droite*
rock concert *le concert de rock* m
room *la chambre* f
rugby *le rugby* m

S
sailing *la voile* f
Saturday *samedi*
saw: I saw *j'ai vu*
say: how do you say 'friend' in French?
c'est quoi en français, "friend"?
school *le collège* m, *l'école* f
Scotland *l'Écosse* f
sea *la mer* f
second (2nd) *deuxième*
see v *voir* I see *je vois*
send v *envoyer* I send *j'envoie*
seventy *soixante-dix*
she *elle*
shop *le magasin* m
sing v *chanter*
singer *le chanteur* m, *la chanteuse* f
sister *la sœur* f
sixty *soixante*
skateboarding *le skateboarding* m
I go skateboarding *je fais du skateboarding*
skating rink *la patinoire* f
ski: I go skiing *je fais du ski*
small *petit* m, *petite* f
smaller than *plus petit(e) que*
snow *la neige* f
it's snowing *il neige*
some *des*
sometimes *parfois*
song *la chanson* f
soon *bientôt*
see you soon *à bientôt!*
sorry *pardon*
speak v *parler*
people speak French *on parle français*
sport *le sport* m
sports centre *le centre sportif* m
stadium *le stade* m
stay v *rester*
story *l'histoire* f
strawberry *la fraise* f
street *la rue* f
stupid *stupide*, *bête* m or f
subject: school subject *la matière* f
sugar *le sucre* m
some sugar *du sucre*
summer: in summer *en été*
Sunday *dimanche*
supermarket *le supermarché* m
swim v *nager*, *faire de la natation*
swimming: I go swimming *je fais de la natation*
swimming pool *la piscine* f

T
table tennis *le ping-pong* m
take v *prendre* I take *je prends*
tea *le thé* m
teacher *prof* m or f
ten *dix*
tennis *le tennis* m
text message *le texto* m
thank you (for) *merci (pour)*
that *ça*
the *le* m, *la* f, *les* pl
then *puis*
there is *il y a*
they *ils* m, *elles* f
third (3rd) *troisième*
thousand *mille*
Thursday *jeudi*
tiger *le tigre* m
time: at what time? *à quelle heure?*

to 1 *à* to the cinema *au cinéma* m, to the railway station *à la gare* f
2 (with countries) *en* to France *en France*
3 (to people, houses) *chez* I went to my uncle's *je suis allée chez mon oncle*
toast: some toast (with…) *du toast (avec…)*
together *ensemble*
tomorrow *demain*
too *also*
took: I took *j'ai pris*
Tuesday *mardi*
TV *la télé* f

U
uncle *l'oncle* m
understand v *comprendre*
I don't understand *je ne comprends pas*
usually *d'habitude, normalement*

V
very *très*
video *la vidéo* f
video recorder *le magnétoscope* m
video shop *la vidéothèque* f
visit v *visiter*

W
wait v *attendre*
Wales *le Pays de Galles* m
in Wales *au Pays de Galles*
walk: I go walking *je fais des promenades*
want v *vouloir* I want *je veux*
was: it was *c'était*
watch v *regarder*
water *l'eau* f
we *nous*
weather *le temps* m
what's the weather like? *quel temps fait-il?*
Wednesday *mercredi*
week *la semaine* f
well *bien*
went: *je suis allé* m, *je suis allée* f
I went swimming *j'ai fait de la natation*
what *quoi*
what did you do? *tu as fait quoi?*
what's your address? *c'est quoi ton adresse?*
when *quand*
where *où*
which? *quel* m, *quelle* f
white *blanc* m, *blanche* f
who *qui*
why *pourquoi*
wife *la femme* f
win v *gagner* we won *nous avons gagné*
windy: it's windy *il fait du vent*
winter: in winter *en hiver*
with *avec*
won: I won *j'ai gagné* we won *on a gagné*
word *le mot* m
work v *travailler*
write v *écrire* I write *j'écris*

Y
year *l'an* m
I'm in Year 8 *je suis en cinquième*
yellow *jaune* m or f
yes *oui*
yesterday *hier*
you 1 *tu* 2 *vous* (see p. 144)
young *jeune* m or f
your *ton* m, *ta* f, *tes* pl
youth club *le club* m *des jeunes*

Common instructions in *Voilà! 2*

Phrases

ajoute d'autres détails	*add other details*
au passé	*in the past*
c'est quelle photo?	*which photo is it?*
c'est qui?	*who is it?*
c'est quoi en français?	*what is it in French?*
change le dialogue	*change the dialogue*
combien d'exemples	*how many examples*
complète les phrases	*complete the sentences*
(tu es) d'accord avec	*(do you) agree with*
dans le bon ordre	*in the right order*
écoute et lis	*listen and read*
écoute et répète	*listen and repeat*
écris les mots	*write the words*
écris les phrases	*write the sentences*
écris tes réponses	*write your own answers*
en anglais	*in English*
en français	*in French*
expressions de temps	*time phrases*
fais deux listes	*write two lists*
joue le dialogue	*act out the dialogue*
joue et adapte le dialogue	*act out and adapt the dialogue*
lève la main	*put your hand up*
lis la lettre	*read the letter*
pose les questions à ton/ta partenaire	*ask your partner the questions*
pour chaque personne	*for each person*
recopie les mots	*copy the words*
regarde les images	*look at the pictures*
réécoute...	*listen to... again*
réponds aux questions	*answer the questions*
ton modèle, c'est...	*the pattern for you to base your work on is...*
trouve les paires	*find the matching pairs*
vérifie avec ton/ta partenaire	*check with your partner*
vrai ou faux?	*true or false?*

Single words

aussi	*too, as well*
autre(s)	*other*
avec	*with*
le bon	*the right*
la bonne	*the right*
change	*change*
chaque	*each*
choisis	*choose*
comment	*how*
complète	*complete*
corrige	*correct*
dans	*in*
décris	*describe*
devine	*guess*
le dialogue	*the dialogue*
discute	*discuss*
dit	*says*
donne	*give*
écoute	*listen*
écris	*write*
une erreur	*mistake*
et	*and*
faux	*false*
l' image	*the picture*
un jeu	*a game*
joue	*play, act out*

la lettre	*letter*
lis	*read*
le mot	*the word*
note	*note down*
l' option	*option, alternative*
ou	*or*
le passé	*the past (tense)*
la phrase	*the sentence*
pour	*for*
puis	*then*
quand	*when*
quel(s)	*which / what*
quelle(s)	*which / what*
qui	*who*
quoi	*what*
recherche	*research*
recopie	*copy*
réécoute	*listen again*
regarde	*look at*
relis	*re-read*
répète	*repeat*
la réponse	*the answer*
trouve	*find*
vrai	*true*

Photo credits

Alamy, Dynamic Graphics Group / Creatas p 13 (1), Bruce Coleman Inc. p 13 (5), Foodcollection.com p 26 (6), Ingram Publishing p 26 (7), Andre Jenny p 36 (2), Art Kowalsky p 36 (5), Agence Images p 80 (centre), John Foxx p 82 (1), Philip Wolmuth p 82 (5), images-of-france pp 85, 100 (main), POPPERFOTO pp 90 (right), 91, image100 p 97, BananaStock p 100 (inset), Robert Harding Picture Library Ltd p 117, Big Cheese Photo LLC p 123, Janine Wiedel Photolibrary p 129, Stock Image/Pixland p 133; Anthony Blake Picture Library, David Marsden p 26 (1), Joff Lee p 26 (3); Bananastock E (NT) pp 27 (1), 52 (2); Brendan Byrne/Digital Vision SD (NT) pp 52 (1), 93 (1,2), 137 (2, 3); Martyn Chillmaid pp 3 (1-3), 6 (1-3), 7, 8, 10, 12, 13 (2), 14, 16, 18, 19, 20 (bottom), 22, 26 (main, 5), 28 (1-5,8), 30, 32, 34, 38, 40 (1,2), 43 (1-2), 44, 63, 64, 66, 68, 70, 71, 74, 76, 80 (right), 82 (7), 84, 92, 93 (2), 94, 98 (top right, 1,3,6-9), 99, 104, 106 (main, 1-4,6-8), 107, 108, 109, 110, 111, 119, 127, 131, 136 (1,3); Corbis, Sergio Pitamitz pp 3 (main), 36 (1) Reuters p 9, Kevin Schafer p 13 (4), Archivo Iconografico, S.A p 21, Stephane Cardinale p 46, Manuel Blondeau/Photo & Co. p 55, Charles & Josette Lenars p 58, Dave G. Houser p 96, Stephane Cardinale/People Avenue p 122, V198 (NT) p 82 (8); Corbis Sygma, John Van Hasselt p 11 (top left), B/VAN PARYS p 11 (bottom left), Amet Jean Pierre p 36 (4), Philippe Giraud p 57 (top), Eric Robert p 61; Corel 62, 76, 77, 185, 269, 337, 340, 424, 459, 654 (NT) pp 11(3), 13 (6), 26 (2,4), 28 (6,7), 82 (3), 98 (2,4), 114, 121 (2), 136 (6); Digital Stock 4 (NT) p 81; Digital Vision (NT) p 57 (bottom); Digital Vision TT (NT) pp 27 (2), 65, 137 (1); EMPICS, John Marsh p 73; Das Fotoarchiv, Andreas Buck p 56 (left); French Fotos p 6 (bottom); Gerry Ellis/Digital Vision JA (NT) p 124; Gerry Ellis and Michael Durham/Digital Vision LC (NT) p 13 (2,5); Getty Images, Dag Sundberg/The Image Bank p 56 (right), AFP pp 90 (left), 115; Ingram ILGV1 CD 3, ILV2 CD 4, ILV2 CD 5, ILNV1 pp 11 (4), 82 (4), 136 (2), 98 (5); Jeremy Woodhouse/Digital Vision EP (NT) pp 24, 37 (8); Michael Reed at www.mike-reed.com pp 116, 121 (top); Mini-Europe p 36 (3); Océade p 37 (6); Photodisc 10, 50, 51 (NT) pp 82 (2, 6), 136 (5), 137 (top right); www.photogallery.nu p 40 (3); Stockbyte 33, 34, 35 (NT) pp 20 (2), 26 (8,9), 136 (4); Travel Ink, Barbara West p 37 (7); Travel Library p 20 (top).

Front cover picture: "Tour de France competitor, St Etienne, France by Franck Seguin/Corbis"

Every effort has been made to trace all copyright holders, but where this has not been possible the publisher will be pleased to make the necessary arrangements at the first opportunity.